ARCHITECTURE AND POWER

Architecture and Power

*The Town Hall and the
English Urban Community
c.1500–1640*

ROBERT TITTLER

CLARENDON PRESS · OXFORD
1991

Oxford University Press, Walton Street, Oxford OX2 6DP
Oxford New York Toronto
Delhi Bombay Calcutta Madras Karachi
Petaling Jaya Singapore Hong Kong Tokyo
Nairobi Dar es Salaam Cape Town
Melbourne Auckland
and associated companies in
Berlin Ibadan

Oxford is a trade mark of Oxford University Press

Published in the United States
by Oxford University Press, New York

British Library Cataloguing in Publication Data
(Data available)

Library of Congress Cataloging in Publication Data
Tittler, Robert.
Architecture and power: the town hall and the English urban
community, c. 1500–1640 / Robert Tittler.
p. cm.
Includes bibliographical references and index.
1. City halls—England.   2. Architecture and state—England.
3. Symbolism in architecture—England.   4. Architecture and society—
England.   I. Title
NA4435.G7T5   1991
725'.13'0103—dc20   91–19022
ISBN 0-19-820230-X

Typeset by Rowland Phototypesetting Ltd
Bury St Edmunds, Suffolk
Printed and bound in
Great Britain by Biddles Ltd
Guildford and King's Lynn

For my Parents

Preface and Acknowledgements

My interest in English towns of the sixteenth and early seventeenth century stems less from any specialized training than from reading Peter Clark and Paul Slack's *Crisis and Order in English Towns* in 1975. I took this up casually on the eve of a sabbatical leave in which I intended to work on the reign of Mary Tudor, a conventional, nationally focused, and narrative political history in a familiar vein. But that reading gave me a new and different perspective on the period of my interest, and by the end of the sabbatical year I had begun my own work on English towns of this period.

The more immediate inception of this project on town halls as a way of looking at towns themselves did not come until half way through my next sabbatical leave, in 1982–3. I began that leave with an interest in the economic and social characteristics of Tudor and early Stuart towns, and one thing led to another. The moral seems to be that sabbatical years should not be undertaken with any preconceived plan of work that can't be changed: some projects seem to lie in wait and then pounce on the unsuspecting researcher in their own good time.

Having done some research and a good deal of thinking about the subject in that exciting year, I was able to build upon my perceptions by frequent, if brief, trips back to the archives, and especially to the archives of individual towns. That wonderful device known as the Britrail Pass, added to a still reasonably efficient postal service and much writing ahead, allowed me to schedule a great many dashing visits to county record offices and to individual towns, often every day in the week, for several successive months of May.

It has also been helpful to my thinking on English towns to have taught an undergraduate course in English Urban History to *c.*1700, and to have had students of sufficient indulgence not to revolt in the face of offerings which were experimental and sometimes excessively spontaneous. A few graduate students followed, keeping me on my toes with an endless supply of questions to which I had then to find answers.

Still, anyone writing on preindustrial English towns while based in a predominantly French-speaking province across the Atlantic needs more than his own ruminations and the promptings of inquisitive students. My debt to others has been enormous. The Social Science and Humanities

Research Council of Canada provided me with the funding—a succession of small grants which financed several Mays in the archives, and then a research grant which provided fuller support between 1987 and 1989—essential to almost every aspect of the project. Not the least of its virtues was the funding for several talented research assistants.

The staffs of Concordia University's Vanier Library, the Senate House Library of London University, the Records of Early English Drama project based in Toronto, the National Register of Archives in London, and especially the Institute of Historical Research, my home away from home, provided support which was unfailingly sympathetic, supportive, and professional. The archivists and staffs of an even thirty county and town record offices visited between 1982 and 1988 proved willing and able to accommodate the requirements of a perpetually tight schedule, and often to follow up by post. Ms Iona Farrell of the Concordia Computer Centre lent me the word processors on which I wrote much of the text, and graciously sent replacements when my prose jammed up the works. Donna Whittaker solved sundry mysteries of word processing.

For expert research assistance, both in compiling basic information and in checking bibliographic notes and references, I am grateful to Michael Berlin, Louise Craven, Alasdair Hawkyard, Leslie Milne-Smith, and Susan Moore, working in London, as well as to my Concordia students, Kurt Clausen, Janis Housez, and Sherri Mason.

For advice on specific towns or issues I am thankful for the help of Ian Andrews and Derek Beamish (Poole), James Boutwood (Thaxted), P. W. Boreham (Dartford), Richard Butterfield (Totnes), V. H. Deacon (Much Wenlock), Audrey Douglas (Cumberland and Westmorland), Ray Grange and Margaretha Smith (Beverley), David Guy (Walsall), Richard Hogarth (Kidderminster), Marjorie Hallam (Titchfield), Elizabeth Holland (Bath), Bruce Jones (Cockermouth and Penrith), Ian Lancashire (playing sites), Sally-Beth MacLean (drama), Revd Raymond Moody (Burford), and Clive Wainwright (civic furniture).

Though they all said it wouldn't be, reading a chapter or giving advice on large portions of a manuscript is indeed always a chore. The following gave generously of their time and wisdom: Geoffrey Adams, Christopher Chalklin, Lynn Courtenay, Ian Gentles, Robert Goheen, Alexandra Johnston, Derek Keene, David Lloyd, Carl Lounsbury, Stephen Macfarlane, Marjorie McIntosh, Thomas A. Markus, Michael Mason, David Pelteret, Stephen Porter, Daniel Woolf, and Keith Wrightson. None of these good people should be held accountable when I blundered in spite of their counsel. In a more general way, I have been greatly stimulated by conversations and correspondence with Ian Gentles, Norman Jones, Michael MacCarthy-Morrogh, Stephen Macfarlane, and Stephen Porter (none of whom should be held accountable either!).

Finally, I am more than grateful to my wife, Anne, and to Andrew and Rebecca, for their patience, tolerance, making do and looking the other way, all too often. I owe the greatest debt of all to my parents, Professor Emeritus Irving A. Tittler and Mrs Sylvia Tittler, to whom this volume is joyfully dedicated. They'll know why.

R.T.

Montreal
20 July 1990

Contents

List of Plates

List of Tables

Map

Abbreviations

Bailey, *Minutes of Boston*	John F. Bailey (ed.), *Transcriptions of the Minutes of the Corporation of Boston*, 5 vols. (Boston, 1980–3)
BIHR	*Bulletin of the Institute of Historical Research*
BL	British Library
Bodl.	Bodleian Library
DoE	Department of the Environment, Royal Commission on the Historical Monuments of England, National Monuments Register
Ec. HR	*Economic History Review*
Grady, 'Thesis'	Kevin Grady, 'The Provision of Public Buildings in the W. Riding of Yorkshire' (Leeds Univ. Ph.D. thesis, 1980)
HMC	Historical Manuscripts Commission
Leland, *Itinerary*	Lucy Toulmin Smith (ed.), *The Itinerary of John Leland*, 5 vols. (1907–10)
P and P	*Past and Present*
Pevsner, *BoE*	Nikolaus Pevsner, *Buildings of England*
PRO	Public Record Office
C	Chancery
DL	Duchy of Lancaster
E	Exchequer
Req.	Requests
STAC	Star Chamber
REED	*Records of Early English Drama*
RO	Record Office
TRHS	*Transactions of the Royal Historical Society*
VCH	*Victoria County History*

The place of publication can be assumed to be London when not given.

Every architectural work can be regarded as a sign of the power, wealth, idealism and even the misery of its builders and their contemporaries.

Wolfgang Braunfels, *Urban Design in Western Architecture, Regime and Architecture, 900–1900.*

I

Introduction: The Town Hall in England
*c.*1500–1640

Something valuable has been lost in the movement of professional historians away from the physical evidence of the past. For all its obvious virtues, our near exclusive preoccupation with written or spoken sources has overwhelmed a consciousness of the physical record, the built environment of past societies, which was so central to the likes of Gibbon, Burckhardt, and Henry Adams. What each of these worthies saw in the physical record of Rome, Florence, and Mont Saint-Michel and Chartres respectively could only in part have been reconstructed or inferred from the written document. This is a perspective which many contemporary historical studies neglect at their peril for, as the architectural historian and theorist Sigfried Giedion has noted,

> Everything in [architecture], from its fondness for certain shapes to the approaches to specific building problems . . . reflects the conditions of the age from which it springs. It is the product of all sorts of factors—social, economic, scientific, technical, ethnological. However much a period may disguise itself, its real nature will show through in its architecture.[1]

Of course this study does not endorse a return to those earlier epochs of historical enquiry nor, just as obviously, does it suggest that we abandon the prime reliance on the written record upon which the historical discipline rests. It does, however, hope to re-emphasize the importance of the built environment, and perhaps to support some recent efforts to move the mainstream of historical investigation at least of some issues back toward such considerations. It aims to do this not with references to the grand epochs which lured Gibbon *et al.*, and which one could not approach in quite the same manner today, but rather in regard to the much more manageable microcosm of the local community. Indeed, if the

---

[1] Sigfried Giedion, *Space, Time, and Architecture, the Growth of a New Tradition*, 5th edn. (Cambridge, Mass., 1967), 19. The concept is not only Burckhardtian in tone but also in descent. As he tells us elsewhere (p. 2), Giedion studied under and considers himself a disciple of Burckhardt's pupil Heinrich Wölfflin. Other particularly helpful observations on the historiographic traditions linking history and art history or architecture may be found in Donald J. Olsen, *The City as a Work of Art, London, Paris, Vienna* (New Haven, Conn. 1986) and the earlier formulation of Olsen's view in his 'The City as a Work of Art', in Derek Fraser and Anthony Sutcliffe (eds.), *The Pursuit of Urban History* (1983), 264–85. See also John Gloag, *The Architectural Interpretation of History* (New York, 1975) esp. ch. I.

visual perspective has any value for contemporary historical interpretation, this seems the most obvious application.

In so far as such an effort has been extended by historians of Early Modern England, it has been applied particularly to the built environment of the countryside rather than of the town.[2] There is much irony in this, for surely buildings are much more central to the definition of what is urban than to what is rural. Such characteristic structures as the marketplace, tenement, theatre, inn, school, shambles, workshop, and civic hall all emanate first and chiefly from the requirements of urban society. Yet most of these elements remain to be investigated, both in the narrow sense of their reality as building types or in their wider social, political, or cultural context. Only a few have begun to take up this task. Peter Clark, whose book on the English alehouse is a useful paradigm of the genre and an able examination of his subject as a social institution, proves a happy exception to this neglect, as does Stanford Lehmberg with his study of the cathedrals.[3] For a slightly later period Peter Borsay's observations on a variety of urban environmental elements, including promenades, race courses and assembly rooms, has also been especially important,[4] though none of these studies treat the physical structures as the prime objects of interest. In addition, Alec Clifton-Taylor's popular presentations on specific towns rest on firm scholarship and bear a number of interesting suggestions, as does the more detailed analysis of Vanessa Parker on King's Lynn.[5]

Attention to civic, as opposed both to private and to ecclesiastical buildings, is even more scant for this era, and indeed for any era of English history up to the eighteenth century. One prominent, though still regrettably unpublished, exception to this observation is Kevin Grady's doctoral thesis on the public buildings of the West Riding of

[2] Amongst the more successful of such efforts in recent years are Mark Girouard, *Life in the English Country House* (Harmondsworth, 1978, 1980); Malcolm Airs, 'Some Social and Economic Aspects of Country House Building in England, 1500–1640' (Oxford Univ. D.Phil. thesis 1972) and *The Making of the English Country House, 1500–1640* (1975); Lawrence and Jeanne C. Fawtier Stone, *An Open Elite?, England, 1540–1880* (Oxford, 1984); Lawrence Stone, *The Crisis of the Aristocracy, 1558–1641* (Oxford, 1965), esp. ch. 10; Maurice Barley, *Houses and History* (1986); Maurice Howard, *The Early Tudor Country House, Architecture and Politics, 1490–1550* (1987); W. G. Hoskins, 'The Rebuilding of Rural England, 1570–1640', *P and P* 4 (1953), 44–59, reprinted in *Provincial England, Essays in Social and Economic History* (1963) and also parts of *The Making of the English Landscape* [1967] 2nd edn. (1989) and *English Landscapes* (1973).

[3] Peter Clark, *The English Alehouse, a Social History, 1200–1830* (1983): Stanford E. Lehmberg, *The Reformation of Cathedrals, Cathedrals in English Society, 1485–1603*. (Princeton, 1988).

[4] Peter N. Borsay, 'The English Urban Renaissance, Landscape and Leisure in the Provincial Town, c.1660–1770' (Lancaster Univ. Ph.D. thesis 1981); 'The English Urban Renaissance, the Development of Provincial Urban Culture, c. 1680–1760', *Social History*, 5 (May, 1977) 581–603; 'The Rise of the Promenade', *British Journal for Eighteenth Century Studies*, 9 (1986), 125–40; *The English Urban Renaissance: Culture and Society in the Provincial Town, 1660–1770* (Oxford, 1989).

[5] Alec Clifton-Taylor, *Six English Towns* (1985) and *Six More English Towns* (1986); Vanessa Parker, *The Making of King's Lynn: Secular Buildings from the Eleventh to the Seventeenth Century* (1971).

Yorkshire.[6] Another is *The History of the King's Works* compiled by Colvin *et al.*, which provides a monumental study of royal building, some of which may be described as civic.[7] But almost anything else on the subject which has made its way to print for this period tends to be extremely local and specialized in focus, and often equally obscure in terms of publication. For methodological paradigms we do best looking elsewhere, to other historical epochs or even to other national traditions.[8]

This study of the town hall and the English urban community grew primarily out of (but not away from) an interest in English towns of the sixteenth and seventeenth centuries. The choice of the town hall also emanated from a wider interest in the built environment as a historical source. Such an approach promised insights into several problems identified by current research on English urban history of this era: insights which it was hoped might extend the limitations of conventional written records alone. First, then, this study aims to contribute to our knowledge of English towns in the chosen period: their political and social development, financial and administrative organization, economic activity, and even cultural and ceremonial observances.

Second, and more particularly, this project stems from the (initially) casual observation that the number of town halls in the realm began to grow substantially from about the time of the Henrician Reformation. More systematic examination bore out this initial impression, and raised the thought that this may well have been the most concentrated period of civic building before at least the Georgian era. This activity seemed likely not to be coincidental, but rather to indicate some important development in the needs and priorities of those who governed these towns. Pursuit of the hall itself, a presumed indicator of other phenomena, thus seemed a fruitful endeavour.

Third, as a building type which appeared in virtually all types of towns, and whose geographic incidence coincided with the distribution of towns themselves across the map of England, the hall promised an explicitly broad and comparative approach to issues which have most often been

---

[6] Grady, 'Thesis'.

[7] H. M. Colvin, D. R. Ransome, and J. Summerson (eds.), *The History of the King's Works*, 6 vols. plus one vol. of plans (1963–1982), esp. iii pt I (1975), and iv pt. II (1982), covering the period 1485–1660.

[8] Some illustrative examples for England include Christopher Chalklin, *The Provincial Towns of Georgian England, a Study of the Building Process, 1740–1820* (1974); T. A. Markus (ed.), *Order in Space and Society, Architectural Form and its Context in the Scottish Englightenment* (Edinburgh, 1982); Robin Evans, *The Fabrication of Virtue: English Prison Architecture, 1750–1840* (Cambridge, 1982); Michael Ignatieff, *A Just Measure of Pain, the Penitentiary in the Industrial Revolution: 1750–1850* (1978); Malcolm Seaborne, *The English School, its Architecture and Organization, 1370–1870* (1971); Jeffrey Richards and John M. Mackenzie, *The Railway Station, a Social History* (Oxford, 1986); George W. Dolbey, *the Architectural Expression of Methodism* (1964); and, though it deals with the edifice as an end in itself, Colin Cunningham, *Victorian and Edwardian Town Halls* (1981).

examined by means of the case-study of one or a very few towns. While the value of the strict case-study approach to local history has been ably demonstrated by such pioneering works as Margaret Spufford's examination of three Cambridgeshire villages,[9] it was considered equally useful to examine a single phenomenon, in this case a building type, over a wide variety of towns. Still, the reader will observe that as, for instance, with Paul Slack's inspiring study of plague in the same period,[10] case-studies have indeed found their place in the consideration of particular issues.

Fourth, just as the characteristic appearance of breakfast bars and television rooms in our homes today reveals a great deal more about the development of family life than the raw, vital statistics on population, so may the physical characteristics of these buildings permit an additional and quite different perspective on the town from most classes of written documents, though these, too, have also been used as exhaustively as possible.

Finally, as the seat of civic government, the hall seemed likely to show how a particular building type could represent such intangible concepts as power, authority, and legitimacy within the community. Here it has been fruitful to draw upon the work which certain anthropologists have carried out on the interpretation of symbols in the social setting. Clifford Geertz in particular has urged us to delve beneath surface appearances of actions or material objects in the effort to appreciate how such forms may have been understood in common by members of particular communities or societies. Indeed, the search for symbolic as well as literal meaning in apparently mundane objects and practices, Geertz's technique of 'thick description',[11] has now been widely adopted by those, historians as well as anthropologists, seeking to understand the meaning of social activities and the material objects associated with them.

Amongst their other uses, as Geertz himself has demonstrated, such sets of 'symbolic' forms' may readily be employed to investigate the governing role of ruling élites in particular societies. It is precisely these forms, Geertz tells us, the 'crowns and coronations, limousines and conferences—that mark the centre as [the] centre'.[12] Geertz himself has applied the study of such symbolic forms to the understanding of royalty, and has done so in historical societies as diverse as fourteenth-century

[9] Margaret Spufford, *Contrasting Communities, English Villagers in the Sixteenth and Seventeenth Centuries* (Cambridge, 1974).

[10] Paul Slack, *The Impact of Plague in Tudor and Stuart England* (1985).

[11] Clifford Geertz, 'Thick Description: Toward an Interpretive Theory of Culture', in Geertz (ed.), *The Interpretation of Cultures, Selected Essays by Clifford Geertz* (New York, 1973), 21.

[12] Clifford Geertz, 'Centers, Kings and Charisma: Reflection on the Symbolics of Power', in Joseph Ben-David and Terry Nichols Clark (eds.), *Culture and its Creators* (Chicago, 1977) 152. See also C. Geertz, *Negara: The Theatre State in Nineteenth Century Bali* (Princeton, NJ, 1980); C. Geertz, *Islam Observed, Religious Development in Morocco and Indonesia* (New Haven, Conn. 1968); C. Geertz, H. Geertz, and L. Rosen, *Meaning and Order in Moroccan Society* (Cambridge, 1979).

Java, nineteenth-century Morocco, and, more familiarly, sixteenth-century England. Yet his approach seems potentially as useful in examining the non-hereditary ruling élite of English towns as of other cases. This 'architecture and power' study, an analysis of the town hall's role in the English urban community, seems an appropriate application of that approach.

There are, then, a number of good reasons to pursue a study of English towns and urban development from the viewpoint of civic halls, but why do so for the years $c.1500$–1640? Beginning a few decades prior to the break from Rome, a study beginning in $c.1500$ provides bench-marks for activity concerning halls extending beyond the Reformation. Termination at the approximate outbreak of the Civil War, with its frequent disruptions of normal administrative practices, rounds out what seems a distinct and self-contained period in the development of English towns and urban institutions.

In between these milestones came decades marked, as is well known, by a great population increase, rapid social and considerable geographic mobility, significant economic adjustments, and severe problems caused by some or all of these factors. These all bore heavily on urban society: a good many of them bore more heavily on urban society than on agrarian. In addition, the chosen period seems to mark the culmination of some important urban political and administrative developments, including the commonplace establishment of self-governing institutions and of ruling oligarchies within them, whose inceptions may be traced to the High Middle Ages.[13] The resolution of these tendencies during and after the Civil War and Interregnum helped set the stage for a subsequent era of English urban life, one which was politically more controlled, economically more stable, socially more secure, and culturally more polarized, but also (at least at some levels) more sophisticated. *This* era has been characterized by Peter Borsay, following his work on political cultural traditions, as the 'English Urban Renaissance'.[14]

The subject of the town hall is thus presented as a tool in the service of the urban historian, applied here to a distinct and important stage in urban history. Like most unfamiliar tools, this methodological crowbar, intended to pry beneath the surface of the town charter, by-law, and minute book, requires some guidance before it may be taken in hand. What, for example, do we precisely mean by the 'town hall'? Were such buildings numerically significant enough in this period to help shed light on contemporary urban politics and society? How does the town hall of the post-1500 era compare, in terms of numbers and functions, with civic

[13] Summarized in Robert Tittler, 'The End of the Middle Ages in the English Country Town', *Sixteenth Century Journal*, 18/4 (1987), 471–87.
[14] Borsay, *The English Urban Renaissance* and Borsay, 'The English Urban Renaissance' (thesis).

halls of an earlier period? These are all questions which must be addressed at the outset.

Let us begin with definitions. When John Leland, that wonderfully observant traveller and topographer of the 1540s, referred to the *domus civica* (as in 'The market place in Sarisbyri is very fair and large and . . . in a corner of it is *domus civica*') he employed a descriptive term which he obviously understood himself, and which in the end proves useful enough.[15] But Leland never considered it necessary to define his usage for posterity and the subject of his tag is poorly served in the quotidian usage of his contemporaries.

Thus the records yield up a bewildering variety of labels which make it very difficult to determine whether a particular edifice did indeed function as the '*domus civica*'. These not only included the 'town hall', probably the most literal translation of Leland's Latin, but also 'town house', 'market house', 'tolsey', 'tollbooth', 'guild-hall', 'yeldehall', 'moot hall' and 'mote hall', 'boot hall' or 'booth hall', 'court hall', or even 'chequer house'. Some of these names held multiple connotations. Thus, for example, the term 'market hall' might be nothing more than a roofed-over market area with no true rooms at all. It might also refer to an open-sided market structure which at some time supported one or more true storeys in which public business in addition to marketing itself could be conducted. By the same token, a 'town house' may simply be a dwelling owned by the town or a private dwelling in a town, while a 'tolsey' or 'tollbooth' or 'boothall' might merely be a small edifice used more or less exclusively for collecting tolls and other such perquisites. Yet all five of these terms were frequently labels for true town halls as well. Written usage must obviously be corrolated with some additional evidence before the true function of the edifice may be known with certainty.

Sometimes, as with 'yeldehalls' in southern England, usages appear to be regionally specific.[16] 'Tolsey', said by the *Oxford English Dictionary* in its earlier forms of 'tolsel' or 'tolzey' (this last still common in the sixteenth century) to be an 'ancient name' for a 'guild-hall' in both England and Ireland, is most familiar in Oxfordshire, Gloucestershire, and Wiltshire: Burford, Bristol, Tewkesbury, Gloucester, and Devizes provide useful examples. 'Tolbooth' or its etymological variant 'tollbooth', said by the same authority to be common in Scotland as well as in England, seems

---

[15] Leland, *Itinerary*, i. 259 *et passim*.

[16] This apparent variant of 'guild-hall' seems especially common in those areas of southern England (from Chippenham in Wiltshire to Blandford Forum in Dorset and Great Dunmow in Essex) where the hard 'g' became softened in the Middle English period almost to serve as a vowel. See e.g. H. Kurath. S. M. Kuhn, and J. Reidy (eds.), *The Middle English Dictionary* (Ann Arbor, 1950–   ) vol. 'G–H', 110–11, s.v. *gild(e)*. My thanks for this note and much else on the derivation of related terms to Dr David Pelteret.

chiefly to have been employed in the northern counties. Durham, Howden, Knaresborough, Morpeth, Ripon, Rotherham, and Whitby speak to this. Yet the town hall was sometimes known as a 'tollbooth' in parts of East Anglia as well, as in Beccles and East Dereham. 'Boothall', for which the *OED* unaccountably and misleadingly gives no usage prior to 1712, seems to have taken hold in the West Midlands and the West Country well within our period, as in Evesham, and again in Gloucester and Tewkesbury.

How can we account for this multiplicity of usage? First, some of these terms originated with literal and functionally accurate descriptions of earlier buildings on particular sites. Such structures may thereafter have been expanded to serve fully as town halls. For example, a note in the Borough Minute Book of Tewkesbury, dated 15 May 1576, tells us that 'in this year the Tolsey was transformed as it is nowe for the corte keeping'.[17] Other edifices were replaced altogether by new buildings for use as town halls with the original name living on even after the change in function. This probably accounts not only for much of the usage of 'tolbooth', 'tolsey', or 'booth hall', but also for the additional term 'market cross'. In extension of its original meaning this often came to denote the canopied polygonal structure, often with a partly vestigial central shaft, which one finds in the West Country or the Cotswolds, of which more will be said in Chapter 2,[18] or even the true hall with full meeting rooms above, as with the Wymondham, Swaffham, or Sevenoaks 'market crosses'.[19]

Yet such apparently self-explanatory and functional labels are not always accurate indications of origin and we must use them only with great caution. An excellent example of this is the innocent looking 'guild-hall', with its 'yield(e)hall' variants. In fact, this may or may not derive from a descriptive term having to do with the hall of a religious or economic guild. The Old English noun *gi(e)ld* or *gyld* was linked with the Old English verb *gielden*, meaning 'to yield [!], pay, render', etc.[20] This could refer to payments to a guild as if for dues or mutual benefits, but it could as easily refer to payment to some other authority in the sense of taxes or tribute, indeed, as 'yield', and as in *wergild* or *danegild*. Though we find references to 'guild-halls' even in Anglo-Saxon times, the original meaning of the term, and thus its derivation, in some cases remains unclear. It

---

[17] Gloucestershire Co. RO, MS TBR/A1/1, fo. 11ʳ.

[18] Examples may be found at Witney, Oxon. (still standing) and in the three Somerset towns of Glastonbury (drawn in the nineteenth century by Buckler, BL, Add. MS 36381, fo. 269), Nether Stowey (BL, Add. MS 36383, fo. 249), and Shepton Mallet (BL, Add. MS 36383, fo. 161).

[19] Wymondham still stands; 'W.H.K.', *An Account of Swaffham Markets and Fairs* [1832] (Swaffham, n.d.) unpag.; Sir John Dunlop, *The Pleasant Town of Sevenoaks* (Sevenoaks, 1964), 86.

[20] J. Bosworth and T. N. Toller, *An Anglo-Saxon Dictionary* with *Supplement* by T. N. Toller and *Enlarged Addenda and Corrigenda to the Supplement*, ed. Alistair Campbell, 3 vols. (Oxford, 1882–1922, 1972), q.v. *gielden*.

appears that it need not necessarily be thought of as a hall which once served a religious or economic guild.[21] Evesham's 'gild hall' existed quite apart from any guild, while in Beverley the hall was known as the 'Hanshouse' (undoubtedly reflecting the influence of Hanse merchants via Hull) until the term 'gildhall' was adopted after c.1580. In both cases the meaning of the term had already lost its guild connotations. 'Guild-hall' meant and was intended to mean 'town hall'.[22]

We seem on somewhat safer ground in taking the label 'moot hall' or 'mote hall' as more explanatory of initial function. These forms presumably denoted a building or site once associated with a moot court of some sort, as in burghmoot, portmanmoot, folkmoot, or witangemoot. Though these terms are widespread in the northern counties (as in Keswick, Alfreton, Clitheroe, Appleby, Barnsley, Leeds, and Wakefield) we also find them in Essex (Maldon and Saffron Walden), Bedfordshire (Elstow and Ampthill), and elsewhere.

Even the term 'hall' itself may cause confusion. It may mean an entire edifice, or (as in the hall of a country house) merely a room within an edifice (which may itself be otherwise labelled). The 'guild-hall' in Helston, Cornwall, for example, was simply a room at one end of a market hall.[23] The 'town hall' of Cirencester uniquely constituted the second storey of the parish-church porch.[24] Stroud's town hall was a room in the upper storey of the 'Market House'.[25] Yet most 'town halls', mercifully, connote entire buildings.

As if this were not enough to try the patience of the historian working from archival descriptions, building labels changed with time and concurrent usages were not uncommon. Many buildings were known interchangeably as 'market halls' and 'town halls', and this we learn to anticipate. But it comes as more of a surprise to learn that 'the New House', 'the Council House', and 'the Guildhall' of Chesterfield were one and the same building, or that Shaftesbury's 'Guildhall', its 'Town House', its 'Common Hall', and its 'Market Hall' were also (probably!) all

[21] B. Thorpe, *Diplomatarium Anglicum Aevi Saxonici* (1865), 605–9; A. H. Smith, *English Place Name Elements*, 2 vols. (Cambridge, 1976), i. 200–2; Max Forster, *Der Flussname Themse und Seine Sippe* (Munich, 1941), 792. My thanks to David Pelteret for this reference.

[22] R. H. Hilton, 'The Small Town and Urbanization—Evesham in the Middle Ages', *Midland History*, 7 (1982), 6–7; and J. Dennett (ed.), *Beverley Borough Records, 1575–1821*, Yorkshire Archaeological Society Record Series, 84 (1933 for 1932), 11 and n. 1.

[23] C. S. Gilbert, *An Historical and Topographical Survey of the County of Cornwall*, 2 vols. in 3 parts (Plymouth, 1817–20), ii, pt.ii, p. 766.

[24] Anon., *The History and Antiquities of the Town of Cirencester* (n.p., 1863), 65; and Buckler drawing of 13 Sept. 1819, BL, Add. MS 36362, fo. 176.

[25] P. H. Fisher, *Notes and Recollections of Stroud, Gloucestershire* [1871, 1891] (1989), 61–4; N. Pevsner and D. Verey, *BoE, Gloucestershire*, i (1970), 431; *VCH, Gloucestershire*, xi (1976), 104; Bodl., Rawlinson MS B 323, fo. 209ᵛ.

one.[26] More often than not, unfortunately, such distinctions remain ambiguous, and we cannot always be entirely certain whether our documents mean to describe one or several distinct buildings. In sum, then, each of these many terms refers to our town hall or civic hall (Leland's *domus civica*) at least some of the time, and each may offer helpful clues to the functional origins of the buildings so named. But not always!

Most important for the present study is to establish a working definition which satisfies these vagaries of terminology and which can be employed consistently throughout. The terms 'town hall' and 'civic hall' have been taken synonymously to mean that edifice characteristically regarded by contemporaries as the seat of whatever degree of autonomous civic administration a particular town may have enjoyed.[27] Here the townsmen carried out their public business. Here their administrative officers normally presided, their courts and assemblies normally convened, their fees and fines were normally rendered, their apprenticeships and freedoms were registered and, in short, their perquisites of government, however defined in particular communities, came chiefly to be exercised. Here too, were ordinarily kept the paraphernalia associated with such activities: the town mace, seal and plate, town chest and records, the characteristic furnishings of the courts and assemblies held within.

Having issued such a definition, one must hasten to acknowledge its intentional breadth and the variation which it admits from one instance to another. It is not only relegated to towns enjoying the full liberties conventionally found in the royal charter of incorporation by this period, but also to that much larger number whose self-governing institutions and other characteristics justify the definition which we have agreed to employ. Part of this breadth is necessitated by the common practice whereby townsmen shared their hall with such other authorities as the manorial lord, or the courts of assize and quarter sessions. It was also quite possible for a single town to utilize more than one building for a town hall, or for functions usually associated with the town hall. There are thus more halls dating from this period than there are towns acquiring them.

If this definition is sufficient to allow us to proceed, we must turn to the question of evidence. Relatively few such buildings have survived from

[26] P. Riden and J. Blair (eds.), *History of Chesterfield* (Chesterfield, 1980), v. 246–7; and for Shaftesbury, Buckler drawing of 1822, BL, Add. MS 36361, fo. 165 and depositions of Morgan Senyor (aged 68 in 1608), William Swifte of Melcombe (aged 72 in 1608), and Christopher Raynorre of Shaftesbury (aged 80 'and upwards') recorded in PRO, E 134/5 James I, H.22.

[27] The word 'town' has also been taken in rather a specific way: a community distinct from a village and meeting the criteria laid out in Peter Clark and Paul Slack, *Crisis and Order in English Towns, 1500–1700* (1972), 3–4 and, more fully, in *English Towns in Transition, 1500–1700* (Oxford, 1976), 2–6.

the era in question. A search of published scholarship on town halls in their political and social context, not to mention from the purely architectural point of view, yields so little that one may well wonder if the subject can reasonably be taken up for serious study. Indeed, even the best of writings on Tudor and Stuart building, by the likes of W. G. Hoskins on the rebuilding of rural England, or of Marc Girouard, Malcolm Airs, or Maurice Howard on the country house, or of Howard Colvin *et al.* on royal building, barely hint at *civic* construction.[28] Christopher Chalklin, the authority on civic building and society in a slightly later period, found little of interest in such construction between the Reformation and the eighteenth century. His description of the market and town halls of the era in question as 'small and cramped structures', though often entirely accurate, holds out little promise of greater things.[29]

These sober portents inspired an effort to compile a sequential census of civic halls built, substantially renovated, purchased, or converted to such use during the chosen period. A census of this sort promised some intrinsic value of its own even if it led no further, but it also seemed likely to provide a data base from which to assess a full spectrum of issues regarding the urban community. Most immediately, it would provide reassurance that, *pace* Hoskins, Colvin, Chalklin, and others, there was actually a subject here to pursue.

A variety of sources proved essential to this effort, and indeed—though additional sources serve to support particular chapters and will be identified in turn—these serve as the foundation evidence for the whole study. The method adopted was first to fix upon a serviceable list of towns. The best such list proved to be that of markets compiled by Alan Everitt in his seminal work of 1967 on market towns and marketing.[30] Yet this list of markets was not entirely accepted as a list of towns themselves. Some towns listed therein proved to have functioned as towns during only part of the time-span which his essay shares with the present study. These had to be treated with great care, while a few minor (and marginal) additions (for example Elstow in Bedfordshire, Fordwich in Kent, and Castle-Cary in Somerset) had to be made along the way.

Nevertheless, armed with such a list, it proved possible to attack the problem county by county. For halls still extant, Sir Nikolaus Pevsner's 'Buildings of England' series proved invaluable, as did the records and reports of the Historical Monuments Commission. These were searched

[28] See n. 2 above.

[29] Christopher Chalklin, 'The Financing of Church Building in the Provincial Towns of Eighteenth Century England', in Peter Clark (ed.), *The Transformation of English Provincial Towns, 1600–1800* (1984), 284.

[30] Alan Everitt, 'The Marketing of Agricultural Produce', in Joan Thirsk (ed.), *The Agrarian History of England and Wales*, iv *(1500–1640)* (Cambridge, 1967), 468–75.

with care, county by county and town by town, and were often examined on site. For defunct structures the task of course proved more difficult and the results less precise. Here any sources which came to hand proved fair game when they were sufficiently documented or could otherwise be verified. Published town and county histories, of course including the *Victoria County Histories*, were combined with old travel books (broadly defined and starting with Leland) and local history society publications as the most valuable printed sources. Of unprinted sources (in addition to the modern reports and records of the Historical Monuments Commission noted above) collections of drawings (discussed in Chapter 2), surveys, rentals, property deeds, chamberlains' accounts, borough minute and assembly books, and similar local archives proved particularly useful, though of course neither they nor any other known sources could ever justify claims of comprehensive coverage.

In the end, this effort has established with certainty the construction, conversion, or substantial rebuilding of 202 town halls, in a total of 178 towns (as some towns acquired more than one), during the period under discussion. These have been listed in the Appendix as the 'Census of Town Halls Acquired in England, 1500–1640'. In addition, close to a hundred and fifty other halls seem at least likely to derive from the same era. Lingering doubt over dating, function, or definition prevents us from adding them in with the rest, and they have not been listed here, though there is every chance that most could be added were documentation more complete. In other words, close to half of the approximately six to seven hundred towns in the realm at this time appear to have built, substantially rebuilt, or purchased and converted a town hall, and some of them more than one such edifice, between 1500 and 1640.

This seemed a most impressive record, but the town hall is obviously a subject with a long past, of which our period forms but a part. In order to place this figure in perspective, it became essential to know where Tudor and early Stuart halls fit with the longer period over which at least some buildings could be traced. Except for the small minority of towns which were prominent at an early stage, that past is considerably obscured. R. B. Dobson was very likely correct to suggest that, because of the small number of survivals and the fragmentary nature of written documentation for the rest, 'it may well be that the history of the town halls of Medieval England can never be written'.[31] Yet despite this generally slippery ground, some general patterns do seem to emerge which permit us to reconstruct at least conjecturally the emergence of English town halls prior to the sixteenth century.

Of those English towns of the senior rank, whose prominence came

---

[31] R. B. Dobson, 'Urban Decline in Late Medieval England', *TRHS* 5th ser. 27 (1977), 7.

early, Exeter is perhaps the most familiar example. Yet its Guildhall, already standing in the year 1160, when it was first cited in a deed, remains atypical in point of age and durability for towns of equal lineage.[32] Perhaps a better example comes from Bury St Edmunds, whose hall dates from about the year 1179, when it was presumably built by townsmen with the permission of the abbot. From that point onwards, until the townsmen took legal possession of the building after the dissolutions, it served for their meetings and assemblies. Ironically, for the abbot continued to own it until the dissolution of the abbey, it also provided a bastion of those rights which they asserted against that ecclesiastical landlord. In the mid-fifteenth century there were several renovations, including the addition of a kitchen and a muniment room. So central was this building to the townsmen's sense of identity and to their hard-won rights of self-government that the building itself seems to have formed the organizing principle of local government between the dissolution of the abbey and the acquisition of the borough's charter of incorporation in the early seventeenth century. That is, by a deed of enfeoffment the townsmen created a legal trust to govern the town itself as 'Feoffees of the Guildhall': an arrangement which endured for the control of the hall itself, if not the whole borough, until 1893.[33]

Such developments were roughly approximated in towns of similar political background, and perhaps even more so when no abbot or other powerful landlord held sway as did the abbots of Bury. Gloucester's Guildhall is first recorded in the year 1192, following closely on the heels of several important privileges of self-government obtained by the townsmen.[34] The extensive privileges accorded the burgesses of Salisbury by successive thirteenth-century bishops led to the construction of a hall in the middle years of that century. This was the building which Leland noted some three hundred years later. It was in turn partially superseded by the four-storeyed Council House constructed between 1579 and 1584.[35] Bristol's Guildhall dates from the fourteenth century and served that community until it was partly replaced by the 'Council House' or 'Tolsey' in Corn Street in 1551.[36]

So far as one can tell, these guild-halls were not halls of religious guilds so often or so much as they were halls purpose-built for at least some

[32] H. Lloyd Parry, The History of the Exeter Guildhall and the Life Within (Exeter, 1936), 1.

[33] Margaret Statham, 'The Guildhall of Bury St Edmunds', Proceedings of the Suffolk Institute of Archaeology, 31 (1970), 117–57; Robert S. Gottfried, Bury St. Edmunds and the Urban Crisis, 1290–1539 (Princeton, NJ, 1982), 3–5, 30–1, 44–5, 86, 103, 156, 184, 186–7.

[34] M. D. Lobel (ed.), Historic Towns, i (Baltimore, n.d.) vide 'Gloucester', 5 and n. 62.

[35] Lobel, Historic Towns, i, vide 'Salisbury', 3–5; VCH, Wiltshire, vi (1962), 87 and preceding plate; and H. Shortt (ed.), The City of Salisbury (Salisbury, 1957) 37–8, 94.

[36] Elizabeth Ralph (ed.), Guide to the Bristol Archives Office (Bristol, 1971), p. ix.

aspects of local civic administration. The builders themselves were usually members of the gild merchant or some other defined group of burgesses endowed with some rights of self-government; sometimes even the manorial lord was the builder. Yet this should not be taken to deny either that halls of religious guilds, such as Lincoln's twelfth-century Hall of the Guild of St Mary,[37] were often erected in part for civic administration or that (even as in London) there was always a clear line of demarcation between the role of such 'religious' guilds or fraternities and the governing structure of particular communities.[38]

Even less may confidently be said regarding civic halls in smaller communities which may often have been slower to develop much autonomy. The halls of many religious guilds may easily be traced to well before the Reformation, especially with the aid of the *Valor Ecclesiasticus* drawn up at Thomas Cromwell's order on the eve of the dissolutions.[39] Certainly some of these served as town halls thereafter. More conjectural for the moment is the thought that civic halls emerged when and where townsmen received substantial privileges from seigneurial authorities, or asserted such privileges on their own, and that the functional development and even labels of such halls closely followed the nature of those privileges. We might thus expect that the common market- and town-hall combinations may have appeared where townsmen received some control over the business of marketing. They might then also have received control of extant market halls (which landlords are known to have constructed at least as far back as the twelfth century)[40] or have been moved to build their own. This may have been the case in Wallingford by 1232, Abingdon by 1327, and Maldon by 1400.[41] By the same token, the boothall, tolsey, or tollbooth forms may often have emerged when burgesses received the right to collect their own tolls and other fiscal perquisites. In all cases the physical structures could be, and undoubtedly were at least some of the time, expanded to meet the developing requirements of 'true' town halls when such expansion became appropriate.

Finally, many halls (especially but not exclusively those termed 'court halls' or 'moot halls') were indeed purpose-built for the holding of courts by the manorial authority of the day. These often came to serve the same

---

[37] Francis Hill, *A Short History of Lincoln* (Lincoln, 1979), 35.

[38] Gervase Rosser, 'The Anglo-Saxon Gilds', in John Blair (ed.), *Ministers and Parish Churches, the Local Church in Transition, 950–1200* (Oxford University Committee for Archaeology, Monograph no. 17, 1988), 32. I am indebted for this note to Dr David Pelteret.

[39] *Valor Ecclesiasticus*, ed. John Caley and Jos. Hunter, 6 vols. (1810–34).

[40] Maurice Beresford, *New Towns of the Middle Ages* (1967), 177.

[41] *VCH, Berkshire*, iv (1924), 432; J. K. Hedges, *History of Wallingford*, 2 vols. (1881), i. 333 and ii. 263; Essex Co. RO, MS D/B3/11/5.

TABLE I. Chronological sequence of town halls built, substantially renovated, or purchased and converted, by decade

Dates	Purpose-built town hall	Building renovated or enlarged	Building purchased for conversion	Other, or uncertain	Total
1500–9	3	1	1		5
1510–19	2	1		1	4
1520–9	1		1		2
1530–9	3	1			4
1540–9	4	1	4	1	10
1550–9	6	1	5		12
1560–9	10	1	3	1	15
1570–9	9	1	7	3	20
1580–9	7	1	1	1	10
1590–9	6	2	1		9
1600–9	12	2			14
1610–19	14	1			15
1620–9	6	2			8
1630–9	5				5
TOTALS	88	15	23	7	133

Sources: Extrapolated from Appendix.

function under the successive authority of the townsmen themselves. Though it may never have developed into much of a town, Abbots Bromley had a 'court leet hall' by the early thirteenth century, and the court leet of High Wycombe met in the Guildhall by 1380 and continued to do so after the incorporation of that town in 1558.[42] Other possibilities include Bedford by the early thirteenth century;[43] Pontefract, Stamford, and Colchester in the fourteenth century;[44] and Halifax, Leeds, Newport (Isle of Wight), Olney (Buckinghamshire), and Henley-in-Arden by the middle of the fifteenth century.[45]

[42] M. A. Rice, *Abbots Bromley* (Shrewsbury, 1939), 21, 86-8, 192; L. J. Ashford, *The History of the Borough of High Wycombe from its Origins to 1880* (1960), 33.

[43] Joyce Godber, *History of Bedfordshire, 1066–1888* (Bedford, 1969), 53.

[44] Grady, 'Thesis', 408; David Roffe, 'Walter Draguin's Town? Lord and Burghal Community in Thirteenth Century Stamford', *Lincolnshire History and Archaeology*, 23 (1988), 44–5; Gurney Benham (ed.), *The Red Paper Book of Colchester* (Colchester, 1902), 8.

[45] Grady, 'Thesis', 344, 375; BL, Add. MS 24789, fo. 122ᵛ, an indenture of 7 Henry IV calling for the building of 'Two shops with Solar for a New Court House for the Bailiffs and Commonaly [*sic*] [of Newport] to hold their Courts in and Corporation Seal'; *VCH, Buckinghamshire*, iv (1927), 430; *VCH, Warwickshire*, iii (1945), 206; W. Cooper, *Henley-in-Arden, an Ancient Market Town and its Surroundings* (Birmingham, 1946), 69, 75, and photo opp. 66 (the building in the photo should not be confused with the Elizabethan market and town hall demolished in 1793).

One may well suspect a roughly cyclical pattern of hall-building, coinciding with the ebb and flow of self-governing privileges in specific towns and undoubtedly extending well back into the Middle Ages. Yet there is insufficient evidence to permit the firm delineation of chronological patterns prior to the fifteenth century. For the years thereafter there does seem to be some substance to Professor Dobson's view that such construction projects became more common, especially amongst the larger towns, in the first six or seven decades of the fifteenth century.[46]

From the last third of the fifteenth century the pace at which town halls turn up anew slackened considerably, remaining slow for more than half a century. Only in the 1530s and 1540s did the roll of England's town halls again begin to increase. Even in the sixteenth century we cannot be as precise as we would like, for many halls may be dated only by regnal association (as 'in Henry VIII's time'), part of a century ('early seventeenth century') or by reference to fixed and known points identified in documentation (for example, a hall not mentioned in a survey of 1555 but cited in a deed of 1586). Yet if we evaluate the dated buildings by decade a pattern emerges, which is shown in Table 1.

In addition, there are halls linked only to chronological periods rather than to precise years, but which are still dated within the boundaries of this study. These are shown in Table 2.

Though theoretically there are enough halls only roughly dated to upset any patterns suggested by those which are so designated, we can at least make some conjectural observations about overall chronological distribution.

Even when we add in early sixteenth-century halls, there appears to have been relatively little activity in the growth of town halls in the first four decades of the period. Only thereafter do we see a slow increase in both constructions and conversions of standing buildings from other uses. The overall pattern of increase carries on through the economically (and otherwise) difficult decade of the 1550s and reaches a peak in the 1560s and 1570s.

It is important to note that the bulk of purchases and conversions, most of them from dissolved ecclesiastical properties, occurs here, several decades after those properties presumably became available for purchase rather than at the point of dissolution itself. This suggests that the addition of halls did not derive simply from the immediate availability of suitable former ecclesiastical buildings. A similar chronology seems to apply to the purchase, by individual townsmen, of what had been

---

[46] Dr Derek Keene has helpfully suggested such a building cycle in conversation. Dobson, 'Urban Decline in Late Medieval England', 7.

TABLE 2. Chronological sequence of town halls, by period

Dates	Purpose-built town hall	Building renovated or enlarged	Building purchased for conversion	Other, or uncertain	Total
16th c.	13		5		18
Early 16th c.	6	1			7
Mid-16th c.	2		10	1	13
Late 16th c.	12			2	14
Late 16th to early 17th c.	3			1	4
Early 17th c.	10		2	1	13
Between 1500 and 1640	2			2	4
TOTALS	48	1	17	7	73

ᵃ The total of halls in Tables 1 and 2 is 206, a few more than the total number of buildings listed in the Census of Town Halls. The difference results from the fact that a few buildings underwent more than one renovation or rebuilding, and are thus counted twice.

Sources: Extrapolated from Appendix.

ecclesiastically held residential property in the towns.[47] We may at least speculate that these purchases came some time after the dissolutions themselves because some initial purchasers of church property resold them at a later time, or because towns themselves were then better organized and better financed to make such purchases.

In any event, the overall peak of the 1570s then dropped to a steady plateau of halls added in the two or three decades thereafter. During this time, as the supply of former ecclesiastical buildings ran thin, conversions ceased almost entirely. Almost all halls which appear here were built from scratch. After the turn of the seventeenth century this stability gave way to a steady rise until another peak in the appearance of halls came in the 1610s. This was followed by a precipitous drop-off which endured for the last two decades of the period under discussion and continued, as Peter Clark and Paul Slack have affirmed, for a decade or two thereafter before reviving in the late seventeenth century.[48]

[47] This has been suggested by W. G. Hoskins, 'English Provincial Towns in the Early Sixteenth Century', *TRHS* 5th ser. 6 (1956), 11; Colin Platt, *The English Medieval Town* (1976), 182–3, and borne out for York by D. M. Palliser, *Tudor York* (Oxford, 1979), 265–6, and for Bury St Edmunds by Janis C. Housez, 'The Property Market in Bury St. Edmunds, 1540–1600' (Concordia Univ. MA essay 1988), 88–100.

[48] Clark and Slack, *Crisis and Order*, 34–5.

One may distinguish in this overall pattern two apparent undulations. The first is marked by a steady increase in halls beginning *c.*1540 and extending at least to the end of the 1570s. The second and more modest spans the first two decades of the seventeenth century, though even the 'crisis decades' of the 1590s witnessed nothing like the low levels at the beginning or the end of the entire period. The drop-off of the 1620s and beyond is the most marked decline of the entire period, though the level of halls appearing by the end is still higher than the level which began the sixteenth century.

Potentially related to this chronological sequence of hall acquisition, and obviously worthy of examination in its own right, is the question of geographic distribution. The map in the Appendix shows this distribution of halls for the entire period under consideration, with the dots numbered to identify particular towns in the sequence in which they appear in the Census of Town Halls.

Before we can consider what this may tell us, an important caveat must be considered. The apparent scarcity of halls in the north and in a few counties elsewhere (including Cornwall, which certainly didn't lack for towns) may be related to the current state of archives upon which identification of halls often rests as well as to the true distribution of halls themselves. For a variety of reasons these areas are not as rich in surviving documentation as others. Some records have remained in the private and less accessible hands of estate offices and solicitors rather than in county or town record offices. In those northern and western areas of historically weaker manorial organization[49] many communities were not well served by the practice of record keeping to begin with, and have been less likely to preserve records which were kept. This factor of documentation renders somewhat tentative any conclusions based on known geographical or sequential distribution. If less is made of these considerations than the reader may hope for, the use of caution in extending argument beyond the support of documentation will have to be excused.

However this may be, close examination of the composite map yields some observations which one may be able to interpret more readily as the arguments of subsequent chapters unfold. For one, the tendency of some closely neighbouring towns to acquire town halls in rapid succession appears by the 1550s with Bristol and Chipping Sodbury, and is repeated

---

[49] This important correlation of terrain with the diverse strength of manorial organization seems first to have been suggested by W. G. Hoskins in *The Midland Peasant* (1957), and also by Joan Thirsk in Thirsk (ed.), *The Agrarian History*, iv, esp. 8–9. Some valuable and suggestive correlations between agrarian regions and political behaviour in general include, *inter alia*, Anthony Fletcher, *A County Community in Peace and War: Sussex, 1600–1660* (1975); David Underdown, 'The Chalk and the Cheese: Contrasts among the English Clubmen', *P and P* 85 (1979), 25–48; and *Revel, Riot and Rebellion, Popular Politics and Culture in England, 1603–1660* (Oxford, 1987).

in several subsequent decades. Cricklade and Devizes both built halls in the 1560s. Coventry and Warwick; Billericay, Great Dunmow, and Maldon; Swaffham and Thetford; Hadleigh and Woodbridge all did so in the 1570s. Maidenhead and Wokingham; Evesham, Droitwich, and Tewkesbury; Stafford and Walsall followed suit in the 1580s. Knaresborough and Leeds in the 1590s; Ashford, Maidstone, and Dover in the 1600s; and Leonard Stanley and Painswick repeated this apparently imitative pattern in the 1620s. This could suggest intense rivalries between such neighbours of the sort which will be considered most appropriately in Chapters 4 and 6 below.

Secondly, when the great increase in halls broke upon the scene from the 1540s through the 1570s, it did so more in the southern, south central, east midlands, and East Anglian regions than in the south-west, the west midlands (at least until the 1580s) or the north. According to the typology of English farming regions worked out especially by Joan Thirsk, the four former areas are for the most part lowland zones of mixed husbandry or wood pasture: areas which had traditionally tended to be more tightly organized and closely ruled by manorial lords.[50] By contrast, gains in the 1590s seem more evenly distributed; the north and other largely upland, open pasture areas acquired as many halls even in that economically distressed decade as in the entire forty years beforehand, but none in the 1620s and only two (both in the 'near north' at that) in the 1630s. This may suggest factors implicit in the nature of particular agrarian regions which may be linked, directly or indirectly, with motivations for civic building.

If we consider the geographic patterns for all hall-acquiring towns throughout our period as a whole, Thirsk's model of agrarian zones continues to provoke speculation. If, for example, we categorize all the towns listed in the Census of Town Halls (see Appendix) according to their location by farming region, and if we allow for the fact that some towns lie in the interstices of different agricultural zones and are thus listed by halves, the following emerges. Thirsk's map of farming regions shows the largest proportion of land given over to upland, open pasture areas, followed closely by lowland, mixed agrarian areas, and more distantly by lowland, wood pasture areas. Our tabulation, however, shows by contrast 86.5 of our towns (or 48.9 per cent) to lie in mixed farming areas, 55 (or 31.05 per cent) in open pasture, and 35.5 (or 20.05 per cent) in wood pasture (the halves lying between two areas).

On the other hand, if our distribution of hall-acquiring towns differs from Thirsk's description of the disposition of agrarian regions, it conforms rather more closely to Alan Everitt's conclusions regarding the

[50] Thirsk, *The Agrarian History*, iv, ch. 1.

distribution of markets (and thus presumably towns) *per se* throughout the realm.[51] This may suggest that the distribution of town halls may merely be more closely related to the simple distribution of towns *per se*, and only at second hand (which is to say, somewhat less directly) to agricultural regions. There may prove to be locational correlations between hall-acquiring towns and administrative or political characteristics which conform to agricultural regions, but these remain to be demonstrated.

In considering the central question of why so many towns built or otherwise acquired halls in our period it will be helpful for several reasons to remember the magnitude of such actions in relation to the small size and relatively meagre resources of almost all the towns concerned. Apart from London—whose unique size, complexity, and character have ruled it out as a helpful part of this study of civic halls and English *towns* (as opposed to metropolises) and whose Guildhall, in any event, took shape well before our period[52]—there were but a handful of towns in our period with a population of over 10,000. The vast majority lay within the 800–1,500 range,[53] which was indeed extremely modest by European standards even of the sixteenth century.

One issue upon which this factor bears directly is the comparability of English towns and their halls to those on the Continent at the same time. Here we face difficulties of scale. Those continental cities which come most readily to our attention through published sources fall within a broad population range of between *c*.40,000 and 200,000 people. This same range would have been well beyond the size of any English town except London if, indeed, London had not already exceeded that range. Yet thirty-four continental cities have been established as falling within that range. Even when we extend the already considerable number of European cities by lowering the bottom of the range to 20,000 we find but one additional English example, Norwich, by 1600, compared with a total number on the Continent estimated as 121.[54] In the Netherlands, for example, there were seven urban centres with a population in excess of 40,000 in 1600, and an estimated 60 per cent of the total

---

[51] Everitt, 'The Marketing of Agricultural Produce', 468–75.

[52] On this subject see Caroline M. Barron, *The Medieval Guildhall of London* (1974). In making the point that London is different in kind, not just in scale, Brian Dietz has noted that 'metropolitan history is not urban history writ large'; Dietz, 'Overseas Trade and Metropolitan Growth' in A. L. Beier and R. Finlay (eds.), *London, 1500–1700, the Making of the Metropolis* (1986), 115.

[53] Clark and Slack, *Crisis and Order*, 4–6; John Patten, *English Towns, 1500–1700* (1978), ch. 3.

[54] P. Bairoch, 'Population urbaine et taille des villes en Europe de 1600 à 1970', *Démographie urbaine, XVe–XXe siècle* (Lyons, 1977), 41, as cited in Paul M. Hohenburg and Lynn Hollen Lees, *The Making of Urban Europe, 1000–1950* (Cambridge, Mass., 1985), 109, table 4.1; Clark and Slack, *English Towns in Transition*, 46: Patten, *English Towns*, ch. 3.

population lived in an urban area: at least three times most estimates for England.[55]

There were undoubtedly close physical similarities between English and continental town halls, and in the role which each played within their communities. Yet it is obvious that the scale, design, furnishing, and finance of reported continental examples will be of a different magnitude altogether from what would apply for their English counterparts.[56]

Taken on their own terms, enterprises like the purchase or construction of an English town hall in the period under discussion seem reasonably comparable in magnitude to such projects in our own time as the construction of a shopping mall in a medium-sized town, or of a civic centre or sports stadium in a small or medium-sized city. Not only are these reasonably comparable projects in terms of scale, but often similarly controversial both in their planning and their fulfilment. They undoubtedly provoked great and sometimes bitter debates in particular communities. They may reveal to us sundry interest groups and factional divisions of the sort which normally lie inconspicuously, and perhaps altogether inchoate, beneath the surface of local society. It seems entirely reasonable that an investigation of hall acquisition in the Early Modern period might well yield similar insights into local attitudes and concerns.

In addition, such an undertaking would obviously have had substantial financial implications for these relatively small communities, communities whose mechanisms for raising building funds were still largely *ad hoc* and uncertain. The examination of town halls might then contribute to our knowledge of 'public' finance in the towns of Early Modern England, and of the political considerations involved in such financial undertakings.

And what of the economic implications? At first glance our chronology of acquisition might suggest correlations between prosperity and civic building activity, but a closer examination, especially with reference to, for example, the 1550s or 1590s, may well show that this was not necessarily the case. We may want to consider, as Robert S. Lopez first suggested for

---

[55] Elizabeth de Bièvre, 'The Decoration of Town Halls in the United Provinces, a Study of Style and Iconography' (Courtauld Inst., London Univ. Ph.D. thesis 1986), 26, and Simon Schama, *The Embarrassment of Riches, Interpretation of Dutch Culture in the Golden Age* (New York, 1987); P. Corfield, 'Economic Growth and Change in Seventeenth Century English Towns', in C. Phythian-Adams *et al.* (eds.), *The Traditional Community Under Stress* (1977), 42; Patten, *English Towns*, 111–12.

[56] Cf. e.g. H. R. Hitchcock, *German Renaissance Architecture* (Princeton, NJ, 1981), 175–89; Bièvre, 'The Decoration of Town Halls'; Katharine Fremantle, *The Baroque Town Hall of Amsterdam* (Utrecht, 1959); Richard A. Goldthwaite, *The Building of Renaissance Florence, an Economic and Social History* (Baltimore, 1980); Gerald Strauss, *Nuremberg in the Sixteenth Century*, 2nd edn. (Bloomington, Ind., 1976), 23–4. Mark Girouard usefully points out many physical similarities between English halls and those at least of transalpine Europe, and emphasizes the common characteristic of civic dignity which lay behind their construction and symbolic importance; Mark Girouard, *Cities and People, a Social and Architectural History* (1985), 52–5.

some continental examples of a slightly earlier date, that non-economic factors may have made it important to have a town hall even at times of less than peak prosperity.[57]

As the town hall was first and foremost a place of government and administration, we will certainly want to ask if there are connections between the chronology of acquisition and trends in the development of civic governing institutions, and whether the needs of such institutions may sometimes even have outweighed financial considerations. Indeed, if we examine the development of spatial arrangement and use within the halls, and the furnishings which evolved in the period, these concerns about political and administrative developments will become all the more vivid. Such an investigation may help us to understand why and when crucial developments in civic government and administration took place, and how the building itself may have been prompted and shaped by such changes. And, following the model offered by Geertz and some of his fellow anthropologists, we may be able to ask how and why civic halls of this type came to serve both symbolically and literally as seats of civic government, and how ruling élites furnished and utilized their halls to enhance such connotations.

Finally, coming as most of them did on the heels of the Reformation and the associated dissolutions of ecclesiastical property, what would the role of the town hall have been in relation to the social and cultural needs of the community? Might it have replaced the guild chapel, the parish church, or even the open market-place as a focal point for social and civic life, somewhat as the shopping mall or civic centre has replaced the corner shop or the inn in our own time? Did it provide space for ritual and ceremony, so crucial to the social cohesion of the community, which had formerly been carried on in the market-place or in ecclesiastical structures? Did its availability and utilization invite new forms of social cohesion or add anything to a sense of civic identity or civic pride? These are all questions upon which a study of the town hall and its role of the life of the pre- and post-Reformation urban community must reflect.

Following these themes, Chapter 2 takes up the architectural development of the building genre itself. Here we are reminded that, as form follows function, we are dealing with physical structures designed to accommodate the affairs of townsfolk and their officials in a particular period. Though it may hold greater interest for architectural historians than others (and might be skipped altogether by the 'pure' historian in a hurry), this discussion identifies for all readers the town hall as a building type in its several forms. Employing the developmental explanation of the

[57] Robert S. Lopez, 'Hard Times and Investment in Culture', in *The Renaissance, a Symposium* (New York, 1953), 19–34.

late S. I. Rigold as a point of departure, it traces the structural evolution of common hall types and examines the question of style. This chapter seeks to establish a baseline of sorts from which we may subsequently observe structural developments resulting from the changing requirements of those who built.

The basic assumption of Chapter 3, which treats the financial implications of acquiring a town hall, is that the construction, purchase, or conversion of a town hall constituted one of the most extraordinary and expensive undertakings which could face an urban community throughout the period. That occasion provides us with a rare view of the financial mechanisms and strategies of such towns, stretched to their limits as they must often have been. We shall seek to explain how towns paid for their halls and see how that evidence informs us about the larger question of urban finance itself.

With Chapter 4 we move into the central thesis of the book: that the decision to construct, renovate, or convert a hall often came about not out of any particular desire for ostentation at a time of surplus building capital, or necessarily even at a time of particular prosperity, but rather out of the need to symbolize a particular administrative reality at a crucial stage of urban *political* rather than economic activity. Chapter 5 will examine how the ruling oligarchies which often came to the fore at this time utilized the town hall as both seat and symbol of their authority, to promote the deference and obedience upon which their position depended. Here, too, furnishings become important in the effort to create the aura of obedience essential to urban rule. Chapter 6 will explore the ways in which the use of the hall by various elements in the community, and the restrictions which ruling élites placed upon its use by others, served to make it an integral part of the secular, civic, and urban cultural traditions emerging in the wake of the Reformation.

2

Structure, Space, and Style

SOURCES

Before we proceed to the role of town halls in the English urban community, we must understand what such buildings looked like: their structural forms, spatial divisions, and characteristic styles. This is not as easy as it may appear, for slightly less than 25 per cent of those buildings built, converted, or substantially rebuilt between 1500 and 1640 still survive at least partially to the present day. (See the 'Census of Town Halls', Appendix.) A few of these have undergone thorough and faithful restoration and some, including Norwich and Burford, still actually host some forms of deliberative or judicial function. Others (for example, Leicester, Titchfield, Elstow, and Burford again) have been converted into museums which succeed in preserving and interpreting past appearances for modern observers. These few allow us to examine in detail the style, layout, and even furnishings which *may* be essentially original.

Yet most surviving halls have been altered repeatedly throughout their long history. Here the halls of Faversham, of which only the support structure remains from the Elizabethan original,[1] or the once magnificent hall of Leominster (see Plate 1)—sold at auction in 1855, dismantled, moved, filled in on the ground floor, and converted first to a dwelling and then to offices[2]—or that of St Albans, itself a Reformation conversion of the House of the Charnel Brotherhood but now both 'preserved' and disguised by the local W. H. Smith,[3] may be more typical.

For nearly all such survivals Sir Nikolaus Pevsner's 'Buildings of England' series provides at least cursory identification, and the files and published volumes of the Royal Commission on Historical Monuments take us even further. Yet we are still dealing here with the minority which may still be described rather than with that majority which fate and past improvement schemes have treated more harshly. To learn something of these, and thus of the whole corpus, we must employ a wide variety of sources.

[1] John Newman, *BoE, North East and East Kent* (Harmondsworth, 1969), 305.
[2] George Fyler Townshend, *The Town and Borough of Leominster* (Leominster, 1863), 327–8; Alec Clifton-Taylor, *The Pattern of English Building*, 2nd edn. (1972), 316.
[3] *VCH, Hertfordshire*, ii (1908), 471–2, 480, and n. 129. The modern version may be compared with the (undated) drawing collected by J. W. Jones in BL, Add. MS 32351, fo. 10r.

Many of these sources are archival and familiar to the trained historian. Deeds to property proximate to civic halls or even to halls themselves may yield descriptions, dates both for construction and major renovations, locational information, and contemporary labels for such buildings. A series of deeds describing the same property over a period of time provides a continuous record of change. Manorial rentals and surveys, especially those carried out by the Crown or the Duchy of Lancaster, or by the Interregnum governments just following our period,[4] are also useful for manorial towns, though such sources are less abundant in the lengthy (and in this regard ineffectively administered[5]) reign of Elizabeth, which is so crucial to the present study. Though these sources seldom provide visual evidence beyond an occasional rough map, they do indicate the location, monetary value, and even functional description of the town's hall. Court cases, in which deponents may provide descriptive references of considerable importance, are uncommon but very useful when they do turn up. Perhaps the most valuable written source remains the financial account, whether kept by the chamberlain, bailiff, mayor, or even church-warden. This provides to the diligent gleaner a great many small refer-ences to building repair and decoration, furnishings and other aspects of structural detail, occasionally to construction itself, and to the functional employment of buildings which have long since disappeared.

Yet the most helpful, if not by any means the most common, guide of all to the structural aspects of defunct halls remains not in verbal form at all, but in the sketch or drawing. These were sometimes done (typically to a ratio of one civic building to several hundred churches!) by travelling antiquaries, topographers, or artistic hobbyists of the eighteenth or nineteenth centuries. The mammoth Buckler collection in the British Library (a few fragments of which rest in the Bodleian as well), whose eighty or so volumes yielded up over a dozen carefully drawn civic halls of the 1500–1640 era sketched in the first half of the nineteenth century, is probably the largest such collection.[6] At their best, such drawings label the subject with caption and date, and sketch in adjacent buildings as well as the site itself. This can facilitate more certain identification, especially when it can be matched with archival descriptions, and it often provides a careful delineation of the structure in question. In some cases the combination of archival and visual evidence of this type provides a satisfyingly complete record of halls which either no longer exist or which have been substantially altered in the interim.

Though it shows the Buckler Drawings in an uncharacteristically

---

[4] Listed, for example, in PRO, *Lists of Rentals and Surveys* (Lists and Indexes, xxv, 1908).

[5] This observation is confirmed in D. L. Thomas, 'The Administration of Crown Lands in Lincolnshire under Elizabeth I' (London Univ. Ph.D. thesis 1979).

[6] The volumes relating, *inter alia*, to the period at hand include BL, Add. MSS 36356–97.

misleading light, the town and market hall of Hemel Hempstead provide an excellent example of how this combination of source materials may be employed. A 1651 survey of former Crown lands carried out by a commission of the Rump Parliament refers to a court baron and court leet being held in a court loft over a market house.[7] Another written source refers to a market house near the churchyard.[8] But the term 'market house', as we have seen, may have a variety of meanings, and these descriptions alone leave it unclear whether Hemel Hempstead had two market halls, one with a court leet and another near the churchyard, or a single hall which met both descriptions. Sure enough, on 24 May 1832, Buckler drew a market hall and shambles with a church tower in the near background, and drew the same building from another perspective in 1838. But, though he showed considerable detail of construction and use in both drawings, he left it uncertain if the townsmen employed the loft for anything but the storage of grain or other agricultural products.[9] The fortunate location of another, probably nineteenth-century, drawing of the same building, collected by J. W. Jones to accompany Clutterbuck's *History of Hertfordshire*, shows us that Buckler unaccountably focused on only one wing of the market hall. Another part, which he rendered only in rough outline, does indicate the clear probability of the court loft described in 1651, along with a wealth of other helpful details of construction, appearance, and spatial delineation.[10]

TYPES

Probably the most authoritative attempt to categorize the structural types of civic hall for the late medieval to Early Modern period has been made by the late S. E. Rigold, former Inspector of Ancient Monuments and a scholar whose acknowledged mastery of his subject must not be weighed by the mere volume of his publication. As far as Rigold was concerned, the English civic hall had by the fifteenth century fallen into two chief types. The first of these he called a 'mutation' of the late medieval house: 'a ground floor hall . . . with a storied chamber at each end' as typified by the guild-halls at Leicester, Coventry (St Mary's Hall), Lavenham, and Canterbury. The second and later class consisted of 'specialized derivatives of the early Medieval first floor hall', ranging from the Ipswich Guildhall and Great Yarmouth Tollhouse, with strong undercrofts and external staircases, to the intermediate (about mid-fifteenth century) form with an internal stair and divided ground floor (exemplified by Fordwich and Milton in Kent), and eventually to the 'typical English town

---

[7] BL, Harleian MS 427, fo. 70. I am indebted to Mr A. D. K. Hawkyard for this reference.
[8] *VCH, Hertfordshire*, ii. 218. [9] BL, Add. MS 36365, fos. 212, 213.
[10] BL, Add. MS 32350, fo. 5.

hall of the sixteenth to the eighteenth century . . . largely carried on
pillars but with internal staircases and a small store or lock-up below'. Of
this genre the Thaxted Guildhall, which he dated to the late fifteenth or
early sixteenth century, seemed to Rigold a particularly early and striking
example (see Plate 2).[11]

It must be said at once that the period of Rigold's interest began at an
earlier point than that with which this study is chiefly concerned, and also
that many of his fundamental views seem well supported by the evidence.
Both ground floor and first floor hall plans do indeed share an ancient
lineage: in structural terms post-1500 halls of both types were but middle
chapters in an already long story. There does seem to be a general
tendency for the civic hall to move from a single hall plan (though not
necessarily with additional chambers at either end) to a more complex
division of space and to more than one floor. And, certainly, the first-floor
hall above an open market space, as in Thaxted, did become the more
common type of town hall constructed in the sixteenth and seventeenth
centuries. Yet it is more difficult to accept the view that this familiar
structural type is a derivative of the earlier medieval first-floor hall (in
which the chambers or 'hall' part rested above ground level on a heavy and
very solid vaulting or undercroft) or that buildings of the Thaxted type
represent the link between the two. Difficult, too, is the effort to derive
Rigold's ground-floor hall from the late medieval dwelling-house.

Rigold presumably reached these conclusions at least in part because of
his primary grounding in architecture rather than local political or social
history, and because he seems to have been writing more for an architectural or archaeological readership. Thus in tracing the typology of civic
halls he focused more on form than on function. His very use of the
biological metaphor 'mutation'—always at the start a random event
unrelated to function—to describe the development of the ground-floor
hall from the medieval dwelling house suggests nothing less. He seems
not to have investigated the distinct possibility that, for reasons of its
functional utility, the combination town and market hall on pillars may
have emerged well before the Thaxted 'prototype', and may even have
coexisted with, rather than emerged from, the 'earlier' first-floor hall. Let
us deal with these questions of function and documentation in regard to
the building types in question to see if they lead to a more satisfactory
classification.

Both of Rigold's types extend well back in time, and both may predate
the development of varieties more familiar in the sixteenth century. But
other characteristics of these proposed types seem more important in the
present context, and also tend to blur the distinctions between them.

[11] S. E. Rigold, 'Two Types of Court Hall', *Archaeologia Cantiana*, 83 (1968), 1–22, esp. 1.

First, whether commissioned by landlords (lay, royal, or ecclesiastical) as court or moot halls or by guilds and fraternities as guild-halls, or even by early boroughs as town halls, Rigold's 'types' would appear to have been chosen because they best met the functional requirements placed upon them: secure and covered spaces suitable for meetings of relatively large numbers of people, capable of some defence, and worthy in size, style, and materials of their builders' dignity. Neither the 'ground floor hall' nor the 'first floor hall with undercroft' would have been particularly intended for marketing. Though a few held shops and many were located in or near the centre of town, most would not have offered trading facilities and virtually none would have done so as a prime objective. Thus the ground floor was walled up in both types and location on a spacious island site for ease of access in marketing, though often the most logical and available site for a public building, would of course have been less important. Indeed, such an exposed situation may have worked against the need for security and even secrecy which these buildings had to provide. Some such halls retained bits of courtyard (such as Leicester)[12] or even garden (as in Newent, Chipping Sodbury, and possibly Henley-in-Arden)[13]—all of which seem to have had carefully controlled access— but they frequently found themselves severely pressed for space by other buildings erected 'shoulder to shoulder' on the building line of the same street. Under these circumstances the characteristic vaults or under-crofts, or even expansion to the loft above, became essential. In extreme cases (for example Exeter[14] and possibly Barnstaple[15]) expansion took place even by extension out over part of the street itself.

When we look at the problem in this light, the functional distinctions made between the ground-floor hall and the first-floor hall with cellars become less significant. From the standpoint of both function and location, in fact, they appear less as two types than as versions of a single type: the closed ground floor, building-line sited edifice, constructed chiefly for purposes of administration or for other essentially non-commercial use. There seems ample reason to consider this as town hall type A, or the 'closed ground floor' type, whose members must at least to

<hr />

[12] This is still extant, but cf. N. A. Pegden, *Leicester Guildhall, a Short History and Guide* (Leicester, 1981), 1.

[13] Photocopy of the 1624 survey of the Manor of Newent, Gloucestershire; Gloucestershire RO, MSS D 2071/E11 and D 2071/L7 (1626). It is possible that the present hall garden at Henley-in-Arden may date to the erection of the building.

[14] Still standing, but cf. photograph in the frontispiece of H. Lloyd Parry, *The History of the Exeter Guildhall and the Life Within* (Exeter, 1936).

[15] C. Wills, *A Short Historical Sketch of the Town of Barnstaple* (Barnstaple, 1855); B. W. Oliver, 'The Long Bridge at Barnstaple', *Transactions of the Devonshire Association*, 78 (1946), 191; Buckler drawing, BL, Add. MS 36361, fo. 76.

begin with have been employed either as 'court halls', 'moot halls' or 'guild-halls' of either merchant or religious guilds (see Plate 3).

In clear contrast to type A halls we have the 'town hall carried on pillars' in which the ground floor remained open on at least three sides. Is this a mere derivative, or can we class it as a type of its own? These buildings, too, were first and most often constructed by manorial lords and merchant (if not usually religious) guilds, but always with at least one eye on the necessities of marketing. They were characteristically sited on islands in the central marketing area of the town (whether square, triangular, widened high street, or other configuration) and apart from any building line or adjacent structures. These sites were both maximally accessible and naturally 'public'. They afforded the greatest access for market-goers, the greatest available space for traders, and the greatest ease of surveillance for market authorities. Though encroachment sometimes faced these structures as well as any other, the press for space was rarely as serious, at least before the advent of vehicular traffic, as for type A.

Not only could market and town officials preside here directly over the marketing area—halls in Titchfield (see Plate 4) and Thaxted seem even to have had open first floor galleries for this purpose[16]—but the space in and around the ground level permitted room for marketing scales and beams, the town stocks, the rendering of verbal announcements and posted notices, the entertainment of players both resident and itinerant, and the casual but essential social intercourse of townsfolk. Few of these same activities could be performed as conveniently or well in and around the typical type A hall, locked in, as it was, to the regular street plan. Indeed this was of less concern to the ecclesiastical or manorial author-ities chiefly responsible for the construction of the ground-floor hall than to the townsmen themselves. It was to the élites of the town that the balance of responsibility for civic building shifted during the course of the sixteenth century.

In point of function and location, then, the pillared or open ground-floor hall seems a distinct type. And, just as the activity of marketing is by no means a mere derivative of other urban functions, so should we view this building type as a parallel rather than a derivative development: hence, we may label this distinct type as type B, the open ground floor, pillared hall (see Plates 1, 2, and 4). But what about the evidence for a sequential development from the closed to the open ground floor? How

[16] The restored Titchfield hall, now part of the Weald and Downland Open Air Museum, illustrates this very well. The view that the first floor front façade of the Thaxted hall was initially open has been put convincingly to me in correspondence by Mr James Boutwood, Assistant County Architect, and suggested in his paper 'Thaxted and its Guildhalls' presented to the Vernacular Architecture Group conference in 1984.

do we deal with Rigold's view that staircases moved from the exterior to the interior (as in Thaxted) as part of that transition? Finally, doesn't the observation that there seem to be fewer type A than type B halls being constructed in the sixteenth century and after also support an evolutionary thesis?

Here we must turn to whatever evidence may be found regarding the origins and development of these various types. As noted above, the type A town hall, whether a ground-floor hall or a hall raised over cellars or croft, may be traced far back into the medieval period. The Exeter Guildhall even predates those discussed by Rigold. It is said to have been standing in the year 1160, and there is no reason to believe that it was the first of its type at that time.[17] Yet while one may easily enough verify the origins of existing buildings, it is quite another matter to prove or disprove the origins of buildings which no longer stand. Type B halls, exposed on at least three sides to the weather and built on sites which became obstructive after the advent of vehicular traffic, have not survived as well, and it is doubtful that any exist today from before the fifteenth century.

But the Northampton Guildhall, extant from at least 1385 and possibly as far back as 1138, is considered originally to have had an open ground floor,[18] and there are archival references either to buildings described as 'market halls' or to halls said to have had marketing space below which date even to the thirteenth century. Professor Beresford assures us that 'in the more prosperous towns [of the thirteenth century] there were even market halls that also served as meeting places for the gild merchant and were probably built at the gild's expense or by seigneurial authorities', and this seems to have been a common continental pattern at the same time.[19] As noted in Chapter 1, Wallingford is said to have had such a hall in 1232.[20] Bedford rebuilt an even earlier hall in 1224 so as to provide marketing space of some sort below and a hall above.[21] Southampton's 'Tudor Merchant's Hall', standing by 1428, was initially pillared at least at the western end,[22] while market halls of unknown date in Hunger-

---

[17] Lloyd Parry, *Exeter Guildhall*, p. vii.

[18] *VCH, Northamptonshire*, iii (1930), 36–7 and John Williams, 'Northampton's Medieval Guildhalls', *Northamptonshire Past and Present*, 7 (1983–4), 5–9.

[19] M. Beresford, *New Towns of the Middle Ages* (1967), 177 and, on continental parallels, Mark Girouard, *Cities and People, a Social and Architectural History* (1985), 52–3.

[20] J. K. Hedges, *History of Wallingford*, 2 vols. (1881), ii. 263.

[21] J. Godber, *History of Bedfordshire 1066–1888* (Bedford, 1969), 54–5.

[22] This has been established by the City Archivist, Miss Sheila Thomson, and expressed by her in a typescript research report which has been made available to me through the generosity of Mr Adrian Rance, Curator of Southampton Museums, and at the initiative of Mr David W. Lloyd. I am indebted to all three for their help. In addition, this view of the original appearance of the Southampton hall, if not the dating, is confirmed by excavations carried out by K. W. White for the Southampton City Council. I am most indebted to Mr White for his communication on this.

ford,[23] and Guildford,[24] presumably pillared, were old enough to be considered ruinous by the sixteenth century. There are therefore very strong indications that type B town (as well as mere market) halls also went well back into the medieval period, far predating the Thaxted 'prototype'.

The theory of staircase evolution also pales before close scrutiny. Even if the Thaxted hall had an internal stair in its time—a time which can be pushed at least a half a century earlier than Rigold would date it[25]—we still find evidence of *external* stairs in such later halls as Wokingham (*c.*1585),[26] Macclesfield (*c.*1595),[27] Bromsgrove (late Elizabethan),[28] and Newent (late sixteenth or early seventeenth century).[29] In northern and western parts of the country external staircases were built well into the seventeenth century, as in Kirkham, Clitheroe, and Liverpool, and when English settlers in the New World wished to build a town hall in Boston, Massachusetts in 1657, they gave it an external stair.[30]

Finally, the observation that type A halls were less frequently constructed in the sixteenth and seventeenth centuries than type B halls may tell us less about some abstract evolution of architectural forms than about critical changes both in the relative importance of marketing and in the identity and requirements of those who built them. As we will have further opportunity to note below, the sixteenth century was characterized in this regard by a greater number of 'autonomous' town governments than by those still under strict manorial control, by an absence of religious guilds or fraternities after the Reformation, and at least arguably by a greater preoccupation with marketing and commerce after the revival of internal trade some time in mid-century. Any and all of these observations, and others besides, may help to account for this shift in preference toward type B halls.

In sum then, if we categorize halls by function and location, most of the

[23] G. Astill, *Historic Towns in Berkshire, an Archaeological Appraisal* (Berks. Archaeological Committee Publication no. 2, Reading, 1978), 30.

[24] E. R. Chamberlain, *Guildford, a Biography* (1970), 82–3.

[25] An archival reference shows 'le Guyldhall' in Thaxted to have been standing by a date between 1456 and 1459, and some have placed the hall's construction before 1400. I am again grateful to James Boutwood for his help regarding this edifice. Essex Co. RO, MS D/DMg M117.

[26] For dating of the building, see depositions in PRO, *Hewes and Michael* v. *Dawbney* (*c.*1598), E 134/Hil. 39 Eliz. no. 4; for the staircase, see BL, Add. MS 36356, fo. 215ᵛ, a Buckler drawing of 5 Sept. 1818 in which the building still had an external stair.

[27] Drawing in C. S. Davies (ed.), *A History of Macclesfield* (Manchester, 1968), frontispiece.

[28] W. G. Leadbetter, *The Story of Bromsgrove* (Bromsgrove, 1949), 86. My thanks to Mrs Jennifer A. Costigan, Deputy Director and Curator of the Avoncroft Museum of Buildings, for bringing this to my attention.

[29] N. Pevsner and D. Verey, *BoE, Gloucestershire*, 2 vols. (Harmondsworth, 1970), ii. 304.

[30] G. H. Tupling, 'Lancashire Markets in the Sixteenth and Seventeenth Centuries', *Transactions of the Lancashire and Cheshire Antiquarian Society*, 58 (1947 for 1945–6), 7–8; a drawing of the first Boston hall of 1657 is reprinted in Bernard Bailyn, *The New England Merchants of the Seventeenth Century* (Cambridge, Mass., 1955), opp. 130.

town halls extant between 1500 and 1640 fall into two distinct types: type A, typified by a closed ground floor, undercrofting, and (usually) a street-line site albeit in or near the town centre, usually constructed to serve as a 'moot hall', 'court hall', or 'guild-hall'; and type B, the hall raised on pillars on at least three sides, usually on an island site in the market-place, and devoted at least in part to marketing along with its other functions. The developmental relationship between the two, if indeed there is one, must be described as parallel rather than derivative. Further, neither emerged by any stretch of the imagination as mere 'mutants', but rather as designs deliberately chosen to meet the functional requirements of their builders.

  Of course it must also be said that some town halls conformed to neither of these models. One should not lightly dismiss Rigold's sugges-tion that the occasionally employed polygonal hall plan may indeed 'owe something to the covered "butter cross", with only a loft above it'.[31] This would reflect an entirely logical functional progression from, (1) the provision of simple marketing facilities around the simple cross shaft; (2) provision of an area under the covered 'butter cross'; and finally, (3) a desire for even more commodious, dry storage areas or secure space for market administration, or both. Perhaps this is why the Wymondham hall of 1617, which Rigold cites, remained a 'market cross' in local parlance long after its loft housed a tiny school room and was also probably used as a town meeting room. It has been suggested that an earlier structure, most likely a 'true cross' without hall space, occupied the same site.[32]

  Further suggestions of such a progression emanate from the West Country where basic crosses—simple but stout shafts mounted on pedestals and ending in cruciform or other finial forms—seem to have evolved to the canopied 'butter cross' structure (as at Nether Stowey,[33] Glastonbury,[34] and Shepton Mallett[35] in Somerset or Castle Combe and Malmesbury in Wiltshire[36]) and then to a 'canopy' adopted to serve as the floor of a small polygonal room or hall, as at Dunster[37] or, to move east and cite Rigold again, Sevenoaks.[38] Here we might have a variety of the type B hall in point of function, but with a somewhat different origin.

  A surprisingly small number of halls represent an apparent hybrid type, where some marketing space was initially included in the ground floor of a

  [31] Rigold, 'Two Types of Court Hall', 1–2.
  [32] Norfolk and Norwich RO, Wymondham Town Book, MS Neville 12.12.66/Q173B, fos. 113–17; Revd S. Martin-James, *Wymondham and its Abbey*, 7th edn. (Wymondham, 1953), 13; C. J. W. Messant, 'The Market Crosses of Norfolk', *East Anglia Magazine*, 2/1 (1936), 29.
  [33] Buckler drawing, 28 June 1936, BL, Add. MS 36383, fo. 249.
  [34] Buckler drawing, n.d., BL, Add. MS 36381, fo. 269.
  [35] Buckler drawing, 19 June 1833, BL, Add. MS 36383, fo. 161.
  [36] Buckler drawing, BL, Add. MS 36390, fo. 27; Leland, *Itinerary*, i. 132.
  [37] Buckler drawing, 28 June 1828, BL, Add. MS 36381, fo. 167.
  [38] Rigold, 'Two Types of Court Hall', 1–2.

more complex building with a meeting hall of some kind above, but where the upper storey was carried on much more than mere pillars. In Aldeburgh, for example, recent analysis shows that the ground floor of what is now (but was not originally) called the Moot Hall held six marketing stalls at one end of the ground floor and other, small but more conventional, rooms at the other with a large hall above.[39] (See Plate 5.) This seems also to have been the pattern at Elstow.[40]

This hybrid type should not be confused with those examples in which originally open ground-floor halls had their open marketing areas closed in by brick or stone at some later date, as at Much Wenlock or Bakewell (see Plate 6). These are of course type B halls in origin and, in these two examples, remained so in form throughout the period of our concern.[41]

A few halls, especially those converted from other uses, fit into no type at all. The Essex town of Maldon adopted a fifteenth-century defensive tower for use as a town hall after acquiring its charters of incorporation in 1554 and, in a slightly revised version, 1555.[42] Stamford built its hall upon a bridge in 1558,[43] and Cirencester persisted in using chambers built for the purpose in the porch of its parish church![44]

Even halls of the more conventional type lent themselves to a wide variety of functional and hence structural combinations beyond the essentials required by meetings, courts, and, in type B, marketing. Wymondham was not alone in using its hall space for a school room. Lock-ups and gaol cells were regular features. Leeds[45] and Uttoxeter[46] combined their halls with common ovens, and when an oven fire destroyed the latter hall, townsmen went ahead and built another hall-and-oven to replace it. To facilitate catering both to civic banquets and to the poor, kitchens were common. Bakewell's hall had a 'St John's Hospital'

[39] Excavations carried out by the restoration architect Michael Gooch of Norwich.

[40] DoE, Historical Monuments Register, 'Bedford Rural District' (Report 1913/11/A, Jan. 1960).

[41] The Wenlock hall seems best interpreted in the DoE Historical Monuments Register, Interim Report made by F. W. B. Charles of Worcester, 16 Feb. 1970; for Bakewell, see Pevsner, *BoE, Derbyshire*, 2nd edn. (1978), 75.

[42] DoE, 'List of Buildings, the Borough of Maldon' (1971), 23 and W. J. Petchey, 'The Borough of Maldon, Essex, 1500–1688' (Leicester Univ. Ph.D. thesis 1972), 6.

[43] William Marrat, *The History of Lincolnshire*, 3 vols. (Boston, 1814–16), ii. 321.

[44] K. J. Beecham, *History of Cirencester and the Roman City Corinium* (1887), 92, and Buckler drawing, 13 Sept. 1819, BL, Add. MS 36362, fo. 176. Hull's council alternated its meetings between its delapidated guild-hall and a council room in Trinity Church until a new hall could be constructed in 1633; Edward Gillett and Kenneth A. MacMahon, *A History of Hull* (Oxford, 1980), 107–8.

[45] Grady, 'Thesis', 375.

[46] The destruction by fire of the former hall, common oven, and bakehouse under the hall, are described in a Duchy of Lancaster survey of 39 Elizabeth, PRO, DL 44/551. The rebuilt Common Hall and 'Furnes or Common Bakehouse' are cited in the (?1658) survey attributed to Peter Lightfoot, Staffordshire RO, MS D 3891/8/1–2. See also PRO, DL 43/Bundle 8/41, a survey of 5 Charles I, describing the 'furnis or Comon Bakinge house wᵗʰ a Chambʳ where in the Court is kept'.

on the ground floor which may still be seen.[47] Painswick's hall had a 'blind house' at the same level,[48] and Dover's *may* have held a grain stock against hard times.[49] Several served for the celebration of feasts and weddings (for example Castle Combe)[50] and, more soberly, many had rooms set aside for armouries.[51] The letting of space for dwellings or for commercial premises was often financially essential and, as we will see below, the growing specialization of 'administrative and judicial space' itself deserves a story all its own. Most of these points will be taken up at length in later chapters.

SPACE AND FUNCTION

Now that we have worked out a classification of hall types and observed some of the ancillary functions served by these buildings, we may turn to some characteristic developments in their furnishing and use of space. Though it remains more appropriate to discuss some of the specialized developments in later chapters, it will be very helpful here to establish some basic patterns for halls of representative size and complexity against which we may measure subsequent changes.

Several factors seem to have contributed to this developmental process: the size of the community and its need for public buildings of this type; its fiscal resources at the time of such need; and the relative access afforded by town officials to their fellow townsmen. We must also consider the possibility that such space will have been shared with other authorities, either the manorial administration, guild authorities, or such superior judicial bodies as the assize courts or quarter sessions. A presentation of representative examples in approximate order of their structural complexity seems the most efficient means of demonstrating such patterns of development and also of presenting the common forms of interplay between function and space.

Perhaps the moot hall at Elstow in Bedfordshire, built at the very beginning of our period in a manorial community which hovered on the threshold between village and town, comes closest to the model of a

---

[47] Pevsner, *BoE, Derbyshire*, 75.

[48] *VCH, Gloucestershire*, xi (1976) 59. Blandford Forum had a similar facility in its 1593 hall, noted in the town's accounts for that building project, Dorset Co. RO, Blandford Forum MSS B5, fos. 12–14.

[49] Kent Archives Office, Maidstone, 'Dover Corporation Record Book, 1603–1673' (uncatalogued at time of consultation) fo. 10ʳ.

[50] G. Poulett Scrope, 'Abridgement of the History of the Manor and Ancient Borough of Castle Combe', *Wiltshire Archaeological and Natural History Magazine*, 2 (1855), 133–58, esp. 158.

[51] e.g. Barking, *VCH, Essex*, v (1966), 217–18; Cumbria RO, Kendal MS WMB/K21, fo. 14; and Barnstaple, North Devon Atheneum, MS 3972, nos. 118, 186. I am greatly indebted to the *REED* project in Toronto for affording me access to the Kendal and Barnstaple records on microfilm, and to Dr Audrey Douglas for steering me through the former.

single, undifferentiated town hall.[52] Most fortunately, the building has recently been restored to an early form. This is a two-storey structure, originally four ten-foot bays long and two bays wide, devoted to six market stalls on the ground floor and a stairwell with a simple ladder leading to the single chamber or 'hall' above. Here were held meetings of the manor court and pie powder courts, and whatever assemblies, formal or informal, were required by the inhabitants. Toward the end of the sixteenth century townsmen added a fifth bay on to the east end to house a new chimney-breast of brick, serving fireplaces which were then built on both floors to provide the building's first heating system. At the same time they fortified the original daub and wattle with brick nogging on the exterior, dug a small cellar under the fourth bay, and replaced the ladder with a proper staircase.

Slightly more elaborate, if smaller overall (23 ft. 8 in. × 31 ft.), was the hall at Fordwich, Kent, built without marketing space as one of two public halls in that small river port.[53] This seems roughly contemporary with the Elstow hall and it, too, has survived to the present. Though we cannot be certain if this arrangement represented the original use of space, a ground-floor storage room and gaol cell now underlie both a panelled council chamber, containing a jurat's bench and mayor's chair, and— interestingly—a small jury room of 8 ft. 3 in. × 7 ft. 9 in.

Also rather basic (if larger in size at 46 ft. × 20 ft. at ground level) was the c.1540 Aldeburgh Moot Hall, well maintained since its extensive restoration in the 1880s and undergoing a second complete restoration at the time of this writing. The single first-storey chamber remains un-differentiated and is still in use to the present (see Plate 5). The ground floor seems originally to have been divided into six small shops, in the manner of Elstow, while a gaol cell running the width of the building took up the south end. A chimney serving two hearths seems to have been present by the end of the sixteenth century and may have been part of the original plan.[54]

---

[52] DoE, Historical Monuments Register, 'Bedford Rural District' (Report 1913/11/A, Jan. 1960); Joyce Godber and T. W. Bagshawe, *Elstow Moot Hall* (Bedford, 1981), 5–13 and frontispiece photo; Bedford Co. RO MS X 435/1, a Grant of Markets and Fairs at Elstow, 1553.

[53] C. Eveleigh Woodruff, *A History of the Town and Port of Fordwich* [1895] (Canterbury, n.d.), 110–13. There was also another civic hall in Fordwich, eventually rebuilt in 1555, but this was known as the 'givealehouse' and is clearly a distinct edifice. Cf. Kent Co. Archives Office, Canterbury, MS U 4/Bundle 8/27. The present building is identified with an appropriate locational description in U 4/Bundle 18/8. Rigold dated at least the reconstruction of the building to the 1540s; Rigold, 'Two Types of Court Hall', 17–18.

[54] H. P. Clodd, *Aldeburgh, the History of an Ancient Borough* (Ipswich, 1959), frontispiece. The architectural analysis carried out for the Historical Monuments Commission dates the building to the sixteenth century and the charter of 1554 refers to the elections held 'in guilhalda': thus a construction date of the first half of the century. DoE, 'List of Special Buildings, District of Suffolk Coastal' (1974), 11; East Suffolk RO MS EE1/B1/3, 22 November 1554. My thanks to the restoration architect, Mr Michael Gooch, for his comments on the building.

Still another instructive example may be found in Much Wenlock, Shropshire, where a five-bay-long guild-hall was constructed in 1540 several feet away from but in line with an earlier gaol cell (see Plate 6). Originally, the hall had an open and paved marketing area below and a single, all-purpose chamber above. But as the town grew and its administrative functions became more complex, the need for more space became obvious. Thus in 1577 the building was extended up to and over the gaol cell. This increased the open marketing area below and created a second chamber, two-thirds the size of the first, on the upper storey. Still later in our period the distinction between the upper rooms became formalized with an extensive refurbishing. The newer room, known as the 'inner room' or 'court room', was designated for the judicial and other, more secretive, functions of local administration, while the original and larger room, alternatively called 'the election ['*thelecon*'] house' or council chamber, remained in use for council meetings and more public occasions. This essential division and extensive furnishings to match remain in force to the present.[55]

Fordwich, Much Wenlock, Aldeburgh, and Elstow thus represent early and undifferentiated examples of their respective types of town hall: Fordwich (type A) built solely for administrative purposes; Wenlock (type B), Elstow, and Aldeburgh (both hybrids) combining a concern for commerce with a 'hall' upstairs. Numerous other halls would match these in size range and relative simplicity.

Yet even in halls of modest size, these basic features could be considerably augmented. Despite our ignorance of its precise dimensions and layout, the Walsall hall, acquired from the Guild of St John at the Dissolution and substantially rebuilt thereafter, gives us a great deal to think about.[56] It included a first-floor parlour and chamber for council business, a second-floor court room and 'solar' or loft, a 'chequer room' or treasury, a buttery, and a kitchen, conjecturally on the enclosed ground floor. Let us look at several of these features not initially found in the simpler examples discussed above.

The parlour's initial function might more easily be inferred etymologically than by casual expectation. It was first a small room in which

---

[55] HMC 13, *Tenth Report*, pt. IV, p. 422, and Much Wenlock Bor. Archives, MS B3/1/1, pp. 144, 450, 537–8. Cf. also Interim Report by F. W. B. Charles as in n. 41 above.

[56] Walsall Bor. Archives, MS 277/251/2; PRO, Exchequer Deposition and Interrogatory of 8 Elizabeth, E 133/1/61; *VCH, Staffordshire*, xvii (Oxford, 1976), 218. In addition to this building, referred to in contemporary documents as the 'Town Hall' or 'Guildhall', the town demolished the old market cross at the top of the High Street and replaced it in 1589 with a shop and market called the High Cross House or, again, Market Cross, which was itself demolished in 1691. This is easily confused with the Town Hall, but apart from the town prison built into it, it was usually let out for private use rather than employed as a public building; Walsall Bor. Archives, MSS 276/133 and 277/119; *VCH, Staffordshire*, xvii. 218–19.

to converse and, in the present context, one in which town authorities could confer privately on official matters. As such a room had sometimes featured in medieval monastic or other ecclesiastical buildings it is possible that the same rooms in buildings like Walsall's hall had retained both name and function in the transition from ecclesiastical to civic use. There were clear parallels in aristocratic country houses at least by the early Tudor period, where private space came to be more greatly valued. Clearly town-hall parlours pre-date the Reformation.[57] We know that Canterbury had one by 1438 and Nottingham had one by 1486,[58] and these cannot have been isolated examples.

Still, it is easy to understand how the demand for such a room would grow with the increasing authority of the mayor and other senior officials in the sixteenth and seventeenth centuries. Especially in larger and more oligarchic communities the addition of parlours both within and outside town halls in these years seems well documented. Such additions not only meant an increase in dimensions, but also an upgrading of style and even of comfort, appropriate to the increasing dignity accorded the mayor in many sixteenth- and early seventeenth-century towns. We know, for example, that Coventry converted a dwelling-house to mayor's parlour in 1574 when there was presumably no room for such a facility in St Mary's Hall.[59] We will return again to this issue in Chapter 5 below.

In Leicester the original three-bay ground-floor hall of the mid-fourteenth century underwent expansion to five bays in the latter half of the fifteenth century, the addition of a second hall, at right angles to the first, c.1490–1500, and the conversion of this last area into the Mayor's Parlour in 1563: all additions following the growing requirements of town government. In 1637 the parlour grew again, at a total cost of £22. 14s. 3d.[60] (See Plate 7.)

Well preserved to the present, the oak panelling, lavish spread of windows along the east wall (looking on to the court and thus shielded from the public gaze on the street side), ornately carved and classical mantel over the fireplace, the almost regal mayor's chair (this given by the incumbent Richard Ince) and the size of the whole (approximately 20 ft. × 33 ft.), leave little doubt regarding the acquired importance of that office. The situation of the room in relation to the rest of the edifice is also significant: it is placed at right angles to the 'head' of the Great Hall itself,

[57] M. Howard, *The Early Tudor Country House, Architecture and Politics, 1490–1550* (1987), ch. 5; *OED, vide* 'parlour'.

[58] Rigold, 'Two Types of Court Hall', 3; W. H. Stevenson, *Records of the Borough of Nottingham*, (Nottingham, 1882–5), iii. 253, cited in *OED*, 'parlour'.

[59] *VCH, Warwickshire*, viii (1969), 144.

[60] T. H. Fosbrooke and S. H. Skillington, 'The Old Town Hall of Leicester', *Transactions of the Leicestershire Archaeological Society*, 13 (1923–4), 38–9, 71–2, and plates I–V; Pevsner, *BoE, Leicestershire and Rutland*, rev. by Elizabeth Williams and G. K. Brandwood (1984), 221–2.

so that the mayor could slip easily between his place of precedence over council meetings in the latter, through the inconspicuous connecting doorway to the former. Though the parlour may have been considered equally important in such towns, as for example Lostwithiel[61] or Walsall,[62] it was undoubtedly a more modest affair in those lesser communities.

The distinction made in the Walsall and even Much Wenlock halls between the council chamber and the court room may not have been absolutely necessary in purely functional terms. Yet here and elsewhere it indicates the growing distinction in governing structure between the two-chambered council, which had become common by the Tudor and Stuart period, and the sundry courts which were presided over by the mayor or similar official. In the manor court from which many town governments derived, both functions were carried on at once (albeit in the more primitive stages represented by such feudal jurisdiction) and in the same room.

Typically, furnishings came also to differ in the two rooms to suit the distinctive activities of each. The court room might (as we will see in Chapter 5) come to include a raised chair for the mayor as judge, eventually a judicial bar of some sort, and a bench or benches ('forms' in Much Wenlock) for the jury. Council chambers would require appropriate furnishings for the two councils common to most towns, and the relatively large numbers who sat on the councils themselves—usually twelve and twenty-four respectively, but sometimes twenty-four and forty-eight or some similar combination—as well as the clerks, recorder, serjeants at arms, and others increasingly attendant at such meetings, meant a room larger than most court chambers.

And, whereas the parlour seems most often to have adjoined the council chamber, the court room came often to have a jury room alongside, as in either the Leicester Guildhall or the combined assize and town hall at Barking, where jurors might deliberate in private.[63] If the layout of the existing hall made it difficult to add or partition off a jury room adjacent to the court chamber itself, it could be located elsewhere in the building. In Leighton Buzzard and Exeter this appears to have been above the moot hall chamber, where it was called the 'jury loft'.[64]

The existence of a 'chequer room' at Walsall reminds us of still another

[61] HMC 55, *Various Collections*, i (1901), 331: lease of 29 Sept. 1663, citing the Mayor's Parlour. This was not found in a search of the Lostwithiel Corporation Papers at the Cornwall Co. RO in June 1985.

[62] Cf. n. 56 above.

[63] A. W. Clapham, 'The Court House or "Old Town Hall" at Barking', *Transactions of the Essex Archaeological Society*, NS 12 (1913), 295–8. The provision of space in the town hall for juries has been treated at greater length in R. Tittler, 'The Sequestration of Juries in Early Modern England', *Historical Research*, 61/146 (1988), 301–5.

[64] Bedfordshire Co. RO, MS KK319 (lease of the jury loft); Lloyd Parry, *Exeter Guildhall*, 8.

distinct and ancient hall function. Town halls served as places where accounts were rendered and assets kept, both of which were essential for local administration and social concord. We have already noted how one root of the word 'guild-hall' refers to this pecuniary concern in relation to the common fund of many communities, and how 'booth hall' and 'tolsey', both alluding to tolls, refer to similar concerns.[65] And, again, the word 'hall' itself becomes virtually anthropomorphized in common usage, whereby accounts were rendered not only 'in' but also 'to' the hall. This might apply whether or not a separate room for such activities existed as, in Walsall, it seems to have done. In Droitwich the whole building seems to have been known as the 'Chequer House',[66] though the Walsall pattern (repeated at Abingdon, for instance[67]) of assigning one room for such a purpose more frequently prevailed.

Of all the rooms in the Walsall hall the kitchen may at first seem the most incongruous, but when one considers the importance of feasts and banquets in urban ceremonial its role becomes obvious. As with the great houses of the aristocracy in the same era, the hall kitchen would have been on or even below the ground floor (partly to minimize the hazard of fire) and connected by stairs or passageway to the rooms in which its servings would be consumed.[68] Kitchens could also be employed when halls were also given over to private celebrations, as was the case in Liverpool,[69] or they may have been used as in Bury St Edmunds, at least in the early seventeenth century, to bake bread for the poor in times of hardship.[70]

Despite what sounds like a highly specialized division of space in the Walsall hall, we do not find here evidence of several other uses which were common, if not essential, to towns of this era: no armoury, no schoolroom, no particular storage space, and, especially surprising, no gaol cell or prison. While we know that Walsall kept a prison in a building known as the High Cross House from 1589, and possibly in earlier buildings on the same site before that,[71] such facilities were extremely common in town halls of all sizes, from modest communities like Ashford, Bridport, Alfreton, Fordwich, Titchfield, and Much Wenlock[72] at one

---

[65] See above, Ch. 1.   [66] *VCH, Worcestershire*, iii (1913), 80.

[67] Berkshire Co. RO, MS D/EP7/83, fo. 74d, a payment for benches 'about the chequer'.

[68] Margaret Wood traces the movement of the kitchen in great houses and other large buildings from an external, detached, position to an internal cellar or ground floor location as a development of the fifteenth century and after, Margaret Wood, *The English Mediaeval House* (1965), 247–55.

[69] J. A. Twemlow (ed.), *Liverpool Town Books*, ii (Liverpool, 1935), 10, 72 n. 2, 74–5, 145–6.

[70] M. Statham, 'The Guildhall, Bury St Edmunds', *Proceedings of the Suffolk Institute of Archaeology*, 31 (1970), 117–57, esp. 127–8.

[71] Cf. n. 56 above.

[72] W. R. Briscall, 'The Ashford Cage', *Archaeologia Cantiana*, 101 (1985 for 1984), 57–68; Dorset Co. RO, MS B3/M2, fo. 1; W. H. Stevenson, 'The Old Court House at Alfreton', *Journal of the Derbyshire Archaeological and Natural History Society*, 38 (1916), 127–30; Woodruff, *History of Fordwich*, 112–13; the Titchfield and Much Wenlock cells are still visible.

end of the urban spectrum to county towns and provincial centres such as
Reading and Hertford near the other.[73]

Of course not all facilities were the same from place to place, and a
distinction should be made between the single-cell 'cage' or 'lock-up' of
most market-town halls and the prison of the larger centres, especially
those, like Reading and Hertford, with sessions or assizes as well as
borough courts. Though terminology may not be an accurate guide in this
case, the first group of labels refers to small and largely temporary holding
areas, which were probably more closely connected in function and
location to the business of the market. This is certainly reflected in
surviving descriptions. The 'lock-up under the stairs' at Stroud,[74] the
cells which may still be seen in the Fordwich, Much Wenlock, or
Titchfield halls, or the 'cage' at Barking,[75] are places of detention from
which felons were taken for trial or for punishment in larger facilities
elsewhere.

The term 'prison' refers more clearly to a place designed for more
lengthy incarceration, as was its apparent synonym, 'dungeon', employed,
for example, in Louth and Kendal[76] or such purely local usages as 'the
grate' at Exeter. Some of these facilities could obviously hold large
numbers of inmates, for in Southwark an entire tenement,[77] in Reading
the main body of a former church,[78] and in Boston a hall chamber and
entire kitchen[79] were converted for use as prisons during the period.
'Houses of correction', a still more advanced facility, came into use by
statute in the late sixteenth and early seventeenth centuries. More will be
said of these structures in Chapter 5 below.

Perhaps it is ironic that the halls in the largest and most important
towns were least likely to include room for prisons, except for the
temporary cell proximate to the court chamber. The reason must be that
the greater need for such facilities in these communities warranted larger
space than the hall could provide. In Exeter, for example, cells were added
at one time or another in at least three different parts of the Guildhall until
such time, in the early seventeenth century, when a separate facility had to
be built to take the place of the rest. Except for four temporary cells which
remained outside the court room itself, all such areas were removed at

[73] Astill, *Historic Towns in Berkshire*, 78; BL, Add. MS 32350, fos. 24ᵛ, 25; the hall of *c.* 1610 was
splendidly drawn by Buckler in the early 19th c. and the ground floor area on the right-hand wing of
the building may well have housed this prison; BL, Add. MS 32350, fo. 43.
[74] P. H. Fisher, *Notes and Recollections of Stroud, Gloucestershire* [1871, 1891] (1989), 64.
[75] Clapham, 'The Court House . . . at Barking', 295–8.
[76] J. E. Swaby, *A History of Louth* (1951), 161; Cumbria RO, Kendal, MS WMB/κ8, fos.
16–17ʳ *et passim*.   [77] D. J. Johnson, *Southwark and the City* (Oxford, 1969), 130–1.
[78] Astill, *Historic Towns in Berkshire*, 78.
[79] Bailey, *Minutes of Boston*, i. 9–11 and M. R. Lambert and R. Walker, *Boston, Tattershall and
Croyland* (Oxford, 1930), 117.

that time.[80] In addition, these greater towns were more likely to be walled, and thus to have available prison space, suitably fortified, in their stone gates. In such cases, of which Oxford's Bocardo was typical, it was highly desirable to keep the noisome air of the cells appropriately distant from the more dignified citizens who more commonly frequented the civic hall itself. Two gates were employed as prisons in the City of York—Monk Bar and Fishergate Bar—along with prison facilities in the former chapel of St George, the lower storey of St Anthony's Hall, and several other prisons maintained by other jurisdictions.[81]

With the reference to York we leave the paradigms presented by towns of Walsall's size and arrive at that select group of England's largest urban centres, except London, in the period. York, Bristol, and Norwich, the three 'miniature Londons' of the north, west, and east respectively, along with Exeter and Newcastle, served as the provincial capitals of England. Having grown in size, independence, and political complexity so relatively early, these would have had civic halls for some considerable time. Especially with the greater availability of appropriate structures following the Reformation, some of them distributed key civic functions amongst several buildings.

York exemplifies this well. Leaving aside all those authorities which coexisted with the city administration itself—the Archdiocese, the King's Council in the North, and the High Sheriff, a distinct official from the two city sheriffs—even city administrative functions were scattered under several roofs. The City Corporation might meet either in the council chamber on Ouse Bridge or in the mid-fifteenth century common hall off Coney Street, where the commons also met. In the absence of suitable space in public buildings or an official mayor's residence until the eighteenth century, much official business simply took place at the private residences of the mayor or other high public officials. Needless to say, the markets in so large a community had long been separate from the administrative and judicial functions of these other buildings. Ceremonial activities too, after the Reformation, extended to the several surviving and commodious guild-halls as well as to the council chamber or common hall.[82]

Other great centres exhibited somewhat more consolidation of space than this. Newcastle's 'town court', used both as a guild-hall and common council room, dated chiefly from the reign of Henry VI, but was pulled down and rebuilt in 1658.[83] Bristol's guild-hall dated from the fourteenth

[80] Lloyd Parry, *Exeter Guildhall*, 4, 13, 70–1, 78, 79.
[81] For the suggestion regarding gatehouse prisons, I am indebted to Dr Stephen Porter. D. M. Palliser, *Tudor York* (Oxford, 1979), 25, 65, 276.
[82] Ibid. 25.
[83] John Bourne, *The History of Newcastle-upon-Tyne* (Newcastle, 1736), 124–5.

century, but the town built a council house and tolsey in 1551 which largely superseded the older building as the chief civic hall.[84] Norwich, too, has been included on the list of halls deriving from our period because of a major renovation: the entire east wing of the fifteenth-century hall was rebuilt after the collapse of the original chamber in 1511.[85]

Though these examples are instructive of civic buildings in the largest of England's provincial urban communities, by far the best example derives from the Exeter Guildhall, parts of which, as has been noted, had stood in the year 1160. This edifice finds a place on our list of post-1500 halls because of the addition in the 1590s of the entire forefront of the building which, extending out over the footpath of the High Street, gives the whole its distinctive character today. This followed other substantial renovations or additions in 1330, 1466, and 1484, but is itself the last substantial modification until our own time.[86]

Though at one point or another in its long history the Exeter Guildhall served about as many functions as a civic hall could, it will be most helpful to try to reconstruct its spatial divisions and their functions as they were in the sixteenth century. The chief pre-Tudor features were the cellar under the hall, used as a dungeon, a 'hall' or 'guild-hall' on the ground floor back, in which most courts were held, and the great chamber in the ground floor front used for meetings of the council and general administration. This latter room also held several locked chests for the storage of armour, muniments, and plate. The first floor included the Chapel of St George, built in 1484–5 and employed in part for the rich pre-Reformation religious rituals which were so integral to civic pageantry at this time. Elsewhere in the building lay the smaller court room for the mayor's court (called the Provost's Court), converted to a prison for women in 1521, a pillory and whipping post, a latrine and cesspool (among the first such amenities recorded in any town), a serjeant's room and two chambers over the guild-hall simply known as the 'high' and 'middle' chambers. On the exterior lay the remains of shops which once lined the south, east, and west walls of the structure, and the guild-hall garden, apparently on the side.[87]

Apart from the normal repairs and redecoration, and the expansion of prison cells in 1521, 1557, and 1576, the chief additions in our period date from the latter half of Elizabeth's reign. These include the redesign of the court hall in the rear of the first floor, the conversion of the 'high'

[84] E. Ralph (ed.), *Guide to the Bristol Archives Office* (Bristol, 1971), p. ix.
[85] Pevsner, *BoE, North-east Norfolk and Norwich* (1962), 259.
[86] Lloyd Parry, *Exeter Guildhall*, 1–3 et passim.
[87] Ibid., chs. 1 and 2.

and 'middle' chambers on the first floor to house extensive muniments, and the 1592–4 reconstruction of the entire front at a cost of nearly £800 spread out over four years:[88] almost four times what it cost to build the entire town hall of Blandford Forum in Dorset at exactly the same time.[89] This vast renovation included the addition of the mayor's parlour, the reconstruction of the greater chamber, and the extension of the distinctive porch to its present position. In size, spatial complexity, grandeur, and cost, the Exeter Guildhall is therefore right at the opposite end of the spectrum from the Elstow, Fordwich, and Aldeburgh halls.

STYLE

Exeter's Guildhall also excels in respect to its style. Taken together, the Elizabethan façade and porch are one of the very few examples of Renaissance neo-classicism in English civic halls prior to the mid-seventeenth century. All but a handful of contemporary halls, even those which would be built anew in the next half century, remained by contrast either predominantly 'vernacular' or quasi-'polite' in a traditionally English Gothic mode.[90]

So far as surviving evidence warrants, it appears that nearly all civic halls built before the mid-sixteenth century, and at least the majority built for a long while thereafter, fit chiefly within the bounds of regional and traditional building. They exhibit an emphasis on utility rather than on aesthetic considerations, they reflect practical rather than theoretic training on the part of their designers, and they bear strong resemblances in both materials and design to other vernacular buildings in their surrounding areas.

From roughly the early Elizabethan period, however, and in those towns where resources matched civic pride and sophistication, we find that this predominance of the regional and traditional is sometimes gently modified by the appearance both of Gothic variations and in a few cases even by flirtation, as at Exeter, with Renaissance neo-classicism or what Maurice Howard has usefully labelled 'the Anticke'. In this regard the design of civil halls followed trends which have been observed in the construction of royal buildings and in the great houses of the landed élite.

[88] Parry computes a total of £782; ibid. 72–7.

[89] Total cost of £198. 11s. 'over and above the helps of timber and carriages given', Dorset Co. RO, Blandford Forum Chamberlains' Accounts, 1564–1750 (uncatalogued), fo. 1.

[90] See esp. the definition of and introduction to the subject provided in R. W. Brunskill, *Illustrated Handbook of Vernacular Architecture* (1971, 1978) and the same author's *Traditional Buildings of Britain, an Introduction to Vernacular Architecture* (1981).

Here a brief employment of shallowly understood Vitruvian principles emanating from the circle of the Duke of Somerset (including, outside Somerset's own family, Thomas Smith, William Cecil, Nicholas Bacon, and other aspiring 'new men' of the day) appeared in the 1550s and 1560s; it gave way barely two decades later to a renewed (and retrogressive) interest in aspects of the English Gothic: the style to which most of the great houses of the later Elizabethan and early Jacobeans made the most explicit reference.[91]

Yet when we discuss the stylistic relationship of civic to private building, we must emphasize the word 'followed'. At its best, a more refined vocabulary in civic halls resulted from the employment of one of a limited number of 'designers' cognizant—through travel, books, or observation of English or even some foreign models—with buildings that transcended the regional and traditional. These figures had gained entrance to the service, if not quite the social milieu, of the great private patrons of building. To that service they brought with them the experience and reputation of acknowledged master craftsmen, often being referred to as 'masters' in that regard, and they gained even greater theoretic knowledge as well as notoriety from working for great magnates who travelled, read, and imitated to an even greater extent.[92] Not surprisingly, for an age typified by a greater expansion in building activities at all levels, these men were in short supply, commanded handsome rewards, and undoubtedly had all the work they could handle almost all of the time. However much groups of townsmen might have wished to build halls worthy of new-found civic pride, a most powerful motive, it remained difficult to compete for the services of, for example, the Smythsons or the Thorpes.[93]

Still, some of the more affluent towns managed to secure the services of men who, if not yet quite 'architects' in the full modern sense of the term, had certainly achieved considerable reputations as 'polite' designers. The contributions of the master mason Walter Hancock (d. 1599), who served as principle mason at Condover Hall in his home county of Shropshire,

---

[91] Howard, *Early Tudor Country House*, ch. 6; Mark Girouard, 'Elizabethan Architecture and the Gothic Tradition', *Architectural History*, 6 (1963), 23–40; Girouard, *Robert Smythson and the Elizabethan Country House* (New Haven, Conn., 1983), 28–39. In so doing, English civic builders also remained aloof from the more sophisticated stylistic tendencies of continental contemporaries.

[92] Airs, *Buildings of Britain, Tudor and Jacobean*, 22–4; Malcolm Airs, 'Some Social and Economic Aspects of Country House Building in England' (Oxford Univ. D.Phil. thesis 1972), 25–6; Howard, *Early Tudor Country House*, ch. 6.

[93] W. G. Hoskins, 'The Rebuilding of Rural England, 1570–1640', *P and P* 4 (1953); Douglas Knoop and G. P. Jones, *The Mediaeval Mason, an Economic History of English Stone Building in the Later Middle Ages and Early Modern Times*, 3rd edn. (Manchester, 1967), 83–4; Airs, 'Aspects of Country House Building', 91–6; Girouard, *Robert Smythson, passim*.

designed the 1596 market hall at Shrewsbury (though not precisely a true
'town hall') at the suggestion of his sometime employer Sir Francis
Newport, and probably shared responsibility on the Stafford hall two
years later, exemplifies this well.[94]

Other known practitioners of more polite,' if not necessarily neo-
classical, style in civic halls of this era include Lawrence Shipway, the
chief designer—possibly with Hancock—of the 1598 Stafford hall, the
Elizabethan Catholic Sir Thomas Tresham and his master mason
William Grumbald, who designed the market hall at Rothwell, Northamptonshire, along with numerous private buildings, and the remarkable
figure of John Abel, deceased at the age of 97 in 1674, who designed the
halls at Kington and Leominster in his home shire of Hereford among his
sundry other accomplishments.

Leaving aside Shipway, of whom little has come to light,[95] Tresham,
Grumbald, and Abel represent important points in the spectrum of
experience. Tresham exemplifies for us the gentleman amateur, precedented to some extent by the Somerset circle or the closely related Sir
Thomas Gresham, but preceding in turn a greater tradition of architectural endeavour which became a frequent aristocratic pastime in years to
come. Tresham travelled widely abroad, collected one of the earliest
architectural libraries in England, and designed, with Grumbald, the
Rothwell Hall according to at least some neo-classical principles. His
employee-associate in this seems to have come from the more practical
and traditional world of building craftsmanship, and undoubtedly provided the voice of experience.[96] Abel began as a carpenter and mason,
and is known to have done some of the actual construction on buildings of
his own design and no doubt on other buildings as well. By the same
token, his buildings still retain the essential timber-framed construction,
with daub and wattle walls, which is so characteristic of traditional
buildings over many parts of England. The use of more polite elements
remained more at the level of a flirtation than any more profound
commitment, and consisted in the main of Ionic or even Corinthian

[94] Pevsner, *BoE, Shropshire* (Harmondsworth, 1958), 266; HMC, 13, *Tenth Report*, App., pt. IV, pp.
423–4 and HMC, *Fifteenth Report*, App., pt. X, p. 60; Shropshire RO, MS 3365/2621 (Francis
Newport to the Bailiffs of Shrewsbury, 11 Nov. 1595); and William Salt Library, MS D(W)1721/1/4,
fo. 179.
[95] William Salt Library, Building Accounts of the Staffordshire Shire Hall, MS D(W)1721/1/4;
VCH, Staffordshire, vi. 201–2.
[96] Sir John Summerson, *Architecture in Britain, 1530–1830*, 3rd edn. (1958), 38–9; Pevsner *BoE,
Northamptonshire*, 2nd edn. rev. B. Cherry (1973), 393, 397–8 and plate 78. Tresham's library
included such continental writers on the subject as Alberti, Vignola, Bullant, Cataneo, Labacco, de
L'Orme, Palladio, Serlio, and de Vries, as well as the early English architectural writer John Shute;
Girouard, *Robert Smythson*, 15.

columns and capitals supporting the still largely traditional hall above.[97]

Yet most towns then constructing halls from scratch were smaller, and rarely so fortunate as to be able to employ the likes of these few. Here vernacular elements continued to prevail, with the gradual absorption of a Gothic vocabulary which some might even consider to have become an unconscious part of English vernacular itself. These traditions may be seen in regard not only to basic design, in which local craftsmen of far humbler standing would have been employed (such as the wheelwright Richard Carpenter of Leonard Stanley, Gloucestershire,[98] 'Good Master Barnabe' by the borough of Wantage,[99] or the bricklayer John Catlyn by Hull),[100] but to other elements of building as well.

Ornamentation, for example, was not common. Save for such rarities as the mayor's chair and parlour fireplace at the very end of our period at Leicester (see Plate 7), its use seems far more didactic than aesthetic or frivolous in intent. There is nothing in the civic building of this period even remotely resembling the eccentric and clever 'delights' or 'devices' which one commonly finds in private aristocratic houses or, for that matter, in the highly polished and ornamented styles of many contemporary halls on the Continent.[101] Thus, for example, the Leominster Guildhall bore inscriptions, but only of a decidedly moral and exhortatory tone,[102] and Wymondham's small 'Market Cross' bore the homely decorative device of wooden spoons to commemorate pride in a local craft.[103]

The question of building materials further supports the emphasis on local and traditional forms in the civic halls in this period, and here one may learn as much from surviving building accounts as from observation of surviving structures. Again with very few exceptions, the materials employed in these edifices are locally derived and almost entirely similar to materials employed in more common and familiar building types. The chief exceptions to this derive from port towns, where we do sometimes

---

[97] *DNB*, vide Abel, John; H. M. Colvin, *Biographical Dictionary of British Architects, 1600–1840* (1978) 43; Colvin, 'The Restoration of Abbey Dore Church in 1633–1634', *Transactions of the Woolhope Naturalists' Field Club*, 32 (1948), 235–7. See also the excellent drawings of Abel's known and suspected buildings in John Clayton, *A Collection of the Ancient Timbered Edifices of England* (1846), unpag.

[98] Revd Charles Swynnerton, 'Stanley St Leonards', *Transactions of the Bristol and Gloucestershire Archaeological Society*, 44 (1922), 256–7, citing from an indenture of 19 June 1619 in the Stanley St Leonards Estate Muniments.

[99] *VCH, Berkshire*, iv (1924), 320.

[100] Gillett and MacMahon, *History of Hull*, 108.

[101] See esp. Girouard, *Robert Smythson*, 18–28. For continental examples, see Ch. 1, nn. 55, 56 above.

[102] Townshend, *Town and Borough of Leominster*, 329.

[103] Messant, 'Market Crosses of Norfolk', 29.

find certain heavy materials being shipped substantial distances or perhaps salvaged from dumped ballast.[104] Though country houses also
tended to use local materials, supplies were also sometimes imported
from considerable distances even in more modest houses,[105] while the
appearance of carved stone, ashlar facings, elegant plaster work, or other
specialized materials common in such buildings was much less frequent
in civic halls. This tended to apply, for that matter, more or less in an
inverse proportion to the size of the town.

An excellent example of this more typical, chiefly vernacular, sort of
building—and of the archival sources one must employ in the quest—
may be drawn from the construction accounts of the Blandford Forum
Town Hall of 1593: a structure erected to replace the 'Old Yeld Hall'
which may have been partially destroyed by fire in 1579. Unfortunately
for the prospect of a purely visual assessment, the 1593 hall itself fell
victim to a later fire in this peculiarly inflammable town, and thus we
can only reconstruct its appearance conjecturally with the aid of the
accounts.[106]

The emerging impression is of a fairly large, undoubtedly rectangular,
two-storey edifice topped by a gabled loft. Though we cannot completely
rule out an open ground floor, as was common to many buildings of this
type, reference to 'lower' and 'upper' halls suggests a structure which can
have had little open space on the ground level. This was, therefore, most
likely a type A hall. Further division of enclosed space is suggested by
reference to a kitchen, probably on the ground floor, and a small 'blind
house' likely to have been on the same level for ease of access. The upper
hall would thus have been left more literally as a hall in the sense of a
single large room for the conduct of public business: assembly meetings,
judicial proceedings, banquets and ceremonies, and other social functions as well. The loft may have been used for storage or even let for
commercial use, though no rental receipts survive in the accounts.

Except for the importation of blue slates from Devon or Cornwall,
readily enough brought through the port of Melcombe Regis, and
hillingstones (that is, roofing stones) of unknown origin carted from
Poole, construction materials derived from a radius of no more than
twenty miles. Reference to materials in the accounts and familiarity with
buildings of the same area suggest timber framing (probably oak, though
for stairs and floors they may have done with elm), and lath and plaster

    104 This observation is based on extensive examination of Port Books for Poole, Weymouth, Lyme
Regis, Southampton, and Plymouth, listed generally in the PRO as class E 190, in which such
shipments are recorded. Cf. also Edwin Welch (ed.), *Plymouth Building Accounts* . . . , Devon and
Cornwall Record Society, NS 12 (1967), pp. xiii–xiv.
    105 Airs, 'Aspects of Country House Building', 137–43.
    106 This and the following paragraphs are based on Dorset RO, Blandford Forum Chamberlains'
Accounts, 1564–1750, fos. 12–14.

filling, along with the slate (unless this was employed for flooring) or hillingstone roofing. The gables and at least some other exterior walls bore a total of fifteen casement windows, making for a large building. Save for such finishing touches as a 'fair lantern' for the lower hall, paving around the exterior, and the completion of lead gutters—these following only after the townsmen had replenished their coffers three years later—construction seems to have begun early in 1593 and been completed by autumn of the same year.

Names of most of the craftsmen (if not necessarily their crafts) and workers are also recorded, and there are a great many more hands at work than one would find in a construction of a more modern era. No fewer than twenty-three men are named, plus eight suppliers of materials, two carters, and sundry 'carpenters', 'workers', 'boys', and the like. Most names appear only once or twice, but there are repeated payments to Thomas Addams (especially early in the accounts: he probably erected the timber framing of the whole at the outset) and the mason Thomas Hellier. The very number of individual payees suggests that a number of contractors had been employed for specific tasks, rather than having a single contractor responsible for the whole.

True to form but most regrettably, no 'plats', plans, contracts, or similarly descriptive documents have survived for the Blandford hall, though they may well have existed, and there is certainly no indication that the design of the whole emanated from a single mind. It is entirely possible that the work began only with a general idea of the final appearance. Hellier, most handsomely and frequently remunerated of all with twenty-three separate payments, is a good bet to have been the master mason, and to have overseen the design of the whole as much as anyone. Yet as there are more total payments for carpentry work and for such supplies as timber, laths, and nails, the master carpenter, probably Addams, cannot be ruled out as a significant force in this regard. It should also be noted that the townsmen engaged in a common practice by appointing one of their own number—John Pitt, frequent mayor, ancestor of two future prime ministers, and apparently the wealthiest citizen—to act effectively as 'clerk of the works', overseeing financial management and much of the progress of the construction itself. Pitt, too, undoubtedly conveyed demands on the design process. In these respects, then, the Blandford hall, of which more will be said in the next chapter, exemplifies contemporary practice in constructing buildings of nondescript—if not necessarily unpleasing—appearance.

Just as Rigold saw the early town hall from the perspective of the medieval baronial hall, the thrust of current scholarship on Tudor and Stuart building leads us to consider town halls from the viewpoint of the great country house. Yet the two building types obviously differed in purpose and any parallels between them are far from exact. Those responsible for civic building were constrained in their planning by factors which, if not entirely distinct, applied to the civic context to a much greater extent than to the private. These factors have a great deal to do with the evident lag in style between the great country houses and sometimes royal buildings, which undoubtedly did set stylistic trends, and the civic buildings of the day, which most certainly did not.

Though a fuller treatment of the subject will be offered below,[107] suffice it to say that the first of these constraints was financial. The more one learns of the fragile financial resources of the early modern town, the more apparent become the financial limitations on the construction of new buildings. Though the great private builders of the day easily spent four and five figure sums on their buildings,[108] no expenditure on a single civic building in this era has come to light for anywhere near a thousand pounds. The great landowners often accumulated debts expressed in even five figure sums, and did so with what strikes us to day as remarkable impunity.[109] Their civic counterparts as building patrons, though, under- took even modest debts only at the risk of extending exactions on fellow townsmen and, as at Poole and other towns, thereby risking civic protest, litigation, and the threat of unrest. Almost inevitably, therefore, local craftsmen, however skilful, building in familiar ways and with local materials, became the most obvious recourse for all but the wealthiest of towns.

The second constraint was the lack of sophistication amongst even the leading townsmen of this island nation: a nation with only a single urban centre of 'international' rank. One simply cannot assume in this era that those conventionally responsible for projecting the construction of civic halls, especially outside coastal communities, were sufficiently familiar with the formal architectural styles or building techniques employed abroad. Even when they did travel, oddly enough, Tudor and early Stuart townsmen don't seem to have looked around them, and had little apparent interest in buildings. A telling example of this, though not in regard to any mere townsman, is the journey to Italy on which the Duke of Northum- berland sent his man John Shute to investigate and report on the state of Renaissance innovations in Italian architecture. Though Shute did go to Italy, and returned to write the first English treatise on Vitruvian prin- ciples (*The First and Chief Grounds of Architecture*, 1563) there is almost nothing in the book itself which speaks of first-hand observation, and little which could not have been extracted directly from a contemporary edition of Vitruvius's own treatise. (An interesting parallel may perhaps be drawn

---

107 Cf. Ch. 3.
108 Lawrence Stone, *The Crisis of the Aristocracy 1558–1641* (Oxford, 1965), 554–5.
109 Ibid., Ch. 9 and Apps. xxi ('Heavy Debtors, *c.*1601') and xxii ('Debtors, *c.*1641').

here between the worlds of architectural style and industrial technology: townsmen of the Tudor century seemed either incapable or unwilling to observe on their commercial travels advanced foreign techniques, for example for the weaving of 'new draperies', the making of paper, or the preserving of fish, but strove to learn these techniques instead by inviting foreign craftsmen to dwell in their midst.)

In addition, and notwithstanding the occasional employment by a town of one of the 'fashionable' designers of the day, men like Hancock and Abel, townsmen outside the few greatest centres simply did not circulate in that society where the names of preferred craftsmen were whispered between baron and earl, as would, for example, the merits of different stockbrokers or horse trainers be whispered in times to come.

Even if the fashionable builder might become known, the 'mayor and his brethren', to use the contemporary term, would obviously have been much more severely constrained in their selection of craftsmen than the aristocratic landowner or the official in charge of the King's Works. In addition to factors of cost and provinciality, it must again be said that the vast majority of sixteenth-century towns were still very small communities indeed, all but a score or so having fewer than 5,000 inhabitants by c. 1600. Except for those crafts, like masonry, whose practitioners were often peripatetic, a preference for hiring craftsmen outside the ranks of fellow townsmen, men in whose close company one would conceivably have to spend a good part of a lifetime, could be expressed only at considerable social peril. Such practice often bore the additional risk of contravening the guild regulations against the employment of 'strangers' not freemen of the town.[110] The normal tendency was undoubtedly for the planners of civic buildings to employ local men to whom, if later practice is any guide, they might often be related.

Finally, while royal and aristocratic builders often had great choice regarding building sites, a factor that could have vast impact on proportion and style, townsmen almost never enjoyed the same luxury. As we have seen, civic halls were almost always constructed in some central and often predetermined area of the town plan. Those built to replace older structures, especially if they were to incorporate market space, had almost always to be situated in the central marketing area of the town traditionally associated with that function. Halls converted or purchased of course remained where they were. The town or market hall of Bridgnorth, however, is considered by local tradition to have been a barn from Much Wenlock that was moved to replace a hall destroyed in the Civil War just after our period.[111]) Structures which were altogether new had obviously

[110] Victor Chinnery, *Oak Furniture, the British Tradition* (1979), 25–6.
[111] Trevor Rowley, *The Shropshire Landscape* (1972), 191.

to be built where space could be found, though there was every probability that this would be in the 'better part' of town, if such choices existed or on a site vacated by the demolition of an earlier building.

For all these reasons and perhaps others as well, civic halls in most— and especially the less prominent—English towns right into the seventeenth century were much more likely to be designed as well as constructed by the best of *local* craftsmen, and often in a highly traditional or at best highly imitative manner, than were the substantial edifices erected by private patrons of means or by the Crown itself.

3
Finance

In considering the financial implications of town halls in our period we will obviously want to know what it cost to build or purchase a hall, how serious an undertaking this was for the towns concerned, and what part these ventures played in the overall economy of such towns. We must ask what role economic considerations played in the decision to acquire a hall. We will want to know, too, whether towns that built or purchased halls acted from a position of economic strength and fiscal security, which might lead us to see the acquisition of halls principally as acts of conspicuous consumption and civic pride, or even whether there is evidence of towns building halls from a less secure financial position. This might lead us to consider other motivations, or to conclude that economic considerations may have been less important than they seem. In the effort to clarify both the narrowly fiscal and the more broadly economic implications of building or purchasing halls, this chapter will treat these points in turn.

As one might assume even from the approximate size and eventual complexity of these halls, their building or purchasing costs could be very considerable. We cannot tell just how much they cost in relation to size because we have no idea of the exact size of any of the buildings for which costs figures are available. Yet a sampling of known costs affords an idea of the range of expenditure involved, and in several cases we can relate this to the actual financial state of the towns concerned.

Table 3 shows absolute costs of some sample buildings. The average annual revenue of each town, where known (last column), has been calculated on yearly balances for five years before and after construction, except at Oxford where, figures being incomplete after 1616, the decade up to the year of construction has been used.

In some contrast to these figures, a recent study by Kevin Grady has estimated costs in the £100 to £200 range for the construction of public buildings in the West Riding of Yorkshire in the seventeenth century.[1] This suggests that there may well be a distinct regional variation in costs and perhaps in the size of such buildings between those in his area and period of study and these largely southern examples from the sixteenth and early seventeenth centuries. Grady's estimate that costs rose only by

---

[1] Grady, 'Thesis', 88.

TABLE 3. Relative cost of selected halls

Building, known components	Dates	Absolute costs £ s. d.	Average annual revenue £ s. d.
Plymouth (type B) Guildhall	1565	146 1 11½	184 2 0
Barking (hybrid type) 2-storey, loft, court rm., lock-up, armoury, market	1567	297 9 8	
Poole (unknown)	1568–70	300 0 0	
Stafford (large, type B) town and assize hall, prison, several rms.	1586–1606	572 3 4	
Blandford Forum (unknown)	1593	c.250 0 0[a]	c.30– 40 0 0
Bridport (unknown) with prison	1593	55 0 0[b]	
Exeter (type A) extensive restoration, rebuilding	1593–6	782 0 0	
Plymouth (type B) house of correction, court and council rms., loft, etc.	1606–7	c.600 0 0	428 3 0
Oxford (type B) 60' × 31', council house, court rm., audit rm., clerk's office, cellar	1615–17	260– 80 0 0	100 0 0
Alcester (type B)	1618(–41)	c.300 0 0	
Marlborough (type B) council rm., market, prison	1630–1	c.400 0 0	125 4 0

[a] Timber and transport were donated *gratis* by local contributors.

[b] The town received free stone from a local patron, but even so this is almost certainly an incomplete figure.

Sources: Plymouth: West Devon RO, MSS Worth 131 and 132, and E. Welch (ed.), *Plymouth Building Accounts of the Sixteenth and Seventeenth Centuries*, Devon and Cornwall Record Society, NS 12 (1967), 1–18, 19–61; Barking: Bodl., Rawlinson MS A 195, Part C, fos. 369–73 and *VCH, Essex*, v (1966), 218, 235. This total is my own sum of itemized expenses given in the Rawlinson document, entitled 'The Boke of the whole charges of the Quenes Majt buildings at Barkinge . . .'. That account itself gives the erroneous total of £425. 9s. 10d.; Poole: the estimate of £300 is based on Poole Bor. Archives, Poole Account Books 1568–78, MS 26(4), fos. 129–30; Stafford: William Salt Library MS D(W) 1721/1/4 fos. 179ff.; Blandford Forum: Dorset Co. RO, MS B5, Blandford Chamberlains' Accounts, 1564–1750, fos. 12–13; Bridport: Dorset Co. RO, Bridport Bor. Archives, MS B3/M15; Exeter: H. Lloyd Parry, *The History of Exeter Guildhall and the Life Within* (Exeter, 1936), 76; Oxford: H. E. Salter (ed.), *Oxford Council Acts, 1583–1626* (Oxford, 1928), pp. lvii, 410–11, *VCH, Oxfordshire*, iv (Oxford, 1979), 331–2; Alcester: *VCH, Warwickshire*, iii. 9; Marlborough: A. R. Stedman, *Marlborough and the Upper Kennet Country* (Marlborough, 1960), 118–20; F. A. Carrington, 'The Old Market House and the Great Fire at Marlborough', *Wiltshire Archaeological and Natural History Magazine*, 3 (1857), 106–14; Wiltshire Co. RO, MS G22/1/205/2, esp. fos. 70–5.

about a third in the seventeenth century also seems an underestimate of the rate of cost increase during the 1500–1640 period in question here, though one must accept that the rate of inflation for the seventeenth century was far less overall than that for the sixteenth.[2] Admittedly, the figures in Table 3 comprise a smallish sample, and it is difficult to claim too much for their typicality. Yet the representative nature of these diverse communities seems significant. Barking hovered on the border between a town and a village. Blandford, Bridport, and Alcester remained small towns: two served chiefly as centres of local marketing, one also as a port. Exeter, of course, ranked with the great centres of the kingdom, while all the rest probably weighed in at somewhat above the average in size and resources, a factor which may account for expenditures slightly higher than Grady's figures for Yorkshire. The evidence of costs alone is thin on the ground for our period and offers nothing more.

Yet if we consider those bare figures along with what can be retrieved of finances in some specific towns, the resulting picture of relative costs becomes more meaningful. Here we observe that towns often spent more or even several times more than a typical year's income. Table 3 shows that Plymouth alone took in more revenue in the year of construction than it paid out in construction costs, but although the total sample is very small, one has the distinct impression that Plymouth was exceptionally well off, both fiscally and economically, in relation to other hall-building towns at that particular time. We can also see that Plymouth built modestly: so modestly that the resulting edifice proved insufficient for the town's needs just forty years on. Plymouth's second hall probably presents a somewhat more typical financial picture, while the larger discrepancy between costs and revenues in Marlborough and Blandford seem by no means unusual. Bridport's annual revenue cannot have been much of anything more than Blandford's, given the similar size and importance of the two towns. Alcester was also a small town to be spending such a sum on its hall. Oxford's revenues for the years just prior to construction were particularly unstable, with year-end balances ranging from £239 in 1609 to just £7 in 1612, excluding the extraordinary events whereby the city sold the Austin Friary for £600 in 1610 and then bought lands in Eynsham for £800 the following year.[3]

Of course comparing costs to annual gross revenues merely provides a yardstick for evaluating those costs relative to the fiscal resources of the moment. By no means should it be taken to suggest that such costs could be met by the simple and direct application of cash on hand. This brings

[2] Ibid. 88; R. B. Outhwaite, *Inflation in Tudor and Early Stuart England* (1969), especially fig. 1, p. 14.

[3] Salter, *Oxford Council Acts*, 399–411.

us to the question of how towns managed the costs incurred in building, converting, or purchasing civic halls in our period.

As we probe these fiscal strategies, we may also consider that the finance of civic halls may serve as a useful paradigm for other civic expenditures which were extraordinary, large, and—unlike costs incurred by flood, fire, or pestilence—planned in advance. These might well include the substantial sums required to seek legislation in Parliament, acquire or confirm a charter of incorporation, provide extraordinary relief in times of plague or particular hardship, carry out other important forms of civic building (schools and true market halls especially), conclude major purchases of property, or engage in litigation. Any or all of these might prove particularly draining of civic resources, and, like civic building itself, could often entail expenditures well in excess of a single year's revenue.

In some cases those town leaders who made the decision to build may have planned several years ahead. We have numerous examples of money collected for civic building or donated towards the same end several years before construction began.[4] But despite the desirability of this foresight and despite the fact that some forms of revenue—the rent roll especially—changed relatively little from year to year, the ability to plan ahead was often curtailed by the extreme and largely unpredictable fluctuations in revenue and expenditure which characterized contemporary urban finances. Most towns thus faced these large construction projects with little or nothing more than the resources of the moment, and some forms of extraordinary funding were almost always essential.

The scope of such funding efforts could be impressively broad. Wokingham applied to its building funds the fines of those who refused to serve in office.[5] Penryn sold jewels belonging to the parish church.[6] Hertford at least tried to sell its market cross[7] and Marlborough, as we shall see, successfully raised £140 by selling its old town hall and an adjoining house.[8] Several towns, including Leeds and Deddington, employed funds which had been set aside for poor relief; the town officials of Leeds reasoned that revenues derived from the new building would

---

[4] This was especially true of donations and bequests. Sir James Watt, for example, gave £26. 13s. 4d. in 1511 to extend and rebuild the Norwich Guildhall, which work was not undertaken and completed until 1535. John Lister gave £100 to rebuild the Guildhall at Hull in 1617, with the work being undertaken and completed in 1633. W. K. Jordan, *The Charities of Rural England, 1480–1660* (1961), 148, 295.

[5] PRO, *Hughes and Michael v. Dawbney*, E 134/Hil. 39, Eliz. no. 4.

[6] R. J. Roddis, *Penryn, the History of an Ancient Cornish Borough* (Truro, 1964), 99.

[7] Hertfordshire RO, Hertford Bor. Records, vol. 33, nos. 3–5.

[8] Wiltshire RO MS G 22/1/205/2, entries for 1631.

benefit the poor in the end.[9] Blandford held a series of 'bailiff's ales',[10] thereby borrowing a traditional church fund-raising device which had come into disfavour at the Reformation.

The laurels for the most organized and energetic fund raising must surely go to another small Dorset borough, the decayed port of Bridport. Here the town council actually expended a small sum (£2. 9s. 11d.) specifically for fund-raising activities, and brought in by subsequent efforts almost exactly enough to build their small hall of 1593. Chief amongst many efforts employed was the methodical canvassing, both in the town and in the surrounding region, of anyone likely to contribute toward the expenses of the hall. A hat passed amongst justices sitting in sessions at Beaminster yielded 25s. 6d; an appeal in Lyme Regis brought in 19s. 11d. plus three pecks of salt; and efforts were made at Whit Sunday, Trinity Sunday, and May Day celebrations in the Bridport area. Successfully solicited in this effort were 'Danby's mariners', 'on Sunday after May Day of strangers we met on the way', 'strangers at the Bull' (a Bridport inn still very much in business), 'Mr. Pitt of Blandford' (who was at the same time in charge of the hall building in his own community), 'Valentine the Carrier', 'Mr. Greenwood of Chard', and 'Captain Moone'. The total collected over what must have been an extended time period came to £53. 7s. 4d.[11]

Some funds came unsolicited in the form of gifts and bequests. The Croydon native Francis Tirrell, who had become a prominent citizen and grocer of London, honoured his place of origin (and himself) with a £200 gift to build a new hall in 1566.[12] The Faversham town and market hall of c.1574 benefited greatly from the bequest of the merchant adventurer Henry Hatch, presumably a native of *that* town, though this was not in the end sufficient to cover all costs of construction.[13] Similarly, John Lister of Hull gave £100 for a meeting place for the town's merchants and governors of Hull in 1617, a sum which (along with Thomas Ferries's bequest for the same purpose) was apparently applied to the construction of Hull's town hall of 1633.[14] And finally Banbury's 1633 hall benefited from William Taylor's gift of £100.[15] Yet if these amounted to substantial

[9] Grady, 'Thesis', 159–60; H. M. Colvin, *A History of Deddington, Oxfordshire* (1963), 6.

[10] Dorset Co. RO, Blandford Chamberlains' Accounts, 1564–1750, MS: B5, fo. 13ʳ⁻ᵛ.

[11] Dorset Co. RO, MS B3/M15; this has been discussed in R. Tittler, 'The Building of Civic Halls in Dorset, c.1560–1640', *BIHR*, 58/137 (1985), 43.

[12] *VCH, Surrey*, iv (1967), 218 and D. W. Garrow, *The History and Antiquities of Croydon* (Croydon, 1818), 61, 191, 353.

[13] E. Jacob, *The History of the Port and Town of Faversham in Kent* (1774), 131–4 and Kent Co. Archives Office, Maidstone MS FA/FAc 9/Bundle 2.

[14] Jordan, *Charities of Rural England*, 295; *VCH, Yorkshire, East Riding*, i. (1969), 433.

[15] *VCH, Oxfordshire*, x (1972), 24 and William Potts, *A History of Banbury* (Banbury, 1958), 143–4.

bequests in a few towns, the overall contribution of private donations to civic building remained distinctly modest overall. Professor Jordan has calculated that only 5.18 per cent of charitable donations made between 1480 and 1660 went to 'municipal betterments', citing the construction of town halls as but one part of that category.[16]

While these examples stand out for their exceptional and sometimes colourful nature, it is not always easy to reconstruct the more regular means of finance. Few civic building accounts have survived, and we have no more than a handful of those on which to base an analysis of costs and revenues. Ironically, they have been rendered even more rare by the common practice of keeping such extraordinary accounts apart from the normal run of town accounts. We have several runs of regular accounts for towns and in years in which we know civic halls to have been built where separate building accounts have not survived. This no doubt derives from the common practice of record keeping whereby such extraordinary expenses were totalled roughly as they occurred at any time during the year, while only the totals were noted and recorded in the annual reckoning. Such sums are often accompanied by the tantalizing note 'as shown by a bill of particulars'. Unfortunately virtually very few such 'bills of particulars' have been found separately from accompanying totals.

Let us make the best use of such surviving documentation by examining the relevant accounts of a few towns in detail. We can then extrapolate general patterns and offer other observations on the basis of those examples. In so doing, we should be aware of the difficulties of employing even those sixteenth- and seventeenth-century town accounts which have survived. In the manner of library collections before Dewey, there is only some uniformity of method. There is also much invention and not a little tendency toward arithmetical error. In many instances, for example, we have a single set of annual accounts covering receipt and expenditure, but we cannot count on this any more than we can be certain that what looks like a complete set of accounts actually does include all categories of revenue and expenditure. Frequently, and especially in the more complex governing structures, accounts for such categories of receipt and expenditure as fines, rents, tolls, wages, property repairs, fee farms, or the sundry functions of the market were recorded separately as they occurred, and then not (as with building accounts) necessarily added together or even recorded with the main accounts at the end of the fiscal year. And, as one might guess, that fiscal calendar varied somewhat from place to place, with Michaelmas the common but by no means the invariable point of annual reckoning.

But despite the cautions imposed by such characteristics of Early

[16] W. K. Jordan, *Philanthropy in England, 1480–1660* (1959), 368, 372, 376–7.

Modern town accounts, they are still valuable and instructive when they turn up. By examining several of the best examples, we can hope to shed considerable light on the costs and strategies involved in civic building, and to observe a surprising variety of experiences. Poole, which (as we can see from Table 3) built its hall between 1568 and 1570; Blandford Forum, which built its 'Yelde Hall' in 1593; Plymouth, which built a guild-hall in 1565 and replaced it with a large hall between 1606 and 1607; Oxford, which purchased its 'lower Guildhall' in 1562 and built a new council house in 1615–17; and finally Marlborough, which built its town and market hall in 1631–3, combine to exhibit a wide range of common financial patterns, as well as a sampling of special efforts. They allow us to assess the impact of civic building on the finances of individual towns.

The decision to build a new town hall in Poole, taken by the mayor and members of the town council with little or no consultation with other townsmen, came at a distinct point of prosperity for that town. Population size had grown steadily but not excessively and the town's housing stock had kept pace. Though unmatched by any particular vitality in local marketing in this geographically isolated community, the chief local enterprise of commerce, both coastal and overseas, had completely recovered from the slump of the 1550s.[17] In a sequence commonly followed elsewhere, the decision to build the hall followed fresh upon the heels of the acquisition of the borough charter in 1568.[18] Even so, there are no indications even in this particularly well documented town of a decision to build before that constitutional landmark.

The decision having been made, the projectors set about financing this undertaking and at the same time began to raise some of the costs of securing their charter as well. (We may estimate the cost of the hall at close to £300, while recorded costs of the charter, which are likely to be incomplete, came to £130.[19]) The very great sum of £500 had already been pledged to support the acquisition of the charter by a consortium of wealthy townsmen who had in turn raised much of that sum from a general levy of 105 rateable inhabitants, in a benevolence of 1568.[20] Now these hard-nosed merchants who ran the town thought they saw an opportunity to feather their own nests at the same time as providing the town with a civic hall. They thus set about raising loan money amongst themselves at an interest rate approaching 10 per cent: a rate which would shortly (in 1572) become the statutory norm for money lending by statute

[17] Tittler, 'The Vitality of an Elizabethan Port: The Economy of Poole, c.1550–1600', *Southern History*, 7 (1985), 96–7 *et passim*.   [18] Cf. below, Ch. 4.

[19] Harry P. Smith, *The History of the Borough and County of the Town of Poole*, 2 vols. (Poole, 1948–51), ii, 95.

[20] Poole Bor. Archives MSS 25(3) fo. 10, 1568; and 63(18), 1568.

and which was thus probably near the going rate for the time. These seventeen creditors were all local merchants and virtually all were also members of the town council. That body, naturally enough, approved the loan, and the lenders had every reason to expect a steady and secure return in the bullish conditions of 1568 and 1569.

Yet in the economically uncertain tenor of the times even these shrewd denizens of the counting-house could miscalculate, and within a very short time it became obvious that the town corporation, as it now was, would have a great deal of difficulty repaying those loans. In 1574 the corporation assessed all rateable inhabitants for another levy, this time to repay the town's debts, though it is not certain that these 191 individuals were actually dunned the sums affixed against their names.[21] If the levy was employed, it failed in its purpose. A grand reckoning of the town's finances carried out in 1578 and reviewing all costs and revenues since 1560 found the town to have a net debt of £314. 10s. 2d. still payable to the seventeen creditors and others, or to their estates.[22]

In a now desperate move to disentangle the town from this web of debt, the councillors, some of the creditors still amongst them, imposed regressive taxes on the sales of grain and beer throughout the town. This promptly elicited a well-organized protest by fifty-six townsmen, lesser merchants, and craftsmen, who decried the lack of consultation in building the hall in the first place, and vigorously opposed the new impositions. So loud were their protests and so obstreperous were their actions in refusing to pay, that the dispute found its way to the Privy Council, which established a committee to investigate on the scene.[23]

This conflict bore overtones of friction between status and occupational groups, and even called forth religious divisions amongst the townsmen. This is especially vivid in the testimony offered the commission by Nicholas Curie, a merchant himself but then only of the second tier in Poole's mercantile ranks, who served as spokesman for the protesters. Curie charged that the efforts to finance the hall had extended to the sale of certain church plate which he felt should have been kept on hand rather than employed 'to pay some merchants' debts . . . so that . . . we have not one communion cup to receive the communion withall but they are driven to borrow one in . . . some tavern at such time when the same is to be ministered'.[24]

---

[21] Poole Bor. Archives MS 26(4), fos. 132–3, 'List of the Names of all the Inhabitants in the Town and Parish of Poole rated with Good Consideration to pay round the redeeming of the Towne oute of Debt'.

[22] Poole Bor. Archives 26(4), fos. 118–30, esp. fo. 129.

[23] Poole Bor. Archives MSS 108(63); 25(3), fos. 100–1; TDW 5.

[24] 'Sir Peter Thompson's Copy of an Ancient Paper Respecting the Cause of Curie against the Mayor', an uncatalogued 18th-c. transcript of a 1582(?) document, generously provided me by Mr Derek Beamish from as yet uncatalogued collections in the Poole Bor. Archives.

In the end, Curie's protests and those of his fellows proved largely ineffective. The corporation was eventually able to extricate itself from the very difficult financial circumstances brought on by the construction of its hall so soon after the enormous costs of securing its charter.[25] This it did partly by simple default on approximately £100 of debt, and partly by levies and even secondary loans.

The episode is particularly instructive of several themes relevant to the present discussion. The members of Poole's ruling oligarchy considered the hall sufficiently important to take the risks entailed—risks of which these merchants must at least have been aware. They did so on their own, with little consultation, and managed thereby to split the town into angrily opposing factions. And, despite their presumed business acumen, they were unable to assess the economic fragility of the town or the likelihood of its supporting the considerable costs entailed.

When we take up the case of Blandford Forum, we turn to the smallest of those towns for which at least a goodly part of building accounts have survived. With a population which probably fell into the 600–800 range,[26] Blandford typifies that common garden variety of market town about which we know so little. An examination of the somewhat incomplete accounts tells us that Blandford's financial resources were as modest as its population. Its rent roll, for example, which seems to have provided the largest portion of regular annual revenues, came to just over twenty pounds in the mid-1590s, and arrears are recorded in several years even against that small sum.[27] But Blandford's size was not always a handicap. It seems to have been sufficiently small to have avoided the polarization in wealth, status, and political power which one certainly sees in Poole and would probably see in most towns of this time. One consequence of this is that it still seems to have been able to command a strong sense of community loyalty and civic concern which could be translated into fiscal resources when occasion demanded.

This was indeed fortunate, for the total costs for building the Blandford Hall seem to have come to about £250—some ten times the town's annual rent roll and probably six or eight times its annual gross revenues—paid out between 1592 and 1597. This works out to £197. 13s. recorded in the

[25] Poole Bor. Archives MS 25(3), fos. 100–1 ('Report of the Commissioners') for 5 May 1582, 17 Dec. 1584, 28 Feb. 1585, 8 May 1586; MS TDW/5, 3 Dec. 1582; and 26(4), fos. 118–32.
[26] Martyn C. Brown has calculated a population of 500–700 in 1562, based on lay subsidy returns and musters. The ensuing decades presumably saw in Blandford the same population growth that was general throughout the realm and certainly in neighbouring towns in Dorset, including Poole, making c.600–800 a fair estimate for the year of building, 1592–3. See Brown, 'Blandford in Elizabethan and Early Stuart Times', *Notes and Queries for Somerset and Dorset*, 30 (1975), 118–19 and Tittler, 'The Vitality of an Elizabethan Port', 96.
[27] Dorset RO, Blandford Forum Chamberlains' Accounts, 1564–1750, MS B5, fos. 15ᵛ–10ᵛ. (Pagination moves from back to front in this volume.)

chief year of building, 1592–3, £17. 9s. 3d. recorded for 1595–6, and £2. 17s. 3d. for 1596–7.[28] In addition, there seem almost certainly to have been further payments made in the intervening years of which record has not survived, bringing the estimated total up to about £250. This sequence of payments suggests that the initial resources on hand for the building ran out before the job had been completed, and that the remaining touches had to wait for the collection of more funds: a pattern which was almost certainly common elsewhere.

In relative terms, this was a very large sum for a town of such modest means. And, although it is difficult to say much with certainty about the town's economic condition at this same time, there are at least indications that this was not a particularly prosperous patch for the townsmen of Blandford. We note that in the year of building roughly a quarter of the rent roll, modest as it may have been, was still unpaid and lay in arrears.[29] And as for the economic base for town finances, we also know that this was a very difficult decade for the realm as a whole and for at least some of the towns of Dorset as well.[30] Blandford's 'port' of Poole, to which there had long been close economic ties, certainly experienced great difficulties in those years, and we find few Blandford merchants noted in the surviving port books covering Poole commerce in the 1590s: fewer, for example, than for the 1570s.[31]

Leaving aside the equally challenging question of motivations for such construction, let us ask here how such a small town, not demonstrably enjoying a period of economic prosperity, supported such an ambitious civic project. The answer for Blandford seems to lie in the spirit of co-operation which characterized its residents, the careful planning which was carried out under the direction of the local merchant John Pitt,[32] chosen specifically to manage this task on the town's behalf, and the ability to avoid unsupportable debts.

The records tell us that the town had collected £189. 8s. 6d., just £8 short of recorded expenditures to that date, by the time of the chief construction in 1592–3:[33] £9. 5s. 4d. in 1590 to buy timber (which if left to season until needed would be an outstanding example of advanced

[28] Ibid., fos. 12–13.

[29] The town received £20. 19s. 8d. in rents in 1593 with £7. 10s. 11d. in arrears; ibid., fo. 11ᵛ.

[30] See esp. Peter Clark (ed.), *The European Crisis of the 1590s* (1985) and, for Dorset in the 1590s, see Tittler, 'The Vitality of an Elizabethan Port', 95, 106–8.

[31] Based on a study of the following Poole Port Books: PRO, E 190: 1571–2: 865/1; 1572: 865/4; 1573–4: 865/5; 1575–6: 865/7; 1578–9: 865/8; 1590–1: 865/22; 1591–: 866/3; 1592: 866/6 and 7; 1593: 866/14; 1594: 866/16; 1595: 866/18; 1596: 867/1; 1596–7: 867/3; 1597: 867/7; and 1599–1600: 867/14 and 17. No other Port Books have survived for Poole in these decades.

[32] Pitt's appointment as 'Keeper of Funds for the New Guild Hall' is noted in 1593, Dorset Co. RO, the Blandford Accounts, MS B5, fo. 11ᵛ. He figures frequently in the accounts thereafter.

[33] See Dorset Co. RO, MS B5, fos. 12–14.

TABLE 4. Funding sources for the Blandford Guildhall, 1590–7

	£	s.	d.	%
Individual gifts (22, from 5s. to £5)	26	7	8	10.3
Group contributions (3)	25	0	4	9.8
Regular civic revenue	61	15	4	24.1
Sale of shambles and old hall	21	12	0	8.4
Sale of building materials	1	2	0	0.4
Fundraising 'ales' (2)	43	14	6	17.0
Loans (1 of £2; 3 of £20)	62	0	0	24.2
Other unknown	14	5	4	5.6
TOTAL	255	17	2	100 (rounded)

Source: Dorset Co. RO, MS B5, fos. 12–14.

planning), £5 in 1592, and the bulk of the sum, £175. 3s. 2d. in the building year itself. A further £72. 14s. 10d. plus a gift of nine oak trees came forth in 1594, £7. 3s. 3d. in 1596, and £2. 17s. 3d. in 1597 for the finishing touches, making a total *recorded* cash collection of £255. 17s. 2d. The sources for these revenues have been summarized in Table 4.

A far greater outlay than this may be seen in the second of the Plymouth halls built in our period, constructed in 1606–7.[34] Though its total announced cost of £794. 8s. 1d. cannot be taken as an accurate figure, entangled as it was with expenses incurred in erecting flesh shambles and buying out two leases of property on the future building site, the approximate figure of £600 for building this hall alone seems about right. Yet because the financial strategy for the whole would probably have been the same even if the hall had been figured in by itself, and also because the form of the documents leaves us little choice, we will have to treat these costs together.

The construction in Plymouth was financed through modest sums collected specifically for the purpose, credit from major builders involved, and personal loans extended by townsmen, in particular the sometime mayor, James Bagg. The resources collected specifically for this hall amounted to £165. 19s. 8d. This included £60 collected in the shire towards the house of correction which had been required by statute (18 Eliz. c. 3, 'An Acte for the setting of the Poore on Worke, and for the avoyding of Ydleness') since the construction of the 1565 hall. The rest of this sum derived without much difficulty from indigenous sources of ordinary revenues: two entry fines for leases of town lands (one of which

[34] The following analysis is based on West Devon RO, MSS: Worth 132, Worth 137: and Welch, *Plymouth Building Accounts*.

was merely for a reversion) and a modest surplus in ordinary revenues from the previous year.[35]

Of the remaining building costs, moneys owed to six master craftsmen for materials and labour came to £131. 13s. This sum was paid out by the end of 1609, or within three years, from town coffers, apparently with no interest recorded. Perhaps the builders, Plymouth men themselves, waived interest altogether, or simply included it in the balance owed. We do not find it in the accounts either for the building itself or of the receivers at the year's end reckoning.

The outstanding balance was borne by James Bagg, to whom, after the £165. 19s. 8d. given in the year of construction, the town still owed £496. 15s. 5d. This was to have been repaid in instalments over five years, but again no indication of interest *per se* appears in the accounts. Bagg was to have received small portions of the principle each year from 1608 to 1612, with the balance to be paid by St Andrew's Day (30 November) in the last year. Though the town was not always able to pay the required portions at the prescribed time, Bagg seems to have received almost all his money by the required due date. The small shortfall between the total obligation and the principal, probably representing the interest, seems to have been met by the town's extension to Bagg of a lease for the marketing area under the new Guildhall in 1612, for which no fine was collected. This was a very lucrative arrangement for Bagg, which would easily have covered the interest on the original loan. A fellow townsman, John Battersbie, had paid £100 for the lease to the town's other market standings in 1607–8.[36]

The lessons to be drawn from Plymouth's experience in building its 1606–7 hall seem to be that borrowing could go a long way towards meeting building costs, and that a town could string its creditors along for several years if, unlike the experience in Poole, they could expect to be paid off in full at the end. It may also have helped considerably that such creditors were themselves townsmen, and thus may have been more willing to be patient on the one hand and to convert some of the indebtedness to advantageous business arrangements on the other.

When we turn to the city of Oxford we find a particularly instructive example of the complexity of contemporary accounting, and also a wealth of material on the context for civic building provided by the local economy. Four distinct city offices each rendered an annual account, and

<hr>

[35] West Devon RO, MS: Worth 132, fo. 172.

[36] In 1610–11 a total of £82 which was to have been paid to Bagg was not paid. In the following year we find Bagg receiving a lease for 'the walk under the guildhall', almost certainly the paved market area, and the space in which payment was supposed to be recorded was left blank. It would thus appear that Bagg received the lease without fine in lieu of the £82 owed to him. West Devon RO, MS: Worth 132, fo. 173; compare with Battersbie's entry fine, Worth 132, fo. 163.

we may celebrate the survival of the annual summary accounts into which
these were combined.[37] Somewhat like Poole, Oxford seems generally to
have been prospering both when it purchased the 'Lower' Guildhall in
1562 and when it constructed the Council House between 1615 and
1617. This 'vigorous, opportunistic, and eventually better-educated
urban community'[38] was regaining something of its earlier, medieval
population levels. Its economy seemed well balanced between the grain
trade and milling industry on the one hand and the needs of the university
community and, by the seventeenth century, those of tourists and visitors
on the other. Notwithstanding heavy civic expenditures between 1587
and 1594, the period between c.1580 and nearly 1620 seems especially
marked by such vigour. Yet even then a perceptive observer might have
noted signs of trouble: most of the city's earlier industries had declined,
its situation in relation to the major trade routes remained less than ideal
despite improvements in Thames navigation, and its fair virtually col-
lapsed during James's reign. Though not as strictly tied to the local
economy as one might assume, Oxford's civic finances had also become
precarious well before the Civil War.[39]

Oxford's 'Lower Guildhall' began its history as a dwelling-house
adjoining the medieval Guildhall. The city leased it in 1541, purchased it
as a freehold in 1562, and expanded and renovated it throughout the late
sixteenth and early seventeenth centuries. By 1577 its size and furnishings allowed it to succeed the decaying castle as the site of the assizes. In
1604 the city improved its lighting by adding new windows in the court
room. Two years later it built a row of shops along the hall's front in an
effort to accommodate more retail traders and thus add to the rent roll,
and in 1611 it rebuilt the porch.[40] Although we know little of the purchase
of the building in 1562 it seems possible that, coming as it did at a
prosperous time, the city could have managed this acquisition largely
through its regular revenues. We also know that the freemen were
regularly assessed a 'Sunday penny' throughout the decades of the 1550s
and 1560s for just such costs.[41]

By the reign of James I the levels of both population and apparent
prosperity had been raised further, both evidently attaining their pre-Civil
War peak. Yet the city's finances in those years were not as stable as its
economy might suggest. Shortfalls accrued in roughly one year out of
every three between 1584 and 1617 and regular borrowing, both from
townsmen and from Londoners, had to be employed to make up the

[37] Salter, *Oxford Council Acts*, pp. xl–xlii, 354–428; *VCH, Oxfordshire*, iv. 140–1.
[38] *VCH, Oxfordshire*, iv. 74.
[39] Ibid. 74, 104–8, 141–3. The improvement in navigation is well summarized in Mary Prior,
Fisher Row, Fishermen, Bargemen and Canal Boatmen in Oxford, 1500–1900 (Oxford, 1982), 112–22.
[40] *VCH, Oxfordshire*, iv. 331.   [41] Ibid. 141–2.

difference. This serves to remind us of the distinctions between the economic resources of the community and the fiscal reserves of its administration, and also of the frequent difficulty of translating from the former to the latter.[42]

In the end, Oxford spent between £260 and £270 for what must have been a modest hall, built almost entirely between March and mid-September, 1617. Interestingly, this expenditure, though moderate enough for the time, was not the only major fiscal undertaking or even the largest of the period. Oxford borrowed £350 to defray costs of confirming its charter at James's accession. Though it sold the property of the Augustinian Friars for £600 in 1610, it used the proceeds of that sale and more besides to purchase agricultural lands in nearby Eynsham for £800 in 1611.[43]

Especially in view of the unstable revenues in those years (the chamberlains ending in the red five of the first ten years of the century, the fair dwindling to virtually nothing, and only the city's receipts from the castle mill keeping the civic finances afloat) this may seem like a heady run of wheeling and dealing. Yet the officials of the day were determined to build a new hall to augment the existing facilities, which had become inadequate. Like the leaders of Poole half a century earlier, they assumed that the strength of the local economy would see them through. True enough, by 1615 they were able to add a considerable amount of accumulated capital to the £260 or £270 required by the Council House without further borrowing. Nevertheless, though gaps in the accounts conceal the full totals, it is clear that the city's revenues dropped off sharply just as the hall came to completion, and that a fiscal decline very similar to that in Poole ensued thereafter.[44] By 1638 the city was virtually broke, and the Civil War, which administered the *coup de grâce*, ran up the civic debt to over £1,000.[45] Though it would be irresponsible to attribute the succeeding fiscal débâcle simply to the costs of building the hall, that project seems to have been Oxford's last hurrah for a long time. Oxford's experience demonstrates once again the essentially fragile and unstable state of contemporary urban finances.

In contrast to the fiscal strategies employed in Oxford, the town leaders of Marlborough relied chiefly on borrowing, but here, too, post-construction finances came to a state of flux and shortfall. This Wiltshire borough built a new town and market hall between 1631 and 1633, partly to supplement the earlier Guildhall which had proved too small for holding the assizes. The new building included marketing space below

[42] This paragraph is based on accounts summarized in Salter, *Oxford Council Acts*, 354–412.
[43] Ibid. pp. xlvii–lvii, 400–2, 410–11.   [44] Ibid. 354–428, *passim*.
[45] *VCH, Oxfordshire*, iv. 143.

and distinct areas for a council 'howse', jury room, and prison elsewhere under the same roof.[46] Despite the evident prosperity of the community at the time of construction, the finances of the town were typically precarious.

In most years roughly two-thirds of Marlborough's regular revenues derived from a rent roll which rose but slowly during the years at hand: from £106 in 1620 to £112 twenty years later.[47] To this the chamberlains could usually cobble together additional moneys from several sources: entry fines for leases (which, as in many towns, could be increased much more readily than the rents themselves), freemen's admission fines, interest on loans of capital (but at low interest rates of 5–8 per cent when 10 per cent was permissible from 1572 and 8 per cent from 1624), and sales of such commodities as timber, corn, and building supplies. These resources allowed gross revenues averaging £167 per annum in the decade prior to the construction (with a low of £128. 14s. 6d. in 1621 to a high of £294. 10s. 10d. in 1628, the highest in the borough's history to that time). Expenditures during the same period averaged £195, ranging from £106 to £282, another all-time high, in 1628. Expenditures were always very close to revenues, exceeding them twice: in 1623 (for the first time since 1587) by £6 and in 1626 by just under £5.

If there was any advanced planning for the expense of this new town hall, it seems likely to have come only the year before, when the relatively large surplus of £27. 8s. 6½d. was applied to repaying a £20 loan, but this was small potatoes. The borough's total expenditures in that first building year, 1631, came to £540. 12s. 5d.; between three and four times the usual, with £350 of this accounted for by the building itself. Against these outlays the borough applied regular revenues, augmented by the sale of the old market cross for the sum of £140, the return of the principal of a £100 on which the town had been taking in 8 per cent per annum, and a loan *to* the town for another £100. With that, the chamberlains closed their books on the year 1631 with an income of £481. 18s. 4d., leaving a shortfall of £55 and debts, presumably including loans not recorded for which there is some independent evidence, amounting to £190. 13s.

Although all but about £50 of the recorded building payments had been made by then, further shortfalls followed in each of the two successive years: £55. 4s. 4d. in 1632 and a whopping £109. 18s. in 1633. By 1634, when revenues finally exceeded expenditures (if only by £1. 1s. 7d.) the chamber found itself in debt for a sum of £229. 11s. 1d. The creditors were all townsmen, apparently either those who lent money for the specific project (John Lawrence and a Mr Yorke) or those who were

---

[46] Stedman, *Marlborough and the Upper Kennet Country*, 118–20; Carrington, 'The Old Market House', 106–14; *VCH, Wiltshire*, xii (1983), 203, 215.

[47] The following analysis is based on Wiltshire Co. RO MS G22/1/205/2.

involved in the building itself and who extended credit for labour and materials (Mr Dringe and Mr Fitchthwaite). The town paid off Dringe and Fitchthwaite in full in 1635, as well as some of its debt to Yorke. Yet remaining debts were not paid off until 1640, and then only by a steady accretion of surplus revenues, the very substantial increase of entry fines on borough property (which brought in £100 for a single fine in both 1639 and 1640), and a few small secondary loans employed to pay off the first batch.

In sum, then, construction of the Marlborough Town Hall was supported chiefly by loans taken by the borough, and repaid over the course of several years thereafter. During this eight-year period of construction and repayment, Marlborough's finances were almost completely tied up. When the years 1635 and 1636 bore the highest food prices since the 1590s[48] and made correspondingly strong demands on the town's charitable resources, Marlborough had no choice but to take out a further £70 in loans for relief of its poor, which it did in 1637. The building of its town hall was the largest single expense Marlborough faced during the entire sixty-eight years (1572–1640) covered by its earliest surviving run of chamberlains' accounts.

These examples and others which have come down to us in less detail suggest several conclusions and raise a few questions about the finance of civic halls. First, of course, is the bald fact of substantial cost, cost which could almost never be met with ordinary revenues alone. Additional strategies therefore became necessary. As we have seen, a great variety of these devices ensued. Some of them were fairly innovative or even unique events in the life of a community; Marlborough, after all, could sell its market cross, or Penryn its jewels, but once.

In addition to the accretion of ordinary revenues the two most important and reliable means at hand were the levy on inhabitants and the recourse to borrowing. The first of these was of course by no means a novel device nor one relegated to the construction of halls. In effect, it had long been sanctioned by Parliament for the collection of subsidy and similar national requirements, and by local fiat for such needs as the costs of incorporation, litigation, and recourse to Parliament.

Public levies for building proved effective in Gravesend in 1573[49] and in Tewkesbury, where some of the costs of a new boothall were raised by a levy of all inhabitants in 1578.[50] In St Albans a levy for an Elizabethan market hall was restricted to the mayor and his brethren, each dunned £19, and to the borough's trade and craft guilds.[51] Yet as we have seen in

[48] Peter Bowden, 'Agricultural Prices, Farm Profits, and Rents' in J. Thirsk (ed.), *The Agrarian History of England and Wales*, iv, fig. 15, p. 627.
[49] Kent Co. Archives Office, Maidstone, MS GR/AC 1, fo. 13.
[50] Gloucestershire RO, MS TBR/AI/1, fo. 12.
[51] St Albans Bor. Records, MS 32, fo. 3.

Poole, levies or similar impositions on the population in general or on substantial parts thereof carried considerable risk of popular opposition. This was perhaps even more likely to be the case in those communities pressed for ship money collections in the later decades of our period. Only in small and relatively unstratified communities, with relatively little polarization of wealth and a high degree of consensus on goals, could they be carried out with confidence.

Borrowing was less likely to incur such divisive reactions, yet it bore its own drawbacks and risks. It sometimes entailed interest rates which proved burdensome, and in that age of notoriously unstable economies we have seen how easily creditors could be left high and dry and the borrowing communities seriously weakened. Still, even in an age without institutionalized credit facilities and despite the risks, it could be arranged without much difficulty and often was.

Although our sampling of evidence is small, it appears that lenders tended to be local men or neighbouring gentry throughout most of our period, well known to the town officials who contracted for their services. This was obviously the case in Poole in the 1560s, where almost all the seventeen lenders to the corporation were local and many of them members of the borough administration. James Bagg, who lent so much to the corporation of Plymouth, was also a townsman: mayor in 1595–6 and 1605–6, MP in 1601 and 1604, privateer, merchant and, for that matter, sometime desperado as well.[52] His fellow lender George Shere seems also to have been a local man, though far less colourful.[53] Yet even when lenders were townsmen or town officials, we should not expect special rates. When Oxford's mayor, Isaak Bartholomewe, lent the town money in James's reign he did so at 12 per cent interest, 2 per cent above the going rate identified in standing legislation. His very influence in local administration seems likely to have enabled him to gain such an advantage. (On the other hand, it must also be said that Oxford's town clerk lent the city a similar sum at only 8 per cent at roughly the same time.[54])

Non-residents also appear, possibly more often in the early seventeenth century than before, and were less likely to be indulgent with tardy repayment. Hertford borrowed £65 from a Mr Bull, who was almost certainly a Londoner or a St Albansite, in 1612,[55] and Oxford borrowed

---

[52] P. W. Hasler (ed.), *The House of Commons, 1558–1603*, History of Parliament Trust, 3 vols. (1981), i. 383.

[53] British Record Society, *Index of Wills Proved in the Prerogative Court of Canterbury, 1605–1619*, 43 (1012), 402   [54] Salter, *Oxford Council Acts*, 382.

[55] Hertfordshire Co. RO, Hertford Borough Records, vol. 20, MS fo. 58ᵛ. Mr Bull could have been one of the Londoners, Randolphe Bull, citizen and goldsmith (d. 1617), or Thomas Bull, citizen and poulterer (d. 1617), *Index of Wills, 1605–1619*, 83, or possibly Thomas Bull of St Albans (occupation unknown, d. 1621), *Index of Wills, 1620–1629*, 48.

£150 from 'Mr Jaye of London' for a non-building expense in 1605.[56] Not only may the public spirit of wealthy citizens have been giving way to personal interest, but there are indications that townsmen in general were beginning to look more frequently to outsiders as sources of capital.

Given these high costs of building and the difficulties of financing, we may readily assume that those towns which undertook such an ordeal had at least reasonable expectation of sufficient prosperity and fiscal stability to support the undertaking. This seems to have been a precondition for the marked advance in *domestic* building which has been observed for the period, and one is tempted to see the spate of civic hall construction as simply a part of this 'Great Rebuilding'.[57] Indeed it is obvious that some and indeed many towns added their halls at times of at least reasonable economic and fiscal capability. Of those cases we have examined, this was certainly so at Poole in the 1560s and Oxford both in 1562 and even more so in 1616. Plymouth also experienced expansion in the 1560s and, although it may well have suffered from the slowdown in cloth exports and domination of London merchants by 1606, possibly at the time of the second hall as well.[58]

But a considerable complement of other towns evidently carried on civic building projects at less favoured times, while even in more prosperous towns like Poole the ability to predict continued prosperity was very limited. Shrewsbury did not demur from rebuilding its guild-hall in 1512 despite abundant evidence for prolonged economic decline both before and for some time after that date.[59] Lincoln, a classic case of late medieval urban decay, was exempted from paying its subsidy throughout the 1510s and was listed on the 1540 Act for the re-edification of decayed towns, but still managed to build a guild-hall c.1520.[60] Barnstaple seems to have been in decline when it built its guild-hall in 1532, as was Portsmouth which followed suit in the same decade.[61] Reading's impoverishment after the dissolutions nevertheless coincided with the

[56] Salter, *Oxford Council Acts*, 388.
[57] W. G. Hoskins, 'The Rebuilding of Rural England, 1570–1640', *P and P* 4 (1953), 44–59. Hoskins's thesis has been challenged with some success by those who propose more intense building later on, but the absolute advance in domestic building which he saw in this period still holds weight. See R. Machin, 'The Great Rebuilding: A Reassessment', *P and P* 77 (1977), 33–56.
[58] Hasler, *The House of Commons*, i. 147.
[59] Shrewsbury was listed in the statute of 1535 for the re-edification of decayed towns; 27 Henry VIII, c. 1.
[60] J. W. F. Hill, *Tudor and Stuart Lincoln* (Cambridge, 1956), 19–25; Lincoln is listed in one of the two 1540 statutes for the re-edification of decayed towns, 32 Henry VIII, c. 18.
[61] S. T. Bindoff (ed.), *The House of Commons, 1509–1558*, 3 vols. (1982), i. 66–7, and *VCH, Hampshire*, iii [1908] (1973), 187, citing a 1526 description of Portsmouth 'in sore ruin and decay' and noting that in 1541 the town's defences had 'clean fallen down'. Barnstaple is listed in the second 1540 statute for the re-edification of decayed towns, 32 Henry VIII, c. 19, Portsmouth in the first, 32 Henry VIII, c. 18.

conversion of its guild-hall in about 1542.[62] The same may be said of
Boston[63] and Coventry.[64]

Stafford[65] and Salisbury[66] both seem to have been economically
distressed when they built halls in the 1580s. The 1590s, by most
accounts the most economically depressed decade of the century, still saw
the construction of ten halls of which two, Appleby and Kendal, were in
the particularly afflicted shire of Westmorland.[67] The Dorset towns of
Blandford, which we have discussed above, and Bridport, which was
recoiling from the slow disintegration of its harbour and hoping to
emphasize its cordage production as well as local marketing, both built
halls in 1593.[68] Hull's financial difficulties delayed the completion of its
1633–6 hall, though it may not have been seriously decayed.[69]

What may we conclude from this forest of examples? Most obvious is
the thought that when we are dealing with the financing of some two
hundred halls over a century and a half, it proves impossible to achieve
blanket generalizations and foolish to try. It seems clear that many hall-
building towns were prosperous, but—in marked contrast to the perceived preconditions for *domestic* building—also that many were not so
well off. Even in those towns whose citizens enjoyed general prosperity,
charitable bequests for 'municipal improvement' of any sort, let alone the
building of halls, remained infrequent. In addition, there were rarely
regular and effective means of bringing private wealth into the town's
fiscal resources and, again in marked contrast to the construction of

[62] C. F. Slade, 'Reading' in M. D. Lobel (ed.), *Atlas of Historic Towns* (Baltimore, n.d.), 6. It must
also be acknowledged that Reading had been prosperous up until the dissolutions, and would be so
again by the Elizabethan period.
[63] A bill was entered into the House of Commons on 1 Dec. 1554 for the re-edification of the town
of Boston, though it got no further than first reading. Leland also saw the town as much decayed in the
1540s. *Journals of the House of Commons* (1803–) i. 38; Leland, *Itinerary*, iv. 114–15, 181–2.
[64] Charles Phythian-Adams, *Desolation of a City, Coventry and the Urban Crisis of the Late Middle
Ages* (Cambridge, 1979), *passim*; and *VCH, Warwickshire*, viii. 162–3; Leland, *Itinerary*, ii. 108.
Coventry was listed on the first 1540 statute for the re-edification of decayed towns, 32 Henry VIII,
c. 18.
[65] Stafford was listed in the first 1540 statute for the re-edification of towns (32 Henry VIII, c. 18),
and a statute of 1559 returned the assizes to Stafford because of the decay which had come to that
town in their absence; a copy of the statute, which is not printed in the *Statutes of the Realm*, may be
found in Staffordshire RO, MS D1323/EI.
[66] *VCH, Wiltshire*, vi. 100, 128–9; K. H. Rogers, 'Salisbury', in Lobel (ed.), *Historic Towns*, 7.
[67] Andrew B. Appleby, *Famine in Tudor and Stuart England* (Stanford, 1978), 106, 109, 166, *et
passim*.
[68] The Bridport market charter of 36 Elizabeth describes in detail the state of the town's decay,
noting that its harbour was blocked up 'by reason of which the same Borough in commerce and
merchandize is diminished and deteriorated and the buildings and edifices of the same Borough are
in great decay, ruin and dissolution'. There was no doubt an element of exaggeration in this, but its
substance is verifiable and thus probably accurate; Dorset RO, MS B3/03, dated 18 Jan. 36 Elizabeth.
A great plague hit the town in 1590, causing hardship for many who would normally have contributed
to the costs of civic projects; see court leet session for 5 Oct. 1590, B3/E2, no. 734.
[69] *VCH, Yorkshire, East Riding*, i. 433.

housing, there is very little private investment in *civic* buildings during
this era. In addition, prosperity could often be short-lived, and borough
fiscal reserves often remained thin at the best of times so that even
the wealthiest towns rarely found lavish surpluses to squander on conspicuous expenditure for its own sake. Finally, it is clear that hall-building
by itself is not a reliable indicator of prosperity.

To some extent, of course, it seems clear that some halls, and especially
those with marketing facilities or those in towns which hosted assizes or
quarter sessions, could bring in at least some income to the town and
some revenue to the civic coffers. At times, where fiscal shortfalls made
the upkeep of civic halls unsupportable from civic revenues, the whole
building of specific rooms within it could be let to a private individual, who
then became responsible for the upkeep and permitted the town to use it
when required. The impoverished borough of Shrewsbury, for example,
let its 'Great House called the Council House' to Roland Barker 'for such
term and interest as the bailiffs and burgeses have in it, he keeping it in
repair and paying all such rents and duties as are payable, and removing
when the Council of the Marches shall come here'.[70]

Some such profits deriving from the use of the hall were very short-
term. Halls were often let for the day for performances, a theme we shall
have more to say about in Chapter 6 below. Although this practice may
have been less common in the seventeenth century, we know, for
example, that a puppet-master named Jones, who paid twelve pence to
hire the Peterborough Common Hall 'for shewing of his puppits and for
shewing other tricks' in 1628,[71] represented a great many entertainers
who did the same throughout the realm. The borough of Leicester
collected a total of £5. 15s. 4d. for the year 1590/1 for performances of the
Queen's Players, the Earl of Worcester's Players, and Earl of Hertford's
Players, and for six additional plays plus a bear-baiting (the last of which
let us hope was held in the court-yard of the Leicester Guildhall rather
than in the council room itself!).[72] But though they provided steady
sources of revenue, these were very small sums and, at least in the first half
of our period, could be offset by the convention of giving gifts to the
players.

Clearly the most important and widest financial benefits of some halls
came either from their shared use by the assizes or quarter sessions or
from the business of marketing. Judicial sessions especially brought a
great multitude of people to the town, not only for the conduct of business

[70] HMC, *Fifteenth Report*, (1899), App., pt X, p. 23.
[71] W. T. Mellows (ed.), *Peterborough Local Administration, 1541–1689*, 2 vols. (Northamptonshire
Record Society, 10, 1939), 49.
[72] Mary Bateson (ed.), *Records of the Borough of Leicester*, iii (Cambridge, 1905), 273.

or in litigation, but also to partake in the public occasion provided by such meetings. This naturally meant a great deal to taverners, innkeepers, alehouse keepers, victuallers, and the like, and it is little wonder that so much energy went into attracting such meetings and providing the necessary amenities for them. A number of halls were put up or renovated with the thought of assizes or quarter sessions in mind, and the right to host such meetings was hotly contested throughout our period and well beyond. In a typical example of such conflict, the Welsh borough of Caernarvon succeeded in spiriting through Parliament in 1584–5 a bill ensuring its retention of quarter sessions, only to have Lord Burghley, representing the rival town of Conway, convince Queen Elizabeth not to sign it. A similar dispute arose between Alnwick and Morpeth in 1597/8.[73]

Marketing, too, provided an important source of revenue. Type B halls, clearly the more common type in our period, included sheltered marketing space at the ground level. In addition to this it was not unusual for interior spaces to be converted to commercial use. In a more general sense, and regardless of whether parts of the hall itself hosted market spaces directly, an improved town and market hall enhanced the commercial capability and reputation of the whole town, and was certainly most valued for that reason.

Yet though these functions seem important for their potential to bring profits to townsmen and revenues to the civic coffers, that income could almost never be raised before construction, in order to defray that cost itself, while benefits derived by specific towns from such activities remained long range and often uncertain. In addition, if any great number of towns built halls in expectation of arresting local economic decline, we would expect to find the sequence of hall-building bunched in those decades of greatest urban decay. And, while some halls were built in, for example, the 1550s, 1590, and 1620s, and while there were others built at still other times when fiscal caution might well have overruled in specific communities, these do not seem to have been particularly intense periods for such activities.

We can only conclude that if some towns built during hard times, perhaps with a thought to bringing a greater flow of business to the community and thus arresting such declines, at least as many others did not fall into these patterns. Though the costs and difficulties of building and the evident high priority placed on this particular form of building speak eloquently of the importance of civic halls, neither the circumstances of finance by itself nor the even broader economic considerations

[73] David M. Dean, 'Bills and Acts, 1584–1601' (Cambridge Univ. Ph.D. thesis 1985), 208. I am indebted to Dr Dean for permission to cite his thesis.

satisfactorily account in themselves for such frequent appearance of civic halls in this period. For more complete explanations, we must look beyond the realms of economics and finance alone.

4

The Civil Hall and the
Autonomous Community

INTRODUCTION

Given the considerable expense and organization involved in building, purchasing, or renovating a town hall, and the unlikelihood that many such buildings would pay for themselves through utilization, the movers and shakers behind such projects must have had very compelling motives. There were a number of factors which prompted such undertakings. This chapter will explore the most common motivations for hall acquisition in our period. It will emphasize that this activity often had much to do with political and administrative developments in English towns and with the requirements of town officials. This understanding of political considerations will also illustrate the political functions of the hall, and the symbolic meanings which it came to hold for contemporary townsmen.

To begin with, it is obvious that some towns simply needed to replace or rebuild existing halls which had become too small, dilapidated, or otherwise decayed. This happened with some frequency, and not only with older halls. We have already seen how the needs of government in the rapidly growing borough of Plymouth rendered its 1565 hall too small even by the opening years of the following century, necessitating a new building in 1606. Here, as in some other towns, part of the pressure to rebuild came from the statutory mandate (18 Elizabeth, c. 3, 1576 and 7 James I, c. 4, 1610) to construct houses of correction. No such facility existed in the earlier Plymouth hall, but this become an integral part of the new structure.[1] In Oxford we see an analogous need for additional space occasioned by the steady growth of the common council throughout the sixteenth century: the 60 to 70 members of *c.*1520 had grown to 80 to 90 in the Elizabethan era and to over 130 by 1630. This effectively rendered the existing meeting place inadequate. Similar needs account chiefly for Oxford's acquisition of the 'Lower Guildhall' in 1562 and then, after several decades of debate and procrastination, its bowing to the necessity

---

[1] Edwin Welch (ed.), *Plymouth Building Accounts of the Sixteenth and Seventeenth Centuries*, Devon and Cornwall Record Society, NS 12 (1967), pp. viii–ix. For an outline of the expansion of Plymouth in this period, cf. C. Gill, *Plymouth, a New History, Ice Age to the Elizabethans*, 2 vols. (Newton Abbot, 1966), ch. 9.

of a new Council House in 1615–17 as described in the previous chapter.[2] The same rationale no doubt applied to the notable expansions of town halls in our period, especially amongst such large and old cities as Exeter and Bristol.[3]

Blandford's 1593 Guildhall replaced a precedessor which had been destroyed by fire in 1570, and was itself destroyed by fire during the next century in that peculiarly combustible town.[4] In other communities very old halls had simply deteriorated to the point where, in the sixteenth or early seventeenth century, they had to be replaced. This reminds us again that numerous towns did build halls well back in the Middle Ages, possibly in the same sort of cyclic rhythm which we see in the Early Modern period, and some of these had come to the end of their natural life-spans. This would apparently have been the case in Abingdon;[5] Liverpool;[6] Norwich, where the collapse of the council chamber in 1511 led directly, if not immediately, to the construction of the large Council Chamber completed in 1535 and still in use;[7] Peterborough, whose 'Old Mote Hall' was torn down in its ruinous state in 1615 and replaced three years later;[8] and Hull, whose old common hall was, by 1633, simply too decrepit to be repaired.[9]

As has been noted in Chapter 1, some towns felt it a pressing matter of pride to keep up with the rival down the road. Our map of halls dating from this era (see Appendix) shows a cluster effect in some regions, as competitive towns followed their neighbours, while a random polka-dot pattern indicating an absence of such motivations prevails in others. This first point is well illustrated in Dorset, where Poole, Shaftesbury, and the newly united borough of Weymouth and Melcombe Regis all built halls between 1568 and 1571, Bridport followed Blandford Forum in 1593, and substantial additions and reconstructions were clustered around the 1610s and 1620s: Lyme Regis in 1612, Cerne Abbas around 1617, Weymouth on its own sometime between 1617 and 1622, Beaminster in 1626, Evershot in 1628, and Shaftesbury again at roughly the same time.[10]

---

[2] VCH, Oxfordshire, iv (Oxford, 1979), 131–3 and see above, p. 63.

[3] Both these large and ancient towns expanded their administrative functions in the sixteenth century and both built additional administrative or council space in the form of halls; see 'Census of Town Halls', Appendix.

[4] John Hutchins, The History and Antiquities of the County of Dorset, corrected by W. Shipp and J. W. Hodson, 4 vols. (1861–70), i, 216; E. L. Jones, S. Porter, and M. Turner, A Gazetteer of English Urban Fire Disasters, 1500–1900 (Historical Geography Research Series, 13, August 1984), tables 3 and 5.

[5] VCH, Berkshire, iv (1924), 433.

[6] J. A. Twemlow (ed.), Liverpool Town Books, 2 vols. (Liverpool, 1918 and 1935), i. 353 n. 3.

[7] Nikolaus Pevsner, BoE, North-east Norfolk and Norwich (Harmondsworth, 1962), 259.

[8] W. T. Mellows, Peterborough Local Administration, 1541–1689, pp. xcvii–xcviii.

[9] E. Gillet and K. MacMahon, A History of Hull (Oxford, 1981), 108.

[10] Robert Tittler, 'The Building of Civic Halls in Dorset, c. 1560–1640', BIHR 58 (1985), 38–9.

In Cornwall both Penzance and its rival Truro built halls in 1615; in Westmorland Appleby (1596) followed Kendal (1592); in Worchestershire Droitwich (1581) followed close behind Evesham (c.1580) and in Yorkshire neighbouring Knaresborough (1592) led Leeds (1598) and possibly Ripon (by 1599) in the 1590s, while Ripon (1611) and Leeds (1615) again came in close succession in a second round of hall building in the 1610s. Despite what one might expect, such competition does not seem to conform to wider patterns of geographic distribution.[11] As these examples indicate, towns in lowland and highland zones seem indistinguishable in this regard. Though other factors would have mattered as much and frequently more, keeping up with the Joneses must be counted a significant motivation for adding halls at this time.

Yet even if medieval town hall building may conceivably have been cyclical, it is hard to imagine that either the simple need to replace obsolete or decayed structures or the desire to emulate neighbouring towns should have been particularly more prevalent at one time than another. True, towns may have found it easier to pay for such undertakings in good times than bad, but as we have seen, the correlation between building and prosperity may at very best be described as imprecise. And even if chronological patterns do bear some correlation to overall economic and demographic circumstances, there are undoubted valleys (especially before 1540) and peaks (especially between c.1560 and c.1590) in the construction or acquisition of halls; they surely demand more of an explanation than the mere replacement of decayed structures or the expression of civic pride in the emulation of neighbours.[12]

In order to pursue this crucial question of motivations, and with it the overriding concern with the role of the town hall in this era, it seems crucial to keep in mind some of the contextual factors in English national and local history which may have had bearing on such projects. In any such survey, the tendency of large numbers of towns in this period— especially the simple marketing centres—to obtain greater self-direction, a tendency apparently supported by the Crown and in Parliament, seems particularly striking and germane.

URBAN AUTONOMY UNDER THE CROWN

To begin with, it now seems clear to many that the sixteenth century saw the net acquisition of a substantial degree of self-government in the towns of England.[13] This appears to have followed not merely in some, especially larger and earlier maturing communities as had previously been

[11] See map in Appendix.   [12] Cf. Table 1.
[13] The point has been made in full in Robert Tittler, 'The End of the Middle Ages in the English Country Town', *Sixteenth Century Journal*, 18/4 (1987), 471-87.

the case, but now perhaps even in the majority of towns throughout the realm.

In this discussion, the acquisition of 'self-government' or autonomy is taken to mean the shift of authority from its traditional locus—the crown and its surrogates, the lay landlords or the church—to groups of townsmen themselves, acting in at least a quasi-corporate capacity. This obviously assumes self-government under the 'constitutional', rather than seigneurial, powers of the crown, but it implies the removal of traditional intermediate authorities at the manorial and even sometimes the county level. The autonomous powers in question typically included collecting some taxes, returning writs, farming payments of fee, electing officers, establishing conciliar assemblies, presiding over the marketplace and its perquisites, administering at least some degree of judicial authority, and holding some lands as a source of revenue.

Of course there will be numerous exceptions to such generalities, and to the effort to date such change-overs to the sixteenth century and after. A substantial number remained firmly under manorial authority. On the other hand, some of the most important medieval towns (Exeter, Gloucester, and Salisbury amongst them) had gained these perquisites even in the twelfth century, and many more, especially in the upper and middling ranks of the urban hierarchy, gained them in the years between then and the start of the sixteenth.[14]

Yet if such attainments are undeniably well precedented prior to the sixteenth century, it would appear that such considerable self-direction, and such 'modern' administrative characteristics as bureaucracy, courts of justice, archives and records, and also civic buildings, became the norm rather than the exception in our period. Chronologically, this seems most evident during the latter five or six decades of the sixteenth century, the very period which also exhibits the distinct surge in the acquisition of so many halls. Typologically, it seems most characteristic of the middling communities, predominantly devoted to marketing of both general and specialized nature, which made up a substantial proportion of English towns at all times prior to industrialization. Geographically, it seems most widespread in the lowland zones of mixed or arable husbandry. These were the areas which held more towns to begin with and in which manorial organization, the common forebear of urban self-government, seems to have been more completely formed.

---

[14] Standard listings of borough charters by which powers were conveyed include A. Ballard, *British Borough Charters, 1042–1216* (Cambridge, 1913); Ballard and J. Tait (eds.), *British Borough Charters, 1216–1307* (Cambridge, 1923); M. Weinbaum, *British Borough Charters, 1307–1660* (Cambridge, 1943). See also the case made for greater self-determination amongst smaller towns of the south-east in the late fifteenth century in Marjorie K. McIntosh, 'Local Change and Community Control in England, 1465–1500', *The Huntington Library Quarterly*, 49/3 (1986), 219–42.

These patterns of change would seem to reflect two powerful, complex, and sweeping forces which may be dated to this approximate period. The first of these is that broad redistribution of land, and of the accompanying wealth and authority, often known by the short-hand (and inadequate) term 'the dissolution of the monasteries and chantries'. The second is the even more complex factor of accelerating economic and demographic activity which seems apparent in the realm as a whole, and in a great many towns, by the middle of the century.

Though the impact of the dissolution and redistribution of ecclesiastical properties has most often been examined with regard to the countryside,[15] it proved extremely important in towns as well.[16] For one, a vast amount of urban property, located in literally hundreds of towns, changed ownership. In addition, the actual lordship of many towns changed hands as well: perhaps as many as a hundred or more of England's six or seven hundred functioning towns at this time had been substantially or wholly under ecclesiastical control before 1536 and had experienced a change-over in control by 1547.[17] In many cases such transfers of control meant business as usual but under new management. In other cases it meant an initial discontinuity of some important services: schools, charitable institutions, the upkeep of roads and bridges, the physical structures and the administrative regulation of the market-place, and the like. When vast numbers of dissolved ecclesiastical properties were sold off by the Crown to individual purchasers, including both townsmen and individual towns,[18] local residents had often been compelled by necessity to fill the sudden vacuum of administration on their

[15] This preoccupation lies at the heart of the 'rise of the gentry/crisis of the aristocracy' controversies of the 1950s and 1960s, conveniently summarized in Lawrence Stone, *Social Change and Revolution in England, 1540–1640* (1965) esp. pt. I.

[16] The first to recognize the likelihood of such a tenurial revolution was probably Colin Platt, in *The English Medieval Town* (1976), 181.

[17] The estimated number of English towns is based on Peter Clark and Paul Slack, *English Towns in Transition, 1500–1700* (Oxford, 1976), 7–8, and the attempt at a more precise count in A. Dyer, 'The Market Towns of Southern England, 1500–1700', *Southern History*, 1 (1979), 125. D. M. Palliser is more conservative with a figure of 500–600, *The Age of Elizabeth, England under the Later Tudors, 1547–1603* (1983), 205. Much higher estimates are offered in Alan Everitt, 'The Marketing of Agricultural Produce', in J. Thirsk (ed.), *The Agrarian History of England and Wales*, iv *1500–1640* (Cambridge, 1967), 467 and T. S. Willan, *The Inland Trade* (Manchester, 1976), 53, 88. My own estimate of pre-Reformation 'ecclesiastical towns' is based on the *Calendar of Patent Rolls* and the Victoria County History series.

[18] e.g. St Albans, Faversham, Newark-upon-Trent, Stratford-upon-Avon, Axbridge, King's Lynn, Leominster, Totnes, Abingdon, and Lichfield. Some difficulties in identifying the purchase of such properties by towns arises through the common practice of employing agents, whose name appears on the patent roll or deed in place of the actual purchaser. Cf. H. J. Habakkuk, 'The Market for Monastic Property, 1539–1603', *Ec. HR* 2nd ser. 10/3 (1958), 362–80; R. B. Outhwaite, 'Who Bought Crown Lands? The Pattern of Purchases, 1589–1603' *BIHR* 44 (1971), 18–33, and Christopher Kitching, 'The Disposal of Monastic and Chantry Lands', in F. Heal and R. O'Day (eds.), *Church and Society in England, Henry VIII to James I* (1977), 119–36.

own (much, in fact, as townsmen had often done before when landlords, including churchmen, had been absentees).[19] In the same vein, merchant guilds and religious confraternities which had informally taken on some administrative roles in the past now moved to acquire formal recognition as principal local authorities in their own right.

Contemporaneous with these events, and integrally related to them, England as a whole experienced economic changes which were broadly based and applied, and deeply challenging to established patterns. Among these changes, the demographic factor seems crucial.[20] The often dramatic impact of net population growth during the course of the sixteenth century created or exacerbated problems of housing, food supply, sanitation, and unemployment. It played—with good reason—on fears of crime, rootlessness, and unrest. Ironically, in many towns it also had offsetting beneficial effects, including a quickening in market activity and a rise in rental values. Such changes profited some interests—those, both private and public, with jurisdiction over market revenues and perquisites of local courts,[21] and those who held rental properties[22]—even as it impoverished others.

What seems especially significant in this context of rapid economic change is the increased stakes involved in the control both of a great many whole towns, especially the simple marketing centres which made up the majority of all towns, and of the many rental properties within towns of all

[19] See e.g. Alan Dyer, 'Warwickshire Towns under the Tudors and Stuarts', *Warwickshire History*, 3/4 (1976-7), 131 and Marjorie K. McIntosh, 'Financing Poor Relief in Tudor England', paper delivered at the North American Conference on British Studies, Toronto, October 1984. I am indebted to Dr McIntosh for a copy of her text.

[20] John Hatcher, *Plague, Population and the English Economy, 1348-1530* (1977), ch. 5; E. A. Wrigley and R. S. Schofield, *The Population History of England, 1541-1871, a Reconstruction* (1981), pt. II and App. 3, esp. p. 528.

[21] The best description of such marketing activity is that of Alan Everitt, 'The Marketing of Agricultural Produce', esp. 502-6, but the chronological placement of expansion from 1570 seems late by two or three decades (cf. below, p. 81). See also Alan Dyer, 'Growth and Decay in English Towns, 1500-1700', *Urban History Yearbook*, 6 (1979), 60-72, and, especially for the seventeenth century, the same author's 'The Market Towns of Southern England'. Dyer clearly recognizes the diversity both of market town types and the economic patterns which may be attributed to them.

[22] Though the question of rental values has usually been studied in the rural setting, see A. F. Butcher, 'Rent, Population and Economic Change in Late-Medieval Newcastle', *Northern History*, 14 (1978), 67-77, and the same author's 'Rent and the Urban Economy; Oxford and Canterbury in the Late Middle Ages', *Southern History*, 1 (1979), 11-43; Palliser, *Age of Elizabeth*, 113-14, 214-15. More classic studies include E. Kerridge, 'The Movement of Rent, 1540-1640', *Ec. HR*, 2nd ser. 6 (1953-4), 16-34; R. H. Hilton, 'Rent and Capital Formation in Feudal Society', in *The English Peasantry in the Later Middle Ages* (Oxford, 1975), 174-215 and 'Some Problems of Urban Real Property in the Middle Ages', in C. H. Feinstein (ed.), *Socialism, Capitalism and Economic Growth* (Cambridge, 1967), 326-37; Platt, *English Medieval Town*, 181-3; W. G. Hoskins, 'English Provincial Towns', 11, and 'The Rebuilding of Rural England' 1570-1640', *P and P* 4 (1953), 44-59; Thirsk (ed.), *The Agrarian History of England and Wales*, iv 1500-1640 (Cambridge, 1967), 294-95, 687-94; Ian Blanchard, 'Population Change, Enclosure, and the Early Tudor Economy', *Ec. HR* 2nd ser. 23/3 (1970), 427-45.

types and sizes. While market revenues and the sundry perquisites of tolls and legal jurisdiction may not have been worth collecting by the lords of many fifteenth- or early sixteenth-century market towns, they grew steadily in value thereafter. By the fourth and fifth decades of the sixteenth century, the same era in which Parliament attended closely to the issue of decayed urban properties,[23] we see by contrast fierce competition for such perquisites and a greatly expanded market for rent-bearing urban properties.[24]

Seigneurial rights in many towns, often thrown on to the market in the aftermath of the dissolutions, were thus readily snatched up by eager investers among upwardly mobile landed or professional (but not, as yet, mercantile) interests. Much in the manner of new landlords in the countryside, these purchasers were anxious to ride the crest of rising profits in justifying their investments, and keen to enjoy the enhanced social standing and political influence which came in the bargain. In contrast to some of their predecessors, they were often efficient administrators, attuned to methodical managerial practices, and aware of legal rights and procedures. Thus fortified, they often tried hard to expand traditional roles or to enforce seigneurial rights which, in less prosperous or competitive days, had ceased to be enforced.[25]

Groups of townsmen, often joined in guilds or confraternities for which relations with seigneurial authority had often been dominated by rivalry for control, also saw in these decades both opportunity and need for greater autonomy. In many cases, especially where there had been absentee landlords or 'soft' administration, such townsmen had informally assumed jurisdiction for themselves and developed their own governing institutions. They could often point to decades of precedents in which they had come, quite informally, to collect their own local revenues,

[23] 26 Henry VIII, cc. 8 and 9; 27 Henry VIII, cc. 1 and 22; 32 Henry VIII, cc. 18 and 19; 33 Henry VIII, c. 36. Interesting precedents may be found several decades earlier in legislation primarily devoted to restoring land to tillage, a strong argument for renewed population growth by the turn of the century, in which the shortages of housing were recognized: 4 Henry VI, c. 19; 6 Henry VIII, c. 5; and 7 Henry VIII, c. 1.

[24] Everitt, 'The Marketing of Agricultural Produce', 502–6. These potential revenues may have been even more intensely coveted because of the frequent legal inability or paternalistic unwillingness of many landlords to raise rents on agrarian properties at the same time; Lawrence Stone, *The Crisis of the Aristocracy, 1558–1641* (Oxford, 1965), 303–7.

[25] Platt, *English Medieval Town*, 181–3. Again, landlords of rural properties have received the lion's share of attention, but the following are suggestive and supportive: Andrew Appleby, 'Agrarian Capitalism or Seigneurial Reaction?' *American Historical Review*, 80/3 (1975), 574–94; Alan Simpson, *The Wealth of the Gentry, 1540–1660* (Cambridge, 1962); Stone, *Crisis of the Aristocracy*, 303–7. The improvement-minded, efficient, and even ruthless landowners of those studies stand in sharp contrast to the picture of pre-dissolution counterparts as described in, e.g., J. Youings, *Sixteenth Century England* (1984), ch. 2. For the administrative laxity of pre-Reformation clerical landlords in particular, see S. E. Lehmberg, *The Reformation of Cathedrals, Cathedrals in English Society, 1485–1603* (Princeton, NJ, 1988), 32.

hold their own courts, select at least some of their own officials, and preside over their own marketing activities. Now, when quickening markets restored the financial value of such perquisites, and when landlords of a new generation—whether new purchasers or not—were anxious to receive their due even in an inflationary era, rivalry over local jurisdiction became both more common and more intense.[26]

There were other reasons as well for townsmen to seek greater autonomy in these decades. Towns of several descriptions all scrambled to recover their former well-being: the established manufacturing centre whose fortunes ebbed before the pull of rural competition,[27] the marketing centre now hard pressed by regional rivalry or by a hinterland where changing agricultural circumstances actually reduced trade,[28] and the port which failed to keep up with commercial rivals (especially London and the chartered companies of the Elizabethan era) or which failed to diversify its trade at a time of shifting consumer demand.[29]

The widespread perception of growing disorder proved an equally compelling motivation. Although once again the bulk of modern scholarship has tended to consider riot and other forms of disorder more often in the countryside than in the towns, townsmen and town officials were by no means strangers to the problem.[30] It is noteworthy that one of the first ordinances issued by the council of the newly incorporated borough of Abingdon called for every household 'to have in redynes a good and sufficient clubbe for the conservacon of the peace'.[31]

These complex circumstances provided ample potential for conflict, with quasi-corporate bodies of townsmen on the one hand and the more traditional landlords on the other frequently at each other's throats over political jurisdiction or property holding. In consequence, town officials were now pressed more than ever to seek formal recognition of the authority which would add strength to their efforts. Failure in this effort could mean fiscal impotence, an inability to reinstitute or perpetuate

[26] Everitt, 'The Marketing of Agricultural Produce', 502–6 and R. Tittler, 'The Incorporation of Boroughs, 1540–1558', *History*, 62/204 (1977), 27–9.
[27] e.g. Lavenham, Gloucester, Sheffield, Lincoln, Taunton, Shrewsbury, Bridgwater, and Coventry.
[28] e.g. Chippenham, Brackley, Stafford, and Northampton.
[29] e.g. Boston, Barnstaple, Southampton, Lyme Regis, and Grimsby.
[30] J. A. Sharpe has usefully asked why urban historians have tended to neglect crime as a subject in the Early Modern period, but he himself has no illusions about the gravity of that phenomenon: Sharpe, *Crime in Early Modern England 1550–1750* (1984), 110–11. See also J. S. Cockburn, 'The Nature and Incidence of Crime in England, 1559–1625, a Preliminary Survey', in Cockburn (ed.), *Crime in England, 1550–1800* (1977), 49–53; B. Sharp, *In Contempt of All Authority* (Berkeley, Calif., 1980), chs. 1, 2; K. Wrightson, *English Society, 1580–1680* (1982), ch. 6; Youings, *Sixteenth Century England*, 209; Roger B. Manning, *Village Revolts, Social Protests and Popular Disturbances in England, 1509–1640* (Oxford, 1988), *passim*.
[31] Berkshire Co. RO, MS D/EP/7/84, p. 163.

social institutions uprooted at the Reformation, and a missed chance, perhaps the last, to obtain a grip on local autonomy.

The importance of tighter control was often as clear to the crown and to Parliament in this period as it was to townsmen themselves.[32] While those central governing institutions furthered this objective in their own ways, townsmen tended to adopt one of three strategies towards the same end: litigation, incorporation, and enfeoffment. All three prove closely and sequentially related to the acquisition of town halls, and thus each warrants some brief attention.

Alan Everitt was the first to observe the marked increase in litigation between landlords and groups of townsmen which emerged in this era. Drawing largely on a single class of records in the Court of Exchequer (E 134), Everitt found something in the order of a hundred examples of such litigation from the 1570s forward, litigation which more often than not sustained the claims of the townsmen. He thus dated this litigious striving for local self-determination, and all that it implied, to the 1570s.[33] But by looking at other classes of court records, including cases in Chancery, Star Chamber, and Requests, we may satisfy ourselves that this spate of contests over jurisdiction may be pushed back to at least two or even three decades earlier.

One of the earliest such cases, and perhaps one of the longest lasting as well, aptly illustrates a number of the points at hand. It began shortly after the year 1540, the year in which William Rede purchased the lordship of the fenland surrounding the town of Beccles, in Suffolk. Formerly belonging to the Abbey of Bury St Edmunds, the Beccles Fen held substantial economic importance for the townsmen, and the territory of the Fen even included some of the lands in the town itself. Oddly enough, Rede's grant and title left the precise terms of his jurisdiction to be determined over an initial five-year period.[34] Not surprisingly, the new landlord hastened to establish his authority and perquisites wherever he could. He appointed his own reeves to collect the sundry fines and profits which the townsmen had assumed for themselves, he raised the rents on some of his properties in the town, and he continually denied the townsmen the exercise of several forms of jurisdiction which they had come to consider their own.

The townsmen met this frontal attack on their presumed rights by

[32] Peter Clark and Paul Slack, *Crisis and Order in English Towns, 1500–1700,* (1972), 21–2; Tittler, 'The Emergence of Urban Policy, 1536–1558', in J. Loach and R. Tittler (eds.), *The Mid-Tudor Polity, c.1540–1560* (1980), 74–93.

[33] Everitt, 'The Marketing of Agricultural Produce', 502–6.

[34] J. S. Brewer, James Gairdner, and R. H. Brodie (eds.), *Letters and Papers, Foreign and Domestic, of the Reign of Henry VIII, 1509–47,* 21 vols. (1862–1910), xv. 175, patent delivered 22 March, 31 Henry VIII.

obtaining a charter of incorporation in 1543,[35] and then—Rede still not giving them their due—by undertaking formal litigation to defend their now chartered rights. In effect, therefore, Rede's efficient and aggressive management of his new-bought lands, lands which had been thrown on to the market first by the monastic dissolutions and then once again by a king anxious to replenish his coffers, proved the stimulus for the townsmen of Beccles to assert their independence from manorial control with the full backing of the law. At least for a time, for the ultimate result of their efforts was short of complete victory, the burgesses of Beccles did manage to ward off the seigneurial restraints which Rede had attempted to reimpose.[36]

A similar and more decisive case may be found in the Worcestershire town of Evesham.[37] Its vivid illustration of many of the points raised above warrants a full description. Shortly after the dissolution of Evesham Abbey in 1540 the Crown sold the lordship and manor of Evesham in two parcels to Sir Philip Hoby: first the house, site, and appurtenances of the abbey itself in July 1542, for the sum of £891. 10s., and then in October 1546, the lordship of the actual town, including 171 tenements or messuages, with shops, houses, and other buildings, for the even larger sum of £1,067. 2s. 11d.: an overall investment on Hoby's part of very close to £2,000![38] Yet Hoby was no fool, and certainly no mere social climber. John Leland, who visited the town at almost the precise time it came into Hoby's hands, found it 'metely large and well buildyd with tymbar', but even more important he found that 'the Market Stede is faire and large. There be divers praty streats in the towne. The market kept at Eovesham is very celebrate.'[39] Thus, mid-Tudor Evesham seems to have enjoyed a degree of prosperity. Though Leland didn't say so, Evesham also had three fairs a year and a population, if we may extrapolate from the ecclesiastical census of 1563, of some 311 families in two parishes, or roughly 1,400 residents: a fairly typical population for a mid-Tudor market town.[40]

A point which Leland failed to note and which Hoby conveniently

---

[35] PRO, C 66/721/m. 10 (10 March 1543).

[36] The litigation, enduring for three generations of the Rede family, may be followed chiefly in three separate cases: *Rede* v. *Baase*, PRO, E 134/4/658, E 123/14/203–5, E 123/12/108–9, and E 123/11/297–8; *Beccles* v. *Gresham*, PRO, C 3/29/109; and *Beccles* v. *Rede*, PRO, C 3/30/4. See also the extensive records of Beccles Fen in the care of the town clerk of Beccles, and conveniently summarized in typescript in National Register of Archives vol. 2988.

[37] The basic story has been related in G. May, *A Descriptive History of the Town of Evesham* (Evesham, 1845), 254–84, in *VCH, Worcestershire*, ii. 374–5, but both accounts call for some correction: see below. A valuable background is provided in R. H. Hilton, 'The Small Town and Urbanisation—Evesham in the Middle Ages', *Midland History*, 7 (1982), 1–8.

[38] PRO, C 66/715/m. 33 and C 66/787/m. 11.   [39] Leland, *Itinerary*, ii. 52.

[40] BL, Harleian MS 595, fo. 211ᵛ. I have used the commonly accepted multiplier of 4.5 persons per family.

chose to ignore, is that Evesham was one of those towns in which the townsmen had come informally to exercise a considerable degree of self-government while still under the nominal jurisdiction of the abbots who had held the manor. In 1482 the abbot of the day had assented to this arrangement, though it may already have been in force. From that time forth the townsmen operated an unofficial but effective and self-perpetuating system of local government. Their chosen officers, still called bailiffs, held the leet court and the 'three weeks court' in the name of the Crown and, for the price of a modest annual payment to the Exchequer, the townsmen received the profits of the market, fair, and courts.[41]

Almost immediately after he had come to possess the manor, Hoby strove to regain the jurisdiction and perquisites which had effectively been abandoned by his ecclesiastical predecessors some sixty years before. He pressed the chief inhabitants to submit for his selection a list of candidates to serve as bailiffs, and worked hard to establish his claims on the feudal and chiefly fiscal perquisites of the market, fairs, and courts.[42] Oddly enough, the townsmen submitted to these claims for some years while Hoby, who died in 1558, and then his heirs and successors, appear to have made at least *some* benevolent gestures towards them.

Yet the chief inhabitants eventually grew impatient with their renewed subordination, and by the middle of Elizabeth's reign they were able to convince the Crown that, in holding a leet court in his own name, Hoby was depriving the Exchequer of revenue. Acting in effect on behalf of the majority of the townsmen, the Crown then sued Hoby in the court of Exchequer.[43] Though that court eventually brought down a compromise judgement in 1586, the townsmen pressed on until, in 1604, they secured from James I a full charter of incorporation, slightly amended by a second charter in the following year.[44] These charters virtually assured independence from the control of the Hoby family in all but name.

In the cases of Beccles and Evesham as in many similar communities, (for example Aylesbury,[45] Tenby,[46] Thaxted,[47] Chippenham,[48]

---

[41] VCH, Worcestershire, ii. 373. See also the various depositions in the lengthy case of Hoby v. Kighley, PRO, E 134/29 Eliz./East. 12.

[42] VCH, Worcestershire, ii. 373–5.

[43] Hoby v. Kighley et al., PRO, E 134/29 Eliz./East. 12.

[44] VCH, Worcestershire, ii. 374–5. The second charter has been translated and printed in full in W. Tindal, The History and Antiquities of the Abbey and Borough of Evesham (Evesham, 1794) and May, Descriptive History, 254–84.

[45] Pakington v. Walwyn, PRO, C 1/Bundle 1371/11 (1553–5).

[46] Queen v. Hastling, Interrogatory and Deposition of 18 Elizabeth, PRO, E 133/Bundle 2/319.

[47] Cf. R. Tittler, 'Incorporation and Politics in Sixteenth Century Thaxted', Essex Archaeology and History, 8 (1976), 224–32.

[48] A dispute over the rights of Sir Henry Sherington to the borough market, c. 1554–8, is narrated in M. G. Rathbone (ed.), A Descriptive List of the Wiltshire Borough Records (Devizes, 1951), 9.

Launceston,[49] and, in the early seventeenth century, Olney,[50] Oswestry,[51] and Walsall[52]) the informal assertion of local autonomy which had taken place during the administration of late medieval lordship came under challenge and led to formal litigation in the changing economic and political circumstances of the post-dissolution era. Some such challenges even came from the Crown, which—out of its concern for strong local government—feared weakened control over recently repossessed Crown lands. Yet most came from a more aggressive and, for lack of a better term, more modern group of individual landlords. These socially aspiring purchasers of former ecclesiastical properties naturally wanted all the control and perquisites to which they considered themselves entitled. The frequent, if not invariable, result of ensuing litigation tended to favour the interests of local autonomy over that of the landlords. In the eyes of the common law, local claims to rule were often better grounded in practice while, as a matter of political reality, local authorities often held out greater promise for maintaining law and order.

As one might expect, contests over specific urban properties are even more thoroughly documented, and again this is true well before the 1570s. Such contests included disputes over such revenue-producing facilities as the rights to a mill in Reading[53] as well as the more common type of dispute over rental properties themselves, as in Worcester (c.1544–7),[54] Sudbury (c.1544–7),[55] Barnstaple (1547–51),[56] or Launceston (1547–51).[57]

A second device by which townsmen sought to augment control over their own communities was the charter of incorporation. While it would be obdurate to insist that formal charters of borough incorporation necessarily created rights anew, rather than merely sanctioning authority already claimed and exercised informally, the very fact that townsmen sought and received royal sanction, and through such a formal and expensive process as incorporation, surely marks an important milestone in the assertion of local autonomy.

When, then, were such charters granted? Here again precedents extend well back in time, for the first towns to be incorporated gained such boons in the mid-fourteenth century. Yet the chronological record

[49] *Tenants of Launceston* v. *Hicks* et al., PRO, Req. 2/Bundle 22/91, *temp.* Mary.
[50] PRO, C 93/9/21, m. 3 (21 James I).
[51] *Lloyd* v. *Morrys*, PRO, STAC 8/198/27, *c.*1610.
[52] E. J. Homeshaw, *The Corporation of the Borough and Foreign of Walsall* (Walsall, 1960), 10–22; Interrogatory and Deposition of 8 Elizabeth, PRO, E 133/1/61.
[53] *Bowyer* v. *Nicholas*, PRO, C 1/File 1101/34–5 (*c.*1544–7).
[54] *Sheldon* v. *Calowe and Ewe, Bailiffs*, PRO, C 1/File 1160/26–7 (*c.*1544–7).
[55] *Smyth, Mayor* v. *Ayloffe*, PRO, C 1/File 1160/61–2.
[56] *Cockeram* v. *Rede and Meryfeld*, PRO, C 1/File 1204/70, (*c.*1547–51).
[57] *Seymer* v. *Monke, Mayor*, PRO, C 1/File 1184/17–20 (*c.*1547–51).

provides a clear pattern which again points to the mid-sixteenth century as the time when the practice began to be general and widespread. After a trickle of only thirteen borough incorporations in the period 1485–1540, we find a virtual torrent immediately thereafter. Excluding mere confirmations, eight towns received incorporation in the last seven years under Henry VIII, 12 in the reign of Edward VI from 1547 to 1553, a striking 24 in the five and a half years of Mary's reign from 1553 to 1558, an additional 46 in the rest of the century under Elizabeth,[58] and a further 47 to 1640. By the early seventeenth century the incorporated borough, with the self-governing powers which became the standard features of such corporations, became a normative form of town government in towns of any significant size, and would remain so right up until the nineteenth century.

Ironically, the not uncommon practice of concealing ecclesiastical properties and assuming jurisdiction informally militated against such formal processes as incorporation, which could well uncover illegal concealments. In Walsall, for example, the mayor and 'his brethren' concealed and assumed jurisdiction over the chantry lands of the Gild of St John, including the Guildhall itself and lucrative rental properties, succeeding in their ruse until 1565. Even after discovery they continued informally but effectively to utilize such lands, until threatened by a new manorial lord in the reign of James I. Only then did the townsmen seek and receive incorporation and secure their possessions.[59] A similar pattern seems to have pertained in Bury St Edmunds, and no doubt other communities as well.[60]

Yet more commonly the effort to gain secure title to former church lands and rental properties, and to hold such lands in mortmain with the right to alienate according to the terms of incorporating charters, remained paramount in the decision to seek incorporation. Indeed, the right to hold land in mortmain was one of the most important aspects of such incorporations and it could well have been difficult for an unincorporated body to sustain such a claim. In some cases the resulting revenue facilitated the refoundation of such institutions as schools which were uprooted in the Reformation (for example Warwick, Louth, Saffron Walden, St Albans, Stafford, Stratford-upon-Avon, and Wisbech). In other instances (such as Colnbrook, Sheffield, and Barnstaple) essential public works were the favoured cause, while in still other towns the process was simply intended to augment the revenue base of the community. Such an infusion of resources (or reclamation, under secular

[58] Summarized in Tittler, 'Incorporation of Boroughs, 1540–1558'.
[59] PRO, E 133/1/61.
[60] Margaret Statham, *Jankyn Smith and the Guildhall Feoffees* (Bury St Edmunds, 1981), 7–11.

aegis, of traditional resources) may have made the difference in some towns between fiscal viability and fiscal collapse. In Boston, for example, lands formerly held by local religious guilds to the value of £526. 16s. 11d. per annum were received by charter for a purchase price of £1,646. 15s. 4d., payable over twelve years, assuring a profit even at stable rental values of over £300 a year.[61] Towns with similar experience include Hull, Worcester, Winchester, Grantham, and Bath.[62]

A third telling sign that many towns came to covet greater autonomy under the Crown in this period is the little explored tendency of townsmen to form legal trusts in order to establish and preserve important perquisites of government. Here the question of revenue properties, and the social services which they helped to support, was even more central. The very essence of the trust or 'use' was to ensure that a self-perpetuating body of townsmen could control sufficient real property to provide the income and authority necessary for the direction either of charitable institutions alone or even the effective government of an entire town.

By the sixteenth century royal policy had swung round behind this legal device as a means of protecting such properties and charitable endowments. We may see this as an integral component of the Tudor concern for maintaining order through the relief of the poor. Having first distinguished between superstitious and secular (that is, charitable) uses (by 23 Henry VIII, c. 10; 27 Henry VIII, c. 10; 37 Henry VIII, c. 4; and 1 Edward VI, c. 14) such policy reached its final expression in the more comprehensive statutes of 1597 (39 Elizabeth I, c. 6) and 1601 (43 Elizabeth I, c. 4). The last of these even established a national system of Charity Commissioners to supervise the appropriate operation of trusts in each shire, though corporate towns often remained exempt from such jurisdiction.[63]

Trusts were usually secured when a group of townsmen collected a sufficient sum to purchase the desired rental properties or charitable endowments from the Crown. This often followed the reversion of such

[61] *Brown* v. *Mayor of Boston* et al., PRO, STAC 3/5/11 and STAC 3/8/18 (1547) especially Brown's petition in the former and the defendant's answer in the latter. Cf. also G. A. J. Hodgett, 'The Dissolution of the Religious Houses in Lincolnshire', *Lincolnshire Architectural and Archaeological Society*, 4 (1951), 83–99.

[62] R. Horrox (ed.), *Selected Rentals and Accounts of Medieval Hull, 1293–1528* (Yorkshire Archaeological Society Record Series, 141, 1983 for 1981), 17; Alan Dyer, *The City of Worcester in the Sixteenth Century* (Leicester, 1973), 217–18; Adrienne Rosen, 'Economic and Social Aspects of the History of Winchester, 1520–1670' (Oxford Univ. D.Phil. thesis 1975), 64–75; John B. Manterfield, 'The Topographical Development of the Pre-Industrial Town of Grantham, Lincolnshire, 1535–1835' (Univ. of Exeter Ph.D. thesis 1981), 7, 51, 58; PRO, E 133/1/61; A. J. King and B. H. Watts (eds.), *The Municipal Records of Bath, 1189—1604* (n.d.), 59.

[63] W. K. Jordan, *Philanthropy in England, 1480–1660*, (1959), 109–13 and Gareth Jones, *History of the Law of Charity, 1532–1827* (Cambridge, 1969), chs. 2 and 3.

lands from ecclesiastical to royal control. The Crown would then sell the
land to two or three townsmen selected by their fellows to receive it.
These receivers then conveyed the same land by formal deed to a group of
named townsmen, usually a dozen or more in number, who thus became
trustees or feoffees for that property. The terms of their authority,
including powers of governance, control of the subsequent rental income,
and the provision to co-opt replacements for themselves, often constituted an effective and 'perpetual' instrument of town government. It
conferred the authority to exercise such powers with the legal force of the
registered deed.

Though in practical terms the powers of the town trust were often
expanded by use well beyond strict legal entitlement, trusts still did not
approximate the authority of a corporate body. The well-preserved
records of the Feoffees of the Guildhall which served to govern Bury
St Edmunds between the dissolution of the abbey in 1539 and the incorporation of 1608, shows their activities in providing for education,
relief of the poor and sick, the administration of town lands and the
market place. But the feoffees possessed no judicial authority, and they
could do little to ward off the political influence of several leading
landowners who resided elsewhere in the shire. Indeed, some of these,
including the Lord Keeper of the Great Seal (1558-79) Sir Nicholas
Bacon, and powerful local gentry such as Sir Robert Jermyn and Sir John
Higham, served as feoffees themselves. Still, trusts were more readily
available than charters of incorporation—even Bacon failed in the effort
to secure incorporation for Bury in 1562—and cost less to obtain. Above
all, they readily filled the vacuum left in local administration after the
dissolutions.[64]

As trusts were not acquired by patent and thus remain absent from such
a convenient source of identification as the Patent Rolls, it remains
difficult to assess precisely how many towns followed this course. Yet in
communities such as Market Harborough, Rotherham, Loughborough,
Tetbury, Sheffield, Torrington, Melton Mowbray, Bridlington,
Chippenham, Stroud, and in scores of others, the town trust came to form
the effective instrument of government. This practice too seems first to
have become common in the sixteenth century.[65]

[64] Statham, *Jankyn Smith, passim* and W. Suffolk RO, MSS H2/6.2, vol. I *passim* and H2/3/1.1; R.
Tittler, *Nicholas Bacon, the Making of a Tudor Statesman* (1976), 150. For an interesting essay on the
role of trusts in the refounding and administration of schools in this era, see Joan Simon, 'Town
Estates and Schools in the Sixteenth and Early Seventeenth Centuries' in Brian Simon (ed.),
Education in Leicestershire, 1540–1940 (Leicester, 1968).
[65] F. W. Maitland, 'Trust and Corporation', in H. A. L. Fisher (ed.), *The Collected Papers of F. W.
Maitland*, 3 vols. (Cambridge, 1911), iii. 321–404; Dorothy Pockley, 'The Origins and Early History
of the Melton Mowbray Town Estate' (Leicester Univ. Ph.D. thesis 1964); Kevin Grady, 'The
Records of the Charity Commissioners, a Source for Urban History', *Urban History Yearbook* (1982),
31-3.

Along with the constitutional milestones represented in many towns by victory in litigation, the attainment of an incorporating charter, or the formation of a town trust, went the accompanying concern for the keeping of records. This may be construed both as evidence of the Cromwellian administrative methods of the 1530s percolating down to the town level, and, more practically, a recognition of the potential legal necessity that records be produced to substantiate legal claims.

Again, while this modern administrative habit was certainly present in some, especially larger or older, towns prior to this time, the sixteenth century seems to have been crucial in making it commonplace. No doubt encouraged by the Henrician directive for the establishment of regular parochial records at the same time, we have here the most common period for beginning the town assembly book, keeping regular financial accounts, writing down ordinances and by-laws, and recording the award of freemen's admissions as regular practices in what appears to be the majority of towns with some measure of self-government. This is conspicuously evident, for example, in Boston, which gained self-government for the first time with a charter of 1545, and which began formal record keeping in the form of a corporation minute book the very same year. Thanks to the publication of this book we can follow the earliest stages of Boston's corporate development from birth itself to full maturity by the following century.[66]

We also find here that even smallish towns came commonly to have a clerk directly responsible for many classes of records: perhaps an outgrowth of the medieval parish clerk. We know that in Boston this official was well rewarded for his services from the very beginning, and that from 1562 he was considered a sufficiently prestigious official to receive a dwelling-house as part of his remuneration.[67] Similar examples are provided in Kendal (1575), Liskeard (1556), and Melton Mowbray (1556) among many others,[68] though the example of Hull by 1464 reminds us that, if it then became more common, this was not an absolute invention of the sixteenth century.[69]

And, as the importance of these records, and especially of governing charters or deeds of trust, grew to be recognized in these communities, so

[66] Bailey, *Minutes of Boston*. The emergence at this time of methodical record keeping in administration was not exclusive to the towns. We see it as well in the central government from the reign of Henry VIII, and even amongst the landed aristocracy during the broad period 1560–1640; G. R. Elton, *The Tudor Revolution in Government: Administrative Changes in the Reign of Henry VIII* (Cambridge, 1953), 415–18 *et passim*, and Stone, *Crisis of the Aristocracy*, 274–85.

[67] Bailey, *Minutes of Boston*, i. 53.

[68] R. S. Ferguson (ed.), *A Boke off Recorde . . . of Kirkbiekendall . . . 1575* (Kendal, 1892), 22–39; Cornwall RO, MS B/Liskeard/203; Pockley, 'Origins and Early History of the Melton Mowbray Town Estate', 134.

[69] Horrox, *Rentals and Accounts of Hull*, 107, 177 n. 89.

do we find a growing concern for keeping them secure, not only from decay, but also from the genuine possibilities of alteration or theft. The reference to charters kept 'in bag or box sealed or in chest locked' became almost a stock phrase in contemporary litigation. Town accounts now attest to the acquisition of such chests, the elaborate distribution of keys to open them or even, as at Bury St Edmunds and Morpeth, to muniment rooms purpose-built for their safe-keeping.[70]

THE SEAT AND SYMBOL OF THE AUTONOMOUS COMMUNITY

As all the factors treated above relate closely to the acquisition, design, and utilization of civic halls in specific communities, we may at last consider the Tudor and early Stuart town hall in its appropriate political context. As one might already suspect, the construction, purchase, or renovation of this particular building type is less often likely to have been a purely random event, brought about by decaying timbers or civic booster-ism, than an integral part of the 'coming of age' in towns throughout the realm at this time. The government of towns, like those of nation-states, also came to require permanent buildings in which to conduct official business, and they appear to have done so at this time more than ever before.

The acquisition of many halls followed the attainment of charters of incorporation. As shown in Table 5, at least 31 of the 87 towns receiving such charters between 1500 and 1640 built or otherwise acquired such halls soon after (or, in one or two cases, so shortly before as to suggest almost certain anticipation of) that constitutional event.

The incorporation of Abingdon, for example, certified by charter in 1556, conferred the right to have a council house along with the long list of other rights and powers set out in full. The town had long been under manorial jurisdiction, and the leet court and view of frankpledge had been held since at least the fourteenth century in the old market hall. Yet this was considered inadequate for the needs of a borough corporation: it was too small, in need of too many repairs, and, perhaps above all, too firmly linked with the authority of the manorial lord to suit the new ruling officials. In consequence, Abingdon's mayor and councillors adapted an increasingly common solution. In 1560 they purchased from William Blacknall, who in turn had purchased it from the Crown, the former Chapel and Hospital of St John the Baptist and converted it to serve as the 'new' Guildhall. Though a few governing functions continued to be

---

[70] Margaret Statham, 'The Guildhall, Bury St Edmunds', *Proceedings of the Suffolk Institute of Archaeology*, 31 (1970), 131; Morpeth Bor. Manuscripts, HMC, *Sixth Report* (1877), App. 537.

TABLE 5. Incorporation and acquisition of town halls

Town	Incorporation date	Hall date
Abingdon	1555	c.1560
Bideford	1573	1575
Boston	1545	c.1545–55
Chipping Sodbury	1538	1558
Droitwich	1554	1581
Great Dunmow	1555	1578
Gloucester	1605 (reincorporated)	1606
Gravesend	1562 and 1568	1573
Hartlepool	1593	c.1560
Hereford	1597	c.1599
Kendal	1575	1592
Lyme Regis	1591	1612
Macclesfield	1595	c.1590s
Maidenhead	1582	mid-1580s
Maidstone	1604 (reincorporated)	1608
Maldon	1554	1576
Newbury	1596	1611
Penzance	1614	1615
Poole	1568	1568–70
Reading	1542	1542
Ripon	1604	1611
Romsey	1607 (reincorporated)	early 17th c.
Saffron Walden	1549	post-dissolution
St Albans	1553	1548–53
Sheffield	1554	by 1571
Sutton Coldfield	1528	t. Henry VIII
Tewkesbury	1575	1576
Tiverton	1615	c.1615
Warwick	1545	post-dissolution
Weymouth, Melcombe Regis	1571	c.1571
Wycombe	1598 (reincorporated)	1604

Source: Martin Weinbaum, *British Borough Charters, 1307–1660* (Cambridge, 1943), pp. xxix–lv.

housed elsewhere, the building came by 1563 to contain the council chambers and court room of the corporation.[71]

Similarly, though at the other end of the realm and nearly a half century later, the charter incorporating the Durham borough of Hartlepool in

[71] *VCH, Berkshire*, iv. 433; *Calendar of Patent Rolls, Philip and Mary*, iii. 380–6; B. Challoner, *Selections from the Municipal Chronicles of Abingdon* (Abingdon, 1898), 30; Agnes C. Baker, *Historic Abingdon* (Abingdon, 1963), 28, 46–7; Berkshire Co. RO, MS D/EP7/83 and 84, *passim*.

1593 also called for the mayor 'to appoint a council house or guildhall for the transaction of their business'. Work on the new hall began by the end of the decade, with the wealthier citizens making an annual contribution to supply at least some of the required building capital.[72] This charter, too, called for a new town hall; though by no means an invariable practice, this seems a clear sign that the leading townsmen who petitioned for the charter (almost always the same men who would be named in it as 'charter' officers of the new corporation) sought to gain royal endorsement for the acquisition or construction of such a building, and to identify that edifice with their own governing authority.

Although Abingdon and Hartlepool are typical of those towns building or acquiring a hall after full incorporation, halls were also obtained after lesser constitutional milestones. Bridport received a charter for a new market in January 1594, a few months after beginning construction of the new hall in anticipation of that grant.[73] Farnham's Hall coincided with the grant of the town to its burgesses in 1566, though this was not an actual incorporation.[74] Alcester's Market and Town Hall, built largely with a £300 donation from Sir Fulke Greville, serving as mayor at the time, followed a charter granting St Giles Fair to the town.[75] The Langport Market Hall, which shared the functions of a town hall with another building built at some unknown time in the same century, also followed the grant of a new market.[76] Newark-upon-Trent gained a Sessions Hall after the grant of the status of JP to certain of the town's officials in 1604: the building served some of the functions of the Town Hall when these officials conducted aspects of town business in the name of the Crown.[77] Wokingham's Town Hall of 1585 followed by two years the confirmation of the town's ancient customs and liberties.[78] And the acquisition of Peterborough's Guildhall followed the creation of the town's governing trust in 1571.[79] Similar milestones may well have been provided by the victory of townsmen in litigation, the purchase of substantial lands and properties from a landlord or the Crown, or simply the prevailing mood of assertiveness deriving from such events. Towns which failed to build or purchase a hall after such occasions often already possessed suitable facilities. In these cases, to be explored at length in the next chapter, structural renovations, new furnishings, or substantial additions were

[72] *VCH, Durham*, iii (1928), 265; Cuthbert Sharpe, *History of Hartlepool* (Hartlepool, 1851), 105.
[73] Dorset RO, Bridport Bor. Archives, MS B3/02–3.
[74] Weinbaum, *British Borough Charters*, p. xxxviii.
[75] *VCH, Warwickshire*, iii. 13.
[76] *VCH, Somerset*, iii. 27; PRO, E 134/42 and 43 Elizabeth, no. 27, m. 6.
[77] Weinbaum, *British Borough Charters*, p. xlvi; PRO, SP 14/54/50.
[78] *VCH, Berkshire*, iii. 226–7; PRO, E 134/Hil. 39, Eliz., no. 4, deposition of Thomas Avis, m. 3.
[79] Mellows, *Peterborough Local Administration*, ii. 193–6.

often undertaken to accommodate and reflect newly certified or augmented authority.

It would also appear that, as in Abingdon and so many other communities, the acquisition of a town hall often followed the dissolution of
ecclesiastical properties.[80] This came about not only because of the
transfer of lordship itself from Church to Crown and then to town, but
also because of the obvious availability of large, appropriately propor-
tioned buildings accompanying such transfers or coming independently
on to the market. In addition, a number of such buildings had long housed
at least some civic and secular functions. As D. M. Woodward has
recently reminded us, Englishmen of the pre-industrial era were past
masters at recycling,[81] and we are of course familiar with the pillage of
church buildings for their building materials by landowners, many of
them newly risen, anxious to construct their own houses. Yet we should
also remember that many buildings were recycled intact, or at most
renovated to reflect civic needs, by town authorities who had come into
their own during these decades.

Most familiar amongst these buildings are the halls of the medieval
guilds which kept the name 'guild-hall' but which now came under the
purely secular aegis of civic authorities. Here, in Leicester, Walsall,
Norwich, Lavenham, Peterborough, Chipping Sodbury, and other such
communities, the break in utilization was not at all sharp. The buildings
and the guilds or confraternities which they had housed had already been
closely linked to town governments. But other forms of ecclesiastical
building were also employed, and these often required much more
definitive changes in use and form.

The Benedictine priory of St Mary in Totnes, Devon, founded in 1088,
was suppressed in 1536 and stripped of its possessions and furnishing.
The townsmen bought it from Edward VI in 1553, gutted the interior of
the refectory, and rebuilt and furnished it as the new Guildhall. Further
renovations ensued in 1624, and some of the furnishings and decoration
from this work may still be seen.[82] The borough of St Albans, where local
government had been seriously retarded by the tight control of the abbot,
received by its 1553 charter of incorporation title to the former House of
the Charnel Brotherhood, and converted it to use as the Borough
Common Hall.[83] Wareham in Dorset rebuilt the deconsecrated Chapel

---

[80] See 'Census of Town Halls', Appendix.
[81] D. M. Woodward, '"Swords into Ploughshares": Recycling in Pre-Industrial England', *Ec. HR*
2nd ser. 38/2 (1985), 175–91.
[82] Information, including brochure published by the Borough of Totnes (n.d.), provided by Mr
R. J. Butterfield, Town Clerk, July 1987. I am grateful to Mr Butterfield for his help. See also notes by
Michael Laithwaite in DoE, 'List of Buildings, S. Hams, Devon' (1978), 43–4.
[83] *VCH, Hertfordshire*, ii. 480–1.

of St Peters for a town hall and school in the 1570s.[84] The list of such buildings is obviously very long: too long for us to overlook the importance of this transfer of public buildings from the spiritual to the secular and civic domain in the Tudor town. It would be fascinating to learn, if only we could, how many MPs sitting for such enfranchised towns may have voted for the various dissolutions of church property with some useful high-street chapel foremost in mind.

So much, then, for the circumstances of hall acquisition. When we turn to the question of motivations, it becomes obvious that these and other halls were not only acquired because of the need for mere office space in which to exercise new constitutional authority. Most town halls built or otherwise acquired in our period were intended to symbolize the attainment of civic authority from seigneurial hands and the exercise of that authority over the community. In both cases, the hall seems often to have been regarded not only as a place of government but also as a semiotic object.

That is to say, in anthropological terms, that the hall appears to have functioned as the 'tangible formulation' of the notion of civic authority.[85] As a semiotic form, it does seem to have marked 'the centre as centre'. Its utilization legitimized the authority of its builders, an authority which, even more than majesty, was indeed 'made, not born'.[86]

Several cases effectively demonstrate this recognition, suggesting a widespread and common understanding of the hall's symbolic position amongst townsmen of the day.[87] We may begin with the townsmen of Banbury, who built a new town hall after the town's incorporation in 1556. The government of the manor of Banbury had been situated at Banbury Castle, and the same venue could very likely have been made available to the new corporation. But the fact of self-government itself demanded the symbolism of a new building, in this case one which was purpose-built for the exercise of civic authority. Hence the newly empowered officers of the corporation forsook the castle of an earlier age, the symbol of feudal authority, for the new civic hall of 1556.[88]

[84] Hutchins, *History and Antiquities of Dorset*, i. 109.

[85] Clifford Geertz, *The Interpretation of Cultures* (New York, 1973), 91.

[86] Clifford Geertz, 'Centers, Kings and Charisma: Reflections on the Symbolics of Power', in Joseph Ben-David and Terry Nichols Clark (eds.), *Culture and its Creators, Essays in Honour of Edward Shils* (Chicago, 1977), 152. See also Raymond Firth, *Symbols Public and Private* (Ithaca, NY, 1973), 15.

[87] The symbolic force of the town hall as a representation of civic authority is by no means dead in the Anglo-American political tradition. In carrying out voter registration in the American federal election of 1984 in the rural state of Vermont, I perceived that several habitually non-registered voters, all of them elderly and poor, had never registered in their lives because it meant entering the town hall to do so. Lifelong residents of their small town, they regarded that edificial symbol of civic authority with more foreboding than reverence, and with not a little fear.

[88] W. Potts, *A History of Banbury* (Banbury, 1958), 103–6.

Other cases may be drawn from the litigation which, as noted above, often formed a part of the process whereby urban communities gained greater independence from seigneurial ties. Again the case of Evesham provides appropriate illustration. Prior to the Reformation, as we have seen, jurisdiction in Evesham had technically been in the hands of the abbot, but was effectively shared by the townsmen in the name of the Crown. Both the semi-annual leet court and the three-week court met in the Town Hall, later called the 'Old Booth Hall' or 'Roundhouse'. When the rights of the abbots devolved, by sale of 37 Henry VIII, to Sir Philip Hoby,[89] he built a new hall for the collection of tolls and the holding of courts (see Plate 3). At the same time, the townsmen considered that their rights had devolved from the Crown. For payment of an annual fee farm they assumed permission to choose their own bailiff and to enjoy all perquisites save fines from the three-week court. When these interests came finally into conflict with Hoby's, as seems virtually inevitable, not only were control of the two courts brought into question, but also possession of what had become two town halls, each (in the eyes of those involved) deeply symbolic of a rival claim to authority. What makes this case particularly unusual is not only the two competing venues of local administration, but the ironic twist which saw the townsmen's claims represented by the old building, and Hoby's by the new.[90]

This contest over rights was by no means relegated to mere litigation. We read in the deposition of witnesses lively accounts of the virtual guerrilla warfare whereby each side attempted to wrest control of the other's hall or defend its own as if the halls had become the capital cities of warring nations. The yeoman Henry Wylles described what seems to have been the first move in these campaigns, in which Thomas Cesar, a gentleman of the Inner Temple who had bought considerable Evesham property from the Hoby family and had helped bring the law case against the townsmen, secured the key to the new town hall and defended it at poignard's point from the attempted intrusion of the town's elected bailiffs.[91] But another deponent, George Hawkins, described how the townsmen later attacked the new town hall while Hoby's steward held court there in April 1585. The attacking townsmen used a cucking stool as a battering ram,

'dryven through the face of the saide Courte . . . before the Steward and beneath the jury . . . And one Arnold Tickridge the sonne of Thomas . . . in the Topp of

[89] J. Amphlett (ed.), *A Survey of Worcestershire by Thomas Habington*, 2 vols. (Worcestershire Historical Society, 1895 and 1899), ii. 75; Hilton, 'The Small Town and Urbanisation, 6–7; PRO, C 66/715/m. 33 and C 66/787/m. 11.

[90] Except where noted, this and the following two paragraphs are based on *Hoby* v. *Kighley*, PRO, E 134/29 Eliz., East. 12, and May, *Descriptive History of Evesham*, *passim*.

[91] PRO, E 134/29 Eliz. East. 12, fo. 15.

the Same and a number of boyes hallinge the same makinge a Greate Clamor and Voyce . . . and Cryinge a Steward a Steward a court a court a jury a jury and the foreman of the Jury shuld be sett by the heles'

while the two serjeants stood at the door with great black staves and iron picks in their hands and 'being charged to serve the Quene [from whom the townsmen claimed their authority] they refused to do so'.[92]

In the end the Barons of the Exchequer decreed a compromise whereby the three-week court remained in the old hall and the leet court was held in the new. But by the time Evesham gained its incorporation, the townsmen had assumed full control over the newer hall and gradually abandoned the old.[93]

Possession of a particular hall, and the customary identification of that hall with particular elements of governing authority, thus seems symbolically important as well, extending even to the common assumption that political jurisdiction *depended* on the locus of command. When riotous townsmen in Waltham, Essex, wished to prevent the holding of the portreeve's court in the reign of Mary, they simply nailed shut the Moot Hall door and considered the job done. It seems to have occurred neither to them nor to the court authorities that the court might simply meet elsewhere. Indeed, it would probably not have been considered a legitimate meeting had it done so.[94] Similarly, when the perpetrators of a virtual *coup d'état* to overthrow and replace the mayor of Liskeard unfolded in 1611, the rebels felt it necessary to proclaim their new mayor in the Guildhall, even though they had to break into the building at night to do so.[95] We must presume that a mayor would not have been recognized as such if proclaimed elsewhere.

Depositions taken in the trial of a disputed parliamentary election in Chichester (1586) provide yet another instance of two civic halls operating in the same town, with a strict and symbolically understood division of function and authority drawn between them. Though the view was implicitly disputed by some deponents, Chichester custom seems to have called for the mayor and the senior guildsmen to have chosen one MP in what was now called the Council Hall, and for the freemen to have chosen the second in the separate building called the Guildhall.[96] A somewhat similar system prevailed in Worcester where members of the two councils, the Twenty-Four and the Forty-Eight, elected MPs in the Council Chamber and had their choice ratified by the freemen at large in the Guildhall.[97]

[92] Ibid., fo. 7.   [93] PRO, E 123/12/fo. 275ᵛ.
[94] PRO, STAC 4/Bundle 6/23.
[95] *Hodge* v. *Hunkyn* et al., PRO, STAC 8/164/10.
[96] PRO, STAC 5/C23/37, deposition of John Cooke.
[97] S. T. Bindoff (ed.), *The House of Commons, 1509–1558*, 3 vols. (1982), i. 237.

The symbolic and practical linking of particular forms of authority with specific civic halls was sufficiently important to invite litigation elsewhere as well. Shaftesbury, like Evesham and Chichester, also had two halls, one old hall of uncertain vintage and one constructed by townsmen around 1568. Though there is at least some evidence that townsmen had been responsible for the upkeep of both, clearly the rights of the manorial lord remained more firmly attached to the older building and, especially after the incorporation of 1604, the jurisdiction of the town corporation with the newer. Not surprisingly, when a dispute over jurisdiction between the lord's steward and the townsmen erupted in 1618 the symbolic weight of their respective halls played a conspicuous part.[98]

It had long been the custom in Shaftesbury, both before and after incorporation, for the newly elected mayor to be sworn by the lord's steward at the regular law-day held annually after Michaelmas. But when the mayor-elect, John Sweetnam, presented himself before the steward, Robert Moore, in the new hall for that purpose, Moore refused to proceed unless he could do so in the old hall instead. In his mind the performance of such a ceremony in the new hall indicated the empty and perfunctory nature of the ritual. Performing the same duty in the old, or lord's hall, implied that the townsmen still had an obligation to come before the lord's steward as of old, to be accepted in the seat of *his* authority, in an act implying homage and obedience.

In the event, Moore stalked out, still refusing to swear Sweetnam. The mayor-elect was sworn instead by the recorder, before the outgoing mayor and most of the chief burgesses, and in the new Guildhall. Cutting off his nose to spite his face, Moore then refused to hold any leet courts lest he be compelled to recognize Sweetham as mayor at such sessions. The principle of recognizing the old hall as the only appropriate place in which a mayor-elect could be sworn to office had become more important to Moore, and presumably also more important to the Countess of Pembroke (his employer as Lord of the Manor), even than holding the annual law-day itself. Similar observations follow from events elsewhere, including such geographically disparate towns as Hythe in Kent and Chesterfield in Derbyshire.[99] They all seem to point to the widespread understanding of the hall not merely as a place of business, but as an edifice irreplaceably symbolic of civic authority, power, and legitimacy.

In light of this, many towns campaigned assiduously to have meetings of quarter sessions or assizes in their town halls, so as to gain both the

[98] The following is reconstructed from *Mary, Countess Dowager of Pembroke and William, Earl of Pembroke* v. *Inhabitants of Shaftesbury*, PRO, E 134/18 James I/East. 1.

[99] *Cramer* v. *Hudson* et al., PRO, E 134/19 James I/Mic. 25; D. F. Botham, 'A History of Chesterfield Market Place' (thesis presented to the Royal Institute of British Architects, April 1974, a copy of which is held at the Derby Central Library, Local History Collection), 13.

prestige and hard currency which came with such meetings. Yet most were also very anxious not to give the appearance that such meetings implied any further external jurisdiction than already existed. Thus even so substantial a centre as Worcester permitted the county authorities to hold sessions in the Guildhall when the accustomed venue fell into disrepair, but the mayor and council made it very clear that such permission came only on sufferance, without implication for the question of jurisdiction.[100] Their hall remained a symbol of *their* authority, and its use by others could not be permitted to indicate any sharing of that hegemony.

The point is further and unconsciously demonstrated in several towns by the common linguistic convention whereby 'the Hall' served as a shorthand reference to the authority of the governing bodies which utilized that edifice. Thus, for example, we find an agreement of 1567 made by the mayor and assembly of the borough of Boston that a new market cross 'shall . . . be mayntenyd and repayrede by the Towne Hall, as to them [sic] shall seem goode'.[101] Similar usage occurred in Windsor and elsewhere as well, [102] while in High Wycombe the term 'Council House' had become synonymous with 'the Mayor and his Brethren' by the same time.[103]

By such force of symbolism, both in political practice and common parlance, did the town hall frequently mark the 'coming of age' for towns which may only a short time before have emerged from the economic status of the village or the legal standing of a manorial community. We have in its construction and use the architectural representation of a more mature stage of civic development, a widely understood symbol of civic authority, power, and legitimacy.

---

[100] Dyer, *Worcester*, 211–12.
[101] Bailey, *Minutes of Boston*, i. 90.
[102] Berkshire RO, facsimile, MS w1/Fac 1, *passim*.
[103] L. J. Ashford, *A History of High Wycombe from its Origins to 1880* (1960), 112.

5
Oligarchy, Deference, and the Built Environment

THE RISE AND FOCUS OF OLIGARCHY

In the foregoing chapter we have examined the ways in which the redrawn relations between townsmen and external authorities—lay, royal, or ecclesiastical landlords in particular—motivated the establishment of town halls, especially in the decades following the 1540s. Now we must turn to the social and political forces within urban communities themselves, and to the interaction of those forces with civic halls.

Although one often speaks informally of 'the urban community', and although corporate charters themselves often referred to the freemanry or some similarly broad constituency, it is essential to keep in mind that both the acquisition of such corporate jurisdiction and its architectural representation were the achievements in most instances not of the community at large, or even the freemanry, but of a distinct minority which came increasingly to dominate urban economic and political life.

This minority often constituted a form of oligarchy and indeed, government by oligarchic rule became a political commonplace in English towns during the course of the sixteenth and seventeenth centuries. Yet despite the emergence of this effective and arguably even appropriate form of local government at this time, oligarchic rule bore with it some inherent faults as a system capable of gaining the deference, and hence obedience, essential for political stability. This chapter will discuss the nature of civic oligarchy, with particular reference to the mayor as its most visible element. It will also take up the associated problem of civic deference. Finally, it will examine the manner in which civic rulers legitimized their authority through, *inter alia*, the arrangement, furnishing, and operation of the civic hall and its associated premises.

Though perfectly appropriate to our usage in its dictionary definition—'government by the few; a form of government in which power is confirmed to a few persons or families'[1]—the word 'oligarchy' has acquired morally negative connotations which obscure for us its application in early modern English towns. At its root, the consolidation of

---

[1] *OED*, 1st edn., *vide* 'oligarchy'.

political power within the urban community arose out of the perennial necessity for some authority to take charge and protect local interests in the face of intensified political and social change. In an era particularly characterized by strong population growth and mobility, widespread unemployment, vagrancy and crime, rising prices, and shifting economic activities, both local interests and the Crown found oligarchy entirely appropriate.

Those who rose to positions of leadership in English towns were those most capable of defending local interests by dint of worldly experience, external influence, local reputation, and, perhaps especially, personal wealth. They might typically be senior merchants or craftsmen (rarely professionals or providers of services until the very end of our period) who sought political power so as to protect the economic viability and social stability of the community. They did so not merely out of civic concern, though this cannot by any means be ruled out, but also out of a concern for the conditions upon which their own livelihood depended. Despite the evidence for some evasion of office, which may possibly have been more common in the early part of our period, most were not at all loath to serve in office and some competed hotly for it.[2]

These were the townsmen who strove for local autonomy from external controls, challenged seigneurial claims, and petitioned for incorporation. It is their names which fill the ranks of feoffees in the town trust, or which we see listed as 'governors' (for example 'the Mayor and his Brethren', 'the chief and common councillors', 'the capital burgesses', 'the wardsmen and aldermen', or simply 'the better sort') of the newly granted corporation. They had the most to protect or to gain by such initiatives and they were best able to support the sundry burdens of office once obtained.[3]

To the modern mind, these ruling élites seem narrowly based, considerably self-serving, and essentially undemocratic. On the other hand, considerable affinity of interest pertained between such leaders and the communities from which they arose, and those common aims were often well and energetically served. In addition, as established élites witnessed the rapid disappearance of families from their midst—through death, sterility, or migration—they had also necessarily to remain open to new members. These they admitted, if not democratically, at least with some

---

[2] Examples of hotly disputed contests *for* high civic office may be found in Totnes in 27–8 Eliz. (PRO, STAC 5/B21/6); Liskeard, *c.*1611 (*Hodge* v. *Hunkyn*, STAC 8/164/10); Carmarthen, *c.*1609–10 (*Attorney General* v. *Bynon* et al., STAC 8/20/14); Doncaster, *c.*1618–19 (*Carver* v. *Carliell* et al., STAC 8/93/5); and Lincoln, *c.*1605 (*Dynnys and Gosse* v. *Berke* et al., STAC 8/121/12). For typical early sixteenth-century reluctance to serve in office see Charles Phythian-Adams, *Desolation of a City, Coventry and the Urban Crisis of the Late Middle Ages* (Cambridge, 1979), 47–8, 250–2, 262.

[3] R. Tittler, 'The Incorporation of Boroughs, 1540–1558', *History*, 62/204 (1977), 224–32.

ease and frequency. In this regard this particular form of oligarchy has been likened to a moving bus: a vehicle which keeps to its appointed route and schedule, but which continually takes on and discharges passengers along the way.

Most civic offices at this time expressed the goals and force of oligarchic rule, but none so clearly as the office of the mayor.[4] The emergence of mayoral office into a position of greater authority and prominence in Tudor and early Stuart towns is both obvious and logical. As no convenient summary of this role exists elsewhere, and as it bears so heavily on the larger themes of this discussion, it will be helpful to describe it briefly here.

Mayoral hegemony followed readily enough from the upheavals in manorial authority and from the social and political stratification so characteristic of the era. It provided a precise focus for the central government's broad and long-standing effort to invest the powers of administration and peace-keeping in local officials. The Crown saw such figures as unlikely to have had their own source of power to fall back upon and therefore as highly likely to be trustworthy.

By the end of the sixteenth century and (in towns with a lengthier tradition of civic autonomy) often long before, the mayor presided over town councils, directed the work of the bailiffs, chamberlains, constables, serjeants-at-arms, alms collectors, ale-tasters, clerks, and other appointed officials, most of whom he would have chosen himself or helped his 'brethren' to choose for office.[5] He sat as clerk of the market, sometimes as coroner, escheator, gaoler, commissioner of gaol delivery, and frequently as JP within the town. He presided over most of the town's courts (as opposed to manorial courts) including the mayor's court—a court of record, variously styled, which heard cases of misdemeanour and felony—the market and pie-powder courts, often a leet court where, as in Kendal or Macclesfield,[6] it devolved from manorial to civic control, and sometimes also over such specialized tribunals as the local admiralty court.

---

[4] The term 'mayor' is employed here generically, in reference to the chief governing officer of the civic, as opposed to the manorial, administration. Though in most cases this official is actually called 'the mayor', such terms as 'bailiff', 'alderman', or even 'governor' were sometimes used synonymously in the language of statute or charter, even though such terms also denoted quite different offices in other contemporary usage.

[5] This and the remainder of the paragraph is based on examination of *Statutes of the Realm*, and a survey of charters of incorporation as they appear in the *Calendar of Patent Rolls*, but see also John G. Bellamy, *Criminal Law and Society in Late Medieval and Tudor England* (Gloucester, 1984), esp. chs. 1, 2; Edith G. Henderson, *Foundations of English Administrative Law* . . . (Cambridge, Mass., 1963), esp. ch. 1, 2; Sidney and Beatrice Webb, *English Local Government, The Manor and the Borough*, 2 vols. (1908), i. chs. 2, 3, 6; and M. Bateson (ed.), *Borough Customs.* 2 vols. (Selden Society, 1904, 1906).

[6] *Calendar of Patent Rolls, Elizabeth*, vii, *1575–8* (1982), item 592 and *passim*; Webb and Webb, *Manor and Borough*, i. 46–7.

By power of statute, proclamation, or local by-law, and both before or during our period, the mayor came to examine on his own account rogues, vagabonds, beggars, players of unlawful games and players of stage plays, apprentices suspected of having broken their indentures, employers or artificers who broke contract with each other, or those who refused to pay the poor rate. He could take testimony on oath and bonds for good behaviour, and he could amerce, fine, distrain, and punish for a variety of transgressions. The responsibility for inspecting weights and measures, bread, ale, cloth, and some other manufactures, firewood and other forms of fuel ultimately fell on his shoulders, though he himself could be fined for failure to live up to most of these obligations.

Most mayors had long enjoyed the right to return writs to the Crown or the central courts. Even in the fifteenth century the mayors of many towns could receive part of the forfeit emanating from several misdemeanours and some of the profits of tolls, fees, fines, and other amercements to the use of the town. In addition, and also by the end of the fifteenth century, mayors enjoyed and exercised some statutory powers of detention. In the decades thereafter they often gained additional powers to commit on their own account, without trial, those who transgressed against common order and morality and even against local by-laws.[7]

Finally, as charters of incorporation in the sixteenth century more frequently conferred upon him the powers of the JPs (and notwithstanding frequent local opposition to mayoral authority), the mayor's position grew more potent still. In Winchester, whose government had become particularly oligarchic, the local antiquary John Trussell defended mayoral authority in the 1640s in terms approaching the concept of divine right.[8]

In these and similar respects, the authority of town government, increasingly oligarchic in form and mayoral in focus, continued to blossom in the period at hand. But authority remains a matter of potential until translated into action, and we cannot merely assume that any particular government reached the limits of its theoretical powers in actual practice. So as to grasp this transition from the potential to the active, we must consider two additional strategies of urban government: the inculcation of civic deference and the application of legitimate

---

[7] Bellamy, *Criminal Law and Society*, chs. 1, 2, *et passim*; 2 and 3 Edward VI, c. 15; 5 and 6 Edward VI, c. 14; 5 Elizabeth, c. 4, sections 13, 14; Bateson, *Borough Customs*, i. 19; Berkshire RO, Abingdon Borough Minute Book, MS D/EP 7/84, fo. 17 (an order of 1590 providing for imprisonment of certain craftsmen violating market laws) and Abingdon's charter of incorporation which permits the mayor to commit the chamberlain to prison if he ends the year in arrears, *Calendar of Patent Rolls, Philip and Mary*, iii. 1555–7, 382; Christopher Harding *et al.*, *Imprisonment in England and Wales, a Concise History* (1985), 56; Tom Atkinson, *Elizabethan Winchester* (1963), 44.

[8] Adrienne Rosen, 'Economic and Social Aspects of the History of Winchester, 1520–1670' (Oxford Univ. D.Phil. thesis 1975), citing Trussell's 'Benefactors of Winchester'.

coercion. Both approaches bore heavily upon the design, furnishings, and use of the civic hall. Let us examine each in turn.

THE PROBLEM OF DEFERENCE

In view of this steady and considerable accretion of power vested in the chief governing authorities of the Tudor and early Stuart town, and especially the mayor, the classic political problem of how more effectively to wield authority and command obedience became more vivid than ever. After all, the men who came to dominate the society and government of English towns lacked the one vital advantage of governance which still pertained elsewhere in English society. In almost all other political units of the realm—the county, hundred, manor, and, at least much of the time, the village—the social foundations of political activity remained agrarian in nature. Here the elements of a traditional, lineage-based, and strongly hierarchical society still endured throughout most of our period.

For all the inroads which had been made upon such thinking by the Tudor state, this was still a world in which Shakespeare's famous speech on order and degree in *Troilus and Cressida*, or his 'for so work the honey-bees' passage in *Henry V* (Act I, Scene ii), rang true for many, where Romans 13 was still common coin, and in which Raleigh's *History of the World* viewed its subject in characteristically hierarchical terms.[9] Though their power to do so was under sustained siege, the landlord, the regional magnate, and, ironically, even the monarch still commanded a great deal of loyalty and respect to their persons simply through inherited deference.[10] Thus did considerations of lineage, kinship, and honour allow the Earl of Arundel to deal with the rebellion of 1549 in his 'country' of Sussex[11] and the Earl of Essex to gather supporters for his revolt in 1601.[12]

The rulers of the town, by contrast, merchants and craftsmen propelled by ability, wealth, and personal ambition, rarely enjoyed anything of the sort: no titles, no hereditary status in a fixed social hierarchy, no regional base of support, and no statutory right to legal or social distinctions. Even

[9] The definitions of 'lineage society' and 'civil society' are seminally presented in Mervyn James, *Family, Lineage and Civil Society, a Study of Society, Politics and Mentality in the Durham Region, 1500–1640* (Oxford, 1974) and, more generally, in his numerous essays now collected in *Society, Politics and Culture, Studies in Early Modern England* (Cambridge, 1986). For the classic exposition of the traditional, hierarchical view of society, see E. M. W. Tillyard, *The Elizabethan World Picture* [1943] (1967).

[10] K. Wrightson, *English Society, 1580–1680* (1982), 58–60; M. E. James, 'The Concept of Order and the Northern Rising of 1569', *P and P* 60 (1973), 49–83; J. Youings, *Sixteenth Century England* (1984), ch. 5.

[11] Lawrence Stone, 'Patriarchy and Paternalism in Tudor England: The Earl of Arundel and the Peasants Revolt of 1549', *Journal of British Studies*, 13/2 (1974), 19–23. Unaccountably, Professor Stone identifies Henry Fitzalan as the *fourteenth* Earl.

[12] James, *Society, Politics and Culture*, ch. 8.

our expectation that deference may have accrued from the reputation of urban family dynasties has been disabused by the fruits of modern research showing the rapidity of geographic mobility in and out of towns.[13] A large proportion of urban office holders is now reliably known to have consisted of newcomers to the community,[14] their descendants readily vacating the ranks of leadership and moving on from the town itself.

Of course, neither the need for such deference nor established efforts made to elicit it were entirely new to the towns of the post-Reformation era, though some such efforts were sharply undermined thereafter. The creation of hierarchy in urban office holding, and the deference which it generated in return, had long been established in the form of the *cursus honorum* so familiar in the older and better established communities.[15]

The same deep roots may be observed in regard to the symbols and trappings of such offices, objects which had long since evolved for their utility in creating deferential behaviour. Such civic regalia as the mayor's mace or staff of office had undergone the transfer of function from the literal (that is, as a weapon) to the symbolic (as an insignia of office and, with the addition of royal arms, of royal authority) well back in the Middle Ages.[16] Thus when the leaders of Elizabethan Faversham commissioned a replacement, they could refer to the making of 'a new ancient staffe'.[17] The elaborate ritualism of civic ceremony was also of course well established by the Reformation. It was often integrally related to such ecclesiastical institutions as religious fraternities and to such religious occasions as the Corpus Christi Day celebration, while its very essence supported the social order and upheld the civic leadership.[18] The whole tenor of contemporary religious practice contributed toward the same obediential end.[19] All these objects and activities helped to impart an

[13] Carl I. Hammer, Jr., 'Anatomy of an Oligarchy: The Oxford Town Council in the Fifteenth and Sixteenth Centuries', *Journal of British Studies*, 18/1 (1978), 1–27, 19–20; Susan M. Battley, 'Elite and Community, the Mayors of Sixteenth Century King's Lynn', (State Univ. of New York Ph.D. thesis 1981), 115–16. See also Rosen, 'Economic and Social Aspects of Worcester', 112.

[14] D. M. Palliser, 'A Regional Capital as Magnet: Immigrants to York, 1477–1566', *Yorkshire Archaeological Journal*, 57 (1985), 11–23; Palliser, *Tudor York* (Oxford, 1979), ch. 4.

[15] e.g. Oxford, Coventry, York, and King's Lynn; Hammer, 'The Anatomy of Oligarchy', 3–4; Phythian-Adams, *Desolation of a City*, pt. III and esp. chs. 8, 9; Palliser, *Tudor York*, ch. 3 and esp. 71–2; Battley, 'Elite and Community', 116–19.

[16] Llewellyn Jewitt and W. H. St John Hope, *The Corporate Plate and Insignia of Office of the Cities and Towns of England and Wales*, 2 vols. (1895), i, pp. xxiii–xl and cf. below.

[17] Kent Co. Archives Office, Maidstone, MS FA/FAc 9/Bundle 2.

[18] Charles Phythian-Adams, 'Ceremony and the Citizen: The Communal Year at Coventry, 1450–1550', in Peter Clark and Paul Slack (eds.), *Crisis and Order in English Towns* (1972), 57–85; and Mervyn James, 'Ritual, Drama and Social Body in the Late Medieval English Town', *P and P* 98 (1983), 3–29.

[19] Susan Brigden, 'Religion and Social Obligation in Early Sixteenth Century London', *P and P* 103 (1984), 67–112; Phythian-Adams, *Desolation of a City*, ch. 11.

awareness of hierarchy and support oligarchic tendencies in earlier urban communities. Together they had helped medieval urban leaders approximate the recognition 'naturally' accorded their counterparts in feudal society.

Yet by the mid-sixteenth century many of the same forces which had begun to undermine established notions of hierarchy and deference in agrarian society came also to apply to the towns.[20] In addition, the greater geographic mobility of the mid- and late sixteenth century placed substantial strains on the keeping of local traditions and on the recognition of established families. The large proportion of newcomers unfamiliar with urban ways to begin with made these strains particularly acute.[21] The severe economic fluctuations in many communities during the sixteenth century, while undeniably creating a greater tolerance for oligarchic rule itself, often created personal and corporate financial instability and thus encouraged an even more rapid turnover in the ranks of the wealthy and secure.

In consequence of all these factors, the need of urban leaders to strengthen the trappings of hierarchy and office remained intense throughout the mid- and late sixteenth century and on into the seventeenth. Efforts to accomplish this end assumed many forms. In social terms one may even see here the immediate origins of the 'high urban culture' which has been identified by Dr Borsay as emerging in the Restoration era: distinctive social customs and pastimes developed by the genteel elements of urban society both to express their status and at the same time to create effective social barriers against the rest. Many of the pursuits which came to characterize that process were mirrored in specific, purpose-built structures which became common in at least the larger Restoration towns: pleasure gardens, public baths, race courses, assembly rooms, and promenades.[22]

In the earlier period of our concern, urban élites in most communities had not yet either the political security or the cultural sophistication to undertake such activities. The trappings of office and status had necessarily to do much more with the establishment of power than with the pursuit of cultural ostentation. The genteel pursuits of Restoration

[20] James, 'The Concept of Order and the Northern Rising'.

[21] An observation made by Hammer, 'Anatomy of Oligarchy', 20, but which is implicit in the evidence for rural origins of townsmen in this era of high mobility; Palliser, 'A Regional Capital as Magnet'; Peter Clark, 'The Migrant in Kentish Towns, 1580–1640', in Clark and Slack, *Crisis and Order*, 117–63; G. D. Ramsay, 'The Recruitment and Fortunes of Some London Freemen in the Mid-Sixteenth Century', *Ec. HR* 2nd ser. 31/4 (1978), 526–40; J. Patten, 'Rural–Urban Migration in Pre-Industrial England' (Univ. of Oxford, School of Geography, reseach paper no. 6, 1973); A. F. Butcher, 'The Origins of Romney Freemen, 1433–1523', *Ec HR*, 2nd ser. 27 1 (1974), 16–27.

[22] P. N. Borsay, *The English Urban Renaissance* (Oxford, 1989); Borsay, 'The English Urban Renaissance: The Development of Provincial Urban Culture, c.1680–1760', *Social History* 5 (1977), 581–603.

townsmen depended on a security in the exercise of power which had not yet been achieved in the Tudor and early Stuart period. The characteristic speech of these earlier townsmen was not yet the cultivated imitation of London society, but the legalistic jargon of the council chamber or even the billingsgate of the market-place. And, if the symbolic structure associated with power was no longer the parish church, chantry chapel, or religious guild's hall as in the fifteenth century, nor was it yet the assembly room, pleasure garden, or promenade of the late seventeenth and eighteenth. Instead it was the town hall. In the evolution of its spatial components, furnishings, design, and in the creation of an elaborate decorum surrounding those who had business within it, the hall was integrally bound up with the urban élite and with the need to create a civic deference which was so essential to that group at that time.

CIVIC DEFERENCE AND THE SEAT OF POWER

We have already noted in Chapter 2 the general characteristic of spatial organization in Tudor and early Stuart town halls. It remains for us now to examine that organization not as a static phenomenon, fixed in place throughout our period, but as evolving in response to changes in the communities which they served. Our general theme must be the manner in which the evolution and delineation of space and even the furnishings within the halls mirrored and enhanced the development of civic political authority throughout the period.

Let us begin by examining the halls of our period against the longer time-frame of which they were a part. At one end of the continuum, throughout much of the Middle Ages, town halls played less of a role in general, and many smaller or less politically mature towns, of which there were many, had been governed without purpose-built civic halls. Manorial court halls, parish churches, or even the open air had often sufficed. Such town halls as were in use in smaller towns especially tended, as we have seen, to be spatially underlineated and multi-functional.

Toward the other end of the continuum, we find that town halls of the Restoration and Georgian periods had been figuratively stretched to bursting by the number and the nature of demands for their use. The increasingly complex functions of local administration had caused functionally specific areas within the halls, starved for space, to hive off from the main building and to gain a roof of their own. The armoury (whose migration elsewhere was hastened by the replacement of traditional weaponry with the infinitely more dangerous gunpowder), the prison house and house of correction, the corn exchange, and even the court house (without assembly chambers) or assembly chambers (without court space) all exemplify this tendency. Some examples of this accelerated need for space falls within our period in larger communities such as Oxford or Norwich. Yet for the most part the sixteenth and early seventeenth centuries mark something of a mid-point in this continuum of spatial development. In this epoch we see town halls becoming the normal place of civic business and administration even in smaller towns and the use of space within such buildings becoming steadily more defined and specific.

As we might expect, the extent to which these trends unfolded seems roughly proportional to the size and complexity of each community, with such developments broadly dependent upon the evolution of particular institutions and offices within the civic governing structure. Towns made extensive efforts to dignify all their governmental offices and, through them, the standing and reputation of the whole community. Because it came in most autonomous communities to be the highest and most prominent office, representing the town both internally and externally, the office of the mayor more often than not proved the particular object of such efforts. It follows that the ruling element in these towns worked hard and creatively to dignify that office, to create a deference for its incumbent which did not 'naturally' accrue to his person, and thus to encourage voluntary obedience to his rule.

This pursuit of 'civic deference' took many forms. A number of studies have made us aware that such high civic office involved considerable expense, and this proved a serious problem in many towns.[23] Though the dispensation of largess itself elicited a considerable degree of respect, it was also essentially still personal expenditure for civic purposes. Though it would be foolhardy to suggest that mayors were ever compensated fully in this era, most towns during the course of the sixteenth century, if not before, came to give the mayor an annual allowance, both to help him makes ends meet in a year of less than full attention to his own business, and to keep up the appearances of dignity while in office. Even in smallish towns such allowances came to as much as £20 in Abingdon in 1582, and to £30 in Beverley in about 1580,[24] even if they also came with the expectation that the mayor would defray expenses of livery, diet, and even payment for some of the minor officers of the town.

The preservation of mayoral dignity proceeded by other means as well. 'Opprobrious words' against him in such towns as King's Lynn, Guildford, and Hull could result in temporary loss of citizenship or

[23] Charles Phythian-Adams, 'Urban Decay in Late Medieval England', in P. Abrams and E. A. Wrigley (eds.), *Towns in Societies, Essays in Economic History and Historical Sociology* (Cambridge, 1978), 174–7; Phythian-Adams, *Desolation of a City*, esp. 258–9, 262, 267; Clark and Slack, *Crisis and Order*, 21–22.
[24] Berkshire RO MS D/EP/7/84, p. 12; ibid. 223; Humberside Co. RO, MS BC/II/4, fo. 3ʳ.

substantial fines, or both.[25] In Hedon it could be punished by a ducking in the 'cucking stool', a punishment often reserved for harlots and licentious women,[26] and in both Boston and Hedon again it could even be met with imprisonment.[27] When Thomas Benson, a Norwich cobbler, was hauled before the mayor's court in the Guildhall of Norwich in June 1607 because he 'did yesterday . . . Bid a turd in Mr. Mayors tethe', we may be sure he was dealt with severely.[28]

Observations of proper dress—robes, usually of scarlet velvet, and velvet tippets of various colours for mayors and similar apparel for aldermen—seems to have been expected of officials in the guild-hall at all times, and, indeed, often in the streets on daily business.[29] In many towns, on holidays or in some cases even regular working days, the mayor was to be met at his house door and accompanied to the town hall by aldermen or councillors dressed in appropriate livery, or even suitors.[30] And, though town offices were very much in the male domain, even the mayor's wife partook of her husband's standing. In Poole she was regaled with the gift of a costly kerchief, after the election dinner in her husband's honour; in some other towns the mayor's wife received a scarlet gown.[31] And, while in many towns former mayors were required to wear their old robes on public occasions, Bristol encouraged mayors' wives to do the same, '*pro honore et reverentia civitatis*'.[32]

As of old, though probably now in a great many more towns, the mayor's office served to focus various ceremonial devices and practices: his mace or similar emblem of his office was borne with him in procession, his election was one of the ceremonial high points of the year and on virtually all civic occasions he sat or walked in the place of honour. In almost all such instances, his presence was intimately bound up with the use of the hall. At least in a metaphoric sense the mayor's stage, manor house, and work-place, it was also the symbol of his authority and, through him, of the dignity and position of the town itself. An investigation of many of these practices bears out their essential link with the hall.

[25] Battley, 'Elite and Community', 267; E. M. Dance (ed.), *Guildford Borough Records, 1514–1546* (Surrey Record Society, 24, 1958), 11; Claire Cross, *Urban Magistrates and Ministers, Religion in Hull and Leeds from the Reformation to the Civil War* (Univ. of York, Borthwick Papers, 67, 1985), 12.

[26] J. R. Bayle, *Early History of . . . Hedon . . .* (Hull, 1895), pp. xliii–xciv; J. W. Spargo, *Juridic Folklore in England, Illustrated by the Cucking Stool* (Durham, NC, 1944), 3–9; Humberside RO, MS DDHE/26, fo. 132ʳ; Bailey, *Minutes of Boston*, i. 80.

[27] Bailey, *Minutes of Boston*, i. 80; Humberside RO, MS DDHE/26, fo. 132ʳ.

[28] David Galloway (ed.), *REED, Norwich, 1540–1642* (Toronto, 1984), p. xxiv.

[29] R. W. Ingram, *REED, Coventry* (Toronto, 1981), 201; Bailey, *Minutes of Boston*, i. 2, 88; Humberside RO, MS BC/II/4, fo. 3.

[30] Dance, *Guildford Borough Records*, 10, 36, 37; Much Wenlock Archives, B3/1/1, p. 367; Humberside Co. RO, MS DDHE/26, fo. 131; Maureen Stanford (ed.), *The Ordinances of Bristol, 1506–1598* (Bristol Record Society, 41, 1990), 29.

[31] This is recorded intermittently from 1512, when the sum of £1 was expended for the purpose; Poole Bor. Archives, MS 23(1) *vide* 1511/12.   [32] Stanford, *Ordinances of Bristol*, 45.

The first named of these practices, the use of the mace of office (like such analogous emblems as the 'ancient' staff at Faversham, the swords and hats 'of maintenance' in Exeter and Carmarthen, or the mayor's oar at Chester) were, as we have seen, not entirely novel in the sixteenth century. Yet there are some important developments in the design and use of the mace during this period which support the themes both of increased mayoral power and the greater identification of such power with the town hall, the building in which such symbols of office were conventionally kept.[33] The chief development in the mace's use seems to have been its evolution from a weapon (held at the staff end by the serjeant-at-mace or the serjeant-at-arms in defence of the king, mayor, or other official) to a symbolic implement (held at the opposite end by the same official) which came to have the royal or sometimes the town's arms engraved on the butt end. Such evolution continued into the sixteenth and early seventeenth centuries, along with the enhanced status of the mayor. The businesslike iron and oak of earlier times now often gave way to ornamented gold and silver.

Of greater importance, the relatively small 'serjeant's mace' yielded to the larger and more purely ceremonial mayor's mace during the sixteenth century and then to an even larger version, the 'great mace', in the seventeenth. Though these might still be borne by the serjeant, they were now carried before him and not only on ceremonial occasions. In some towns the mayor might still bear it himself. Certainly he did so in Chichester when, at the election of his successor, he traditionally held the mace aloft and thanked the electors for having chosen him in the previous year.[34] In Jacobean Shaftesbury the business of projecting the mayor's authority became so important that the mace came to be carried before him every day of the year, except for the four days prior to Mid-Summer's Fair.[35] The mace was more than ever symbolic of the mayor's office and dignity. When dissident townsmen rose up against such authority in late Henrician Carmarthen, they made a special effort to wrest the mayor's mace from the serjeant's grasp.[36] Finally, when in the midst of a dispute between town and cathedral officials in Caroline Winchester the mayor came to the cathedral with his mace of office, the dean bade him leave it outside the door, thus barring this symbol of mayoral, and hence of civic, authority from his precinct. The corporation responded by sending its *three* maces along with the mayor and his brethren to the next Sunday's

[33] Jewett and St John Hope, *Corporate Plate and Insignia*, i, pp. xviii–xl.
[34] Deposition of John Sharwin, PRO, STAC 5/C23/37.
[35] Deposition of Walter Hamon, shoemaker and Serjeant to the Mayor, in *Countess and Earl of Pembroke* v. *Inhabitants of Shaftesbury* (1621), PRO, E 134/18 James I/East. I.
[36] *Mayor and Bailiffs of Carmarthen* v. *Devereux* et al., PRO, STAC 2/Bundle 17/271; cf. the plaintiff's bill.

services.[37] A very similar dispute arose in regard to the right of the Mayor of the City of Chester to carry his sword of office—a frequent analogue to the mace—into the cathedral of that city in the year 1606. In the end, the dispute was referred to the Lord Chancellor himself who, after consultation with the JPs of the shire, permitted the mayor to carry his sword anywhere in the cathedral.[38]

Not surprisingly, whereas earlier maces bore the royal arms or those of the town or its lord, it became common by the end of the Elizabethan period to have the arms or name of the incumbent mayor himself added to a new mace or even sometimes to one which had long been in service. Arundel's fifteenth-century mace came to carry the arms of Henry Fitzalan, twelfth Earl of Arundel, by 1580 (the date of the earl's death), but as mayoral authority emerged from the seigneurial shadow, it acquired the inscription 'Thomas Benett Woolen Draper Mayor 1594' (*sic*) a few years later. St Ives's (Cornwall) first civic mace carried its first mayor's arms in 1641.[39]

By practices of this sort the mace became linked very closely with the authority of the town as represented by the mayor. It became a virtual necessity for a town to acquire a mace upon incorporation, though this could be very costly. After the acquisition of a new charter in 1614 the burgesses of Stafford spent £49. 7s. 2d. on a mace of silver and gold weighing 111½ ounces.[40] It is also clear that in almost all towns, the mace, like most civic plate and regalia, came conventionally to be kept and displayed in the town hall.

Indeed, the evolving importance both of the mace and the mayoral dignity to which it contributed are integrally bound up with the political symbolism of the hall. As we might anticipate, this connection is especially vivid in the ceremonies surrounding mayoral and other civic elections. Thus, when the mayor of Carmarthen and his allies tried in 1609 to unseat a town clerk supported by a rival faction and replace him with one of their own, they not only came into the town hall to do their work, but specifically caused the town's sword and 'hat of maintenance' to be brought in for the occasion.[41] Maces were also often kept on display during the conduct of regular town business, including the conduct of courts and councils. In Macclesfield the connection between the mace and the hall is particularly vivid: a mayor's mace carved in stone appears over the entrance-way to the late Elizabethan guild-hall.[42]

[37] Rosen, 'History of Winchester', 229.
[38] BL, Harleian, 1944, fo. 92.
[39] G. W. Eustace, *Arundel: Borough and Castle* (1922), 255; J. H. Matthews, *A History of the Parishes of St. Ives, Lelant, Towednack and Zennor in the County of Cornwall* (1892), 194.
[40] William Salt Library, MS D(W) 1721/1/4, fo. 90.   [41] PRO, STAC 8/bundle 20/14.
[42] C. S. Davies (ed.), *A History of Macclesfield* (Manchester, 1961), frontispiece.

Of ceremonial occasions, the festivities surrounding the annual election of the mayor occurred with relative uniformity in almost all towns enjoying the presence of such an official. Although electoral practices themselves differed somewhat from town to town, two edifices always figured prominently in the proceedings: the church, in which an election day sermon came to be as regular a feature after the Reformation as the mass had before, and the town hall. In the latter were frequently held the election itself, or some part thereof, the oath-taking, and often the electoral banquet at the end of the day. (As we have seen in the previous chapter, those towns with more than one building serving as the hall often spread the electoral proceedings around accordingly.)

Thus, for example, it was the custom in Cambridge to hold the election in the Guildhall, the election day sermon in the parish church, and then the oath-taking back in the Guildhall again.[43] In Bristol, mayoral elections were held on St Giles's Day, the first day of September. Proceedings began when the outgoing mayor summoned all aldermen, councillors, and sheriffs to the Council House, where three candidates were selected: one by the mayor himself, one by all aldermen who had been mayors, and one by the rest of those assembled. The actual election proceeded on the following day, and the mayor took his oath in the Hall.[44]

What varied the most in such proceedings was the degree of participation in the political process. The roles of different political groups within the community were often emphasized symbolically by where they met in relation to the hall. In Oxford, for example, the Council of Twelve sat in the inner room or Council Chamber of the Guildhall—the smaller and more select space—to select three nominees. The freemen, who had the right to carry out the actual election of one of these nominees but not to partake in the nominating process, were not permitted to enter the Council Chamber on that occasion. They were obliged instead to wait outside in the courtyard behind the Hall, there to make their choice by division. But as if to reaffirm the fellowship of the community, both freemen and Council joined in the annual election dinner thereafter. This was served neither in the Council Chamber nor the courtyard, but in the 'lower Guildhall', the larger and less prestigious chamber of the building, located both symbolically and literally halfway between the courtyard and the Council Chamber of the Hall.[45]

Yet as the example of Hedon demonstrates, this physical separation was not always observed: here voting was restricted to the bailiffs and burgesses, but all inhabitants of the town were summoned to attend

---

[43] J. W. Cooper (ed.), *Annals of Cambridge* 5 vols. (Cambridge, 1842–1908), ii. 279.

[44] Stanford, *Ordinances of Bristol*, 41–2.

[45] H. E. Salter (ed.), *Oxford Council Acts, 1583–1626* (Oxford Historical Society, 1928), p. xxxiii.

1. Leominster Town Hall

2. Thaxted Moot Hall

3. Evesham Booth Hall

4. Titchfield Town Hall

5. Aldeburgh Moot Hall

6. Much Wenlock Guildhall

7. Mayor's parlour
Leicester Guildhall

8. Canopy over Mayor's seat
Totnes Town Hall

9. Mayor's seat-and-settle
Beverley Town Hall

10. Aldermanic bench
Beverley Town Hall

11. Magistrate's or Mayor's table
Beverley Town Hall

12. Court room panelling
Much Wenlock Town Hall

13. Portrait of Robert Jannis
Mayor of Norwich

proceedings in the hall on the Thursday before Michaelmas each year. Similarly, all burgesses attended the proclamation of the new mayor, also in the hall, though there is no indication of a general feast thereafter.[46] In some communities it had even been the practice to permit gentlemen and others, not only from the community itself, but also from the surrounding countryside, to witness proceedings in the town hall. Like the civic processions, this served to display the locus of civic authority to both the community and the 'wider world'. But in 1627 this was resented by the commoners of Chester, who saw the occasion as an infringement on their privileges. An observer of this event related that 'such was the barbarousness and rudenesse of the Commons that the would not permit them to be their, nither wold the give their voyces but continued in an uproare, untill the knights, Esquires and Gentlemen departed ye hall'.[47]

It almost goes without saying that the town hall, and the mayor as its chief presiding officer, also took pride of place in other annual ceremonies, even though these naturally differed from town to town. Especially after the Reformation, many of these had as their principal purpose the glorification of the town itself and the promotion of harmonious relations amongst its residents. Though larger in scale than some such festivities elsewhere, the Shrovetide and Easter Monday celebrations in Chester seem typical in this regard.

The first of these occasions had traditionally centred on a football match between the shoemakers and the drapers. But this led to an early form of 'football hooliganism' and so they were transformed after 1549 to less potentially violent activities: a foot race and a horse race. These were interspersed with ceremonial consumption of bread and ale and then, on Ash Wednesday, of leeks and salt. By the end of the century the 'Ashwednesday Drinking' had developed into a grand banquet, hosted by the drapers, principally devoted to doing homage to the mayor, and naturally held in the Guildhall.[48] By 1625 even these events grew out of hand, and another revision ensued. Thereafter the focus turned even more toward a celebration of the mayor, rendered principally by the three major crafts, all in proper livery. On each of the three days before and including Ash Wednesday liverymen from all three waited on the mayor in a procession from the spiritual centre of the city, the cathedral, to the civic centre, the Common Hall.[49]

The Easter Monday rituals, said to have begun in 1511 but probably of earlier provenance, proceeded much in the same vein. Here the central events were the archery contest or 'shooting' between teams chosen by

---

[46] Humberside Co. RO MS DDHE/26, fo. 131ʳ⁻ᵛ.
[47] BL, Harleian, 29,780, fo. 164.
[48] L. M. Clopper, *REED, Chester* (Toronto, 1979), 234–7, 308, 321.
[49] Ibid. 372–3.

each of the city's two sheriffs. The prize was a breakfast of calves' head and bacon, imparting the name Calveshead Breakfast to the whole event. Having concluded the contest, both teams walked to the Guildhall, where they were joined by the mayor, aldermen, and—at least until 1640—others in the community, to partake 'of the saide brekfaste, in a louinge manner . . . it beinge a conendable [sic] exercize, agood recreation and a louinge assemblye'. As another contemporary description tells us, this was to celebrate under the benevolent, neutral, and august hand of the mayor, 'the comfort, refreshinge and societye of all ye Cittisens'.[50]

The annual St George's Day festivities in Norwich proceeded much in the same vein. It was marked by a sermon in the cathedral and then a feast in the Guildhall: not the much more commodious Blackfriars Hall, with its nave of 125ft by 70ft, but in the much smaller but symbolically essential Assembly Chamber of the Guildhall itself, though it measured but 30ft. by 36ft.[51] Similar festivities, and similar employment of the town hall, were also common, if less well documented, elsewhere.

Ceremonial occasions aside, we may observe even in the quotidian routine of civic government the development of special rooms, furnishings, and emblems within the town hall designed to reflect and to enhance the dignity of mayoral office and, indeed, the town itself.

The appearance and evolution of the mayor's parlour has already been observed, with examples from Nottingham as early as 1486, Southwark c.1550, Leicester in 1563 and again in 1637, and even so modest a community as Lostwithiel by the mid-seventeenth century.[52] Both the furnishings of these rooms and the use of which they had already been put in the monastery—where they seem to have originated—and in aristocratic houses, suggests the function of parlours in the town hall. In the parlour, the etymological cousin of the French verb *parler*, to speak, the mayor could confer with people privately rather than in the glare of the council chamber or the court room. Here also, following the pattern of aristocratic practice, he could retire from the hall itself for greater privacy and personal comfort. Whether employed by the lord in his hall or the mayor in the town hall, the parlour seems certain to have contributed to the sense of deference due its incumbent (see Plate 7).[53]

We must also take note of the mayor's seat, a seat both of honour and of

[50] Clopper, *REED, Chester*, 434; BL, Add. MS 11,335, fo. 23; BL, Harleian, 1944, fo. 26ᵛ.

[51] Galloway, *REED, Norwich*, pp. xxx–xxxi, 23.

[52] For Nottingham: W. H. Stevenson, *Records of the Borough of Nottingham*, 3 vols. (Nottingham, 1885), iii. 253; for Southwark: D. J. Johnson, *Southwark and the City* (Oxford, 1969), 222–3; for Leicester: N. A. Pedgen, *Leicester Guildhall, a Short History and Guide* (Leicester, 1981), 4; for Lostwithiel: HMC 55, *Various Collection*, i (1901), 331.

[53] See the discussions of parlours, and the retreat from the hall to the parlour in the aristocratic house, in Mark Girouard, *Life in the English Country House* (Harmondsworth, 1980), 58–9. See also M. Howard, *The Early Tudor Country House, Architecture and Politics, 1490–1550* (1987), ch. 5.

power, and of its historical development. The apparent evolution of this genre of civic furniture suggests that the mayor's accustomed place of precedence in the council chamber conventionally began as the central place on a long bench or settle set along one wall, with the mayor's 'brethren' sitting in some fixed order on the same bench or settle, at the same height and on either side of the mayor himself. Thus, for example, a seventeenth-century description of the town hall of Preston, Lancashire, still refers to 'an elevated bench where at the three portmotes or the two leet days and the Grand Leet . . . sitts the Mayor, Aldermen, and such gentry as attend those meetings'.[54]

In some instances, especially in larger or wealthier towns, the mayor may have come to sit in a more distinctive position as early as the fifteenth century. The significance of this development as a reflection of mayoral status should not be overlooked. Historians of furniture now recognize that chairs, as distinct from benches, stools, or settles, were more common in the High Middle Ages than had once been assumed.[55] Yet in our period they were still very much 'seats of honour', 'associated with dignity, with formal occasions, with power', likened to the bishop's throne in a cathedral.[56] In houses of middling sorts of people in both Norwich and Oxfordshire, where the question has been considered carefully through the use of household inventories, chairs were still not entirely common at the turn of the seventeenth century,[57] though at least one authority would suggest that only large, comfortable, arm chairs remained rare for this long.[58] The point at which mayors began to be provided with chairs of their own in the town hall is thus of considerable importance as a gauge of their growing dignity and authority. This point seems to have come in the Elizabethan and Jacobean periods.

One of the few surviving early mayor's chairs may be seen in St Mary's Hall, Coventry: the surviving third of a 'triple throne' constructed to seat the masters of the three major guilds of Coventry some time in the

[54] R. Kuerden, *A Brief Description of the Borough and Town of Preston, originally composed between 1682 and 1686*, ed. John Taylor (Preston, 1818), 4–5, as cited in G. H. Tupling, 'Lancashire Markets in the Sixteenth and Seventeenth Centuries', *Transactions of the Lancashire and Cheshire Antiquarian Society*, 58 (1947 for 1945–6), 11.

[55] See esp. Penelope Eames, *Furniture in England, France and the Netherlands from the Twelfth to the Fifteenth Century* (1977), pp. xxi, 181. Compare this with the traditional view expressed in, e.g., Ralph Fastnedge, *English Furniture Styles, 1500–1830* [1955] (1969), 8, or H. Cescinsky and E. R. Gribble, *Early English Furniture and Woodwork*, 2 vols. (1922), ii. 145.

[56] John Gloag, *The Englishman's Chair: Origins, Design and Social History of Seat Furniture in England* (1964), 41; S. W. Wolsey and R. W. P. Luff, *Furniture in the Age of the Joiner* (1968), 69.

[57] Ursula Priestley and P. J. Corfield, 'Rooms and Room Use in Norwich Housing, 1580–1730', *Post-Medieval Archeology*, 16 (1982), 108; Pauline Agius, 'Late Sixteenth and Seventeenth Century Furniture at Oxford', *Furniture History*, 7 (1971), 72, 76.

[58] Victor Chinnery, *Oak Furniture, the British Tradition* (1979), 39. Christopher Hill, on the other hand, dates the replacement of benches by chairs in the homes of the better sort to the Restoration era, though this seems a bit late; Hill, *The Century of Revolution, 1603–1714* (1961), 253.

fifteenth century. This ornately carved piece, looking like a fugitive from a late Gothic choir stall, had been adopted for use as the mayor's chair by the mid-sixteenth century.[59] Some care about the mayor's customary seating may be noted in the description of arrangements made to accommodate the visit to Coventry of the Princess Elizabeth in 1604. No fewer than three seats provided for the occasion, each in a different building, were designated as the mayor's accustomed place: one, obviously a pew, in St Michael's Church, a second in the mayor's parlour, and the throne in St Mary's Hall, though only the last of these was truly a mayor's seat in our use of the term: a place from which the mayor presided over the governing structures of the town.[60]

Yet if the Coventry example remains a distinctive source of local pride, it may also be a bit of a cheat for our purposes, not having been built for mayoral use to begin with and still very much in the Gothic and ecclesiastical mode. In other towns the evolution from the mayor's place on the bench as *primus inter pares* with his brethren to a more distinctive location took different forms during the period under consideration. In most instances, and even when the mayor remained seated on a bench with his fellows, that bench became raised up on a dais or on a step or two. A Star Chamber deponent testifying in 1586 about a hotly disputed parliamentary election in Chichester noted that the mayor 'came down from the bench' to pacify unruly participants in the Guildhall. The mayor himself, George Chatfield, deposed to the same effect.[61] Similarly John Hooker, the Elizabethan historian of Exeter, referred to the serjeant carrying the oath book 'up to the benche where the mayo^r, Recorder and aldermen Do sytt' so that the outgoing mayor could give the oath of office to his successor: a clear reference to a raised bench on which the mayor sat with his brethren.[62]

In a common sequence in the development of civic furnishings and the official dignity which was thereby signified, the bench seating the mayor and aldermen first became decorated or otherwise enhanced, and then the mayor's position grew distinct and eventually free-standing altogether in the form of a true chair. Thus, for example, in Shrewsbury, 'the seate

[59] Herbert Cescinsky, 'An Oak Chair in St Mary's Hall, Coventry', *Burlington Magazine*, 39/223 (1921), 170–7, summarized in Cescinsky and Gribble, *Early English Furniture*, ii. 154–63 and figs. 204, 210; Gloag, *The Englishman's Chair*, 33–4; Eames, *Furniture in England*, 196–7.

[60] Cited in Ingram (ed.), *REED, Coventry*, 364–5.

[61] Deposition of James Cooke, PRO, STAC 5/c23/37, and George Chatfield, STAC 5/c41/1.

[62] John Vowell (*alias* Hooker), *The Description of the Citie of Excester*, 3 vols. (1575), ed. W. J. Harte, J. W. Schopp, and H. Tapley-Soper (Devon and Cornwall Record Society (1919–47), iii. 794. Viewed in a broader perspective, it is remarkable that such elevation of seating came only at this time to English towns outside London, when it seems to have been practised widely elsewhere in Europe much earlier. When in 1420 the Florentine Commune wished to emphasize the power of the Priors over the Podesta and other officials, it forbad the latter to be seated at the same level as the former; Richard Trexler, *Public Life in Renaissance Florence* (New York, 1980), 258.

for the baylyffs [equivalent to the mayor in Shrewsbury] and Aldermen in the Guyle hall . . . was waynskottid in more coomlyer and commendabler order than before' in 1583/4. Just a few months later the hall was 'sylyd within overhedd and newe garnyshyd to saye where baylyffs and Aldermen sytt . . . in bewtyfull and decent order'.[63] In York a dozen 'semely' cushions were brought for the mayor and his brethren to sit on in the Council Chamber in 1562/3, implying that all those officials sat together on one bench. But in 1577/8 the council agreed that a 'mete and convenient chaire' be made for the mayor alone, presumably for the first time.[64] In Totnes the mayor's seats in both Council Chamber and court room were covered with ornate canopies of carved oak (c. 1624) each like a testor over a pulpit, which may still be seen.[65](see Plate 8.)

A particularly significant example of mayoral seating, and one which still survives, was constructed in Beverley in the year 1604 (see Plate 9). Here a three-seat settle was built with the middle seat raised up some seven inches above the level of the attached seats on either side. Local tradition maintains that this was constructed by Roger Mack for £2, at the command of the newly elected mayor, Henry Farrar. Both the date and Farrar's initials are carved into the piece. Contemporary with this rare and possibly unique specimen are two lengthy benches, one of 8ft. 5½in. and the other of 9ft. 1in. in length, meant to accommodate the town's aldermen, while the deputy mayor and the town clerk sat alongside the mayor (see Plate 10). One may surmise that prior to 1604 this latter trio simply sat on the same benches as the aldermen: the aldermanic bench looks almost certainly to be the immediate ancestor of the settle-and-seat.[66]

Another variation of mayoral seat survives at Leicester where, in 1637, the mayor's place on the long aldermanic bench was distinguished by the addition of two engaged columns against the supporting wall, flanking his position. The bench itself had a cushion at the mayor's place alone, and a carved depiction of the royal arms was placed on the wall above and between the columns.[67]

[63] Revd W. A. Leighton, 'Early Chronicles of Shrewsbury, 1372–1606', *Transactions of the Shropshire Archaeological and Natural History Society*, 3 (1880), 295, 299.

[64] A. Raine (ed.), *York Civic Records*, 8 vols. (Yorkshire Archaeological Society Record Series), vi (1948 for 1946), 55 and vii (1950 for 1949), 168.

[65] My thanks to Richard J. Butterfield, Town Clerk of Totnes, for clarifying the origins and providing me with illustrations of these pieces.

[66] No published notice of this piece has been located. I wish to thank Mr Raymond Grange, Borough Tourist Officer, Miss Margaretha Smith, Deputy Tourist Officer, and Mr Arthur Coates, all of Beverley, for facilitating access and permission to photograph Beverley's civic furniture, and Mr Clive Wainwright of the Victoria and Albert Museum for his comments on the same.

[67] Pegden, *Leicestershire Guildhall*, 4; T. H. Fosbrooke and S. H. Skillington, 'The Old Town Hall of Leicester', *Transactions of the Leicestershire Archaeological Society*, 13 (1923–4), 1–72, and *passim*.

In addition to these examples, each representing a different solution to
the problem of distinguishing the mayor's place, we have two finely carved
caqueteuse chairs in the Salisbury Guildhall. The first, dated 1585, was
commissioned and presented by the mayor of the year, Robert Bower, and
the second, nearly an exact replica, was commissioned and presented by
Maurice Green, mayor in 1622. The facts that both bore the city's arms
carved in the lower portion of the back panel, and that each was the
donation of a mayor, present strong circumstantial evidence that each was
intended as a mayor's throne or chair of state.[68] In addition, it is worth
noting that the date of the earlier chair coincides with the completion of a
new council house in Salisbury (itself subsequently destroyed by fire in
1780). That four-storey structure appears to have had at least two rooms
or 'halls' in which the mayor presided, and hence the need for more than
one such chair.[69]

The seating of the mayor thus became an increasingly important
consideration in the furnishing of civic halls and—in an age where battles
over seating precedence in church stalls or assize benches became
important points of honour—perhaps this should not surprise us.[70]

At the same time as these seats appeared in their respective halls, we
have a minor proliferation of another form of civic furnishing, the
magistrate's table. This, too, was more than merely functional. These
large, heavy, oak pieces, meant to remain in place and not to be taken apart
and moved as were earlier trestle tables which were designed for the
aristocratic household, further added to the dignity of town officials,
especially the mayor and his brethren, who sat behind them. In Chichester such a table was sufficiently large and sturdy to support several rioters
who stood upon it in the civil disturbances of 1586:[71] perhaps a reminder
that even this symbol of official authority sometimes failed to convey the
proper authority. A similar table remains in the Guildhall of the
Shropshire market town of Much Wenlock, built in the year 1624 and still
apparently capable of supporting the weight of a good many rioters should

[68] Chinnery, Oak Furniture, 448–9 and plate 1.

[69] VCH, Wiltshire, vi. 87; H. Shortt (ed.), The City of Salisbury (Salisbury, 1957), 58, 94; Wiltshire
RO, MS G23/1/3, fo. 61.

[70] The practice of reserving specific stalls or seats in church for local dignitaries seems to have
become common during the sixteenth century, though a few earlier examples are noted in such larger
towns as Exeter. See W. J. Hardy, 'Remarks on the History of Seat Reservations in Churches',
Archaeologia, 53 (1892), 104, and more generally, Alfred Heales, History and Law of Church Seats, 2
vols. (1872), i, ch. 1. For specific examples, Battley, 'Élite and Community', 207 (re: King's Lynn,
1602); K. R. Adey, 'Aspects of the History of the Town of Stafford, 1590–1710' (Keele Univ. MA
thesis 1971), 97; Bailey, Minutes of Boston, i. 81–2, 463, 643. For assize seating, see Anthony Fletcher,
'Honour, Reputation and Local Office Holding in Elizabethan and Stuart England', in Fletcher and
John Stevenson (eds.), Order and Disorder in Early Modern England (Cambridge, 1985), 98.

[71] John Byrde testified that he 'did see many standinge upon the Table wch was before the Mayor
in the said Comon Hall', PRO, STAC 5/C23/37.

the need arise.[72] A splendid example at Beverley, a town whose contributions to the design of civic furniture were as ingenious as they were durable, has five hinged storage compartments for keeping official documents. These open out from the 94½ in. × 68½ in. top surface (see Plate 11).

Below the rank of the mayor, the members of the two conciliar assemblies which operated, under various names, in most towns also strove to gain dignity and respect in this era. Again such efforts were closely tied to the town hall as the locus of their authority. This same deference extended readily to decorum, ceremony, and furnishings. As with the mayor, all members of the Twelve and the Twenty-Four, as Boston's two councils were called, typified the obligation of aldermen in many towns in having to 'come in decent order in ther gownes like Townes men *of such a corporation* [author's italics] at all tyme and tymes when ther dewties is to be at the guildhall . . . upon forfeit of 12ᵈ'.[73] Concern for proper and dignified speech frequently provoked such by-laws as we see in Abingdon, where the burgesses ruled 'that there shalbe no man[ner] of unsemelye wordes styrred raysed or multiplied with in the Comon Councelle [i.e., the council chamber in local parlance] to the disquietinge of the reste'.[74]

Not only was speech regulated within the walls, but town officials were increasingly anxious that their dignity not be affronted by word of proceedings carried outside: the leakage of news to the public had already been invented! In St Albans, such violations of confidentiality resulted, by 1608, in deprivation of office,[75] but similar strictures were commonly articulated even in the early Elizabethan period.[76] In Bridport, where the hall building shared a common wall with a private tenement, four townsmen were found guilty of eavesdropping on guild-hall proceedings in 1578.[77]

While these constraints were chiefly intended to foster civic deference by the persuasion of habitual use, a more restrictive intent inspired measures both to make the town hall the exclusive preserve of the ruling element and to prevent possible trouble-makers from entering at will. An early sign of this tendency was the 1550 decision to construct in Southwark a 'secret chamber' where the mayor could confer in strict privacy with his 'brethren': in effect a form of mayor's parlour.[78] But the

[72] Much Wenlock Borough Archives, MS no. B3/1/1, p. 537. A similar and contemporary table from Coventry is described and photographed in H. Cescinsky, *English Furniture from Gothic to Sheraton* (Garden City, NY, 1937), 91.

[73] Bailey, *Minutes of Boston*, i. 24 (11 Oct. 1555). Cf. also Leicestershire Co. RO, MS BR III/2 31, a fine of 4d. levied for violation of dress regulations in 1564; Berkshire RO, MS D/EP7/84, fo. 7ᵛ; E. Suffolk RO, MS EEI/EI/1 (unpag.) Humberside Co. RO, MS DDHE/26, fo. 131ᵛ.

[74] Berkshire RO, MS D/EP7/84, fo. 7ᵛ.   [75] St Albans Public Library, MS 152, fo. 94.

[76] e.g. by the Mayor and Burgesses of Abingdon, Berkshire RO, MS D/EP7/84, fo. 9ᵛ.

[77] Dorset Co. RO, MS B3/C83 (unpaginated), a 'Grand Inquest' of 21 April 1578.

[78] Johnson, *Southwark and the City*, 222–3.

mayor and burgesses of Bedford voted in 1562 to exclude anyone from the premises but JPs and town officials, except on official business.[79] In Oxford, by 1563, a core of the more powerful members of the Common Council met secretly in a separate chamber under the council room to prepare business for the council at large, and the mayor and aldermen of Bristol took precisely the same step at almost the same time: in each case a clear sign of restrictiveness even within the government of a single town.[80]

Even ceremonial occasions, which in former times had conventionally been carried out openly before the whole community, now came more often to be held for the ruling élite alone behind the closed doors of the guild-hall. The trend went hand in hand with the proliferation of oligarchic rule and practice in a great many towns at this time. In Hastings this became true of mayoral elections in 1603, a time of economic and social duress:

It is also ordered & decreed by this Assemblie That to avoid the great inconveniences wch by common experience are found to be by reason of the eleccon of the maior of this towne abroad in the publick view of the wholl multitude not only of Inhabitants but also of many strangers assembling at such elecons in the open Hundred place whereby all matters of Counsell is disclosed & may not be kept secret, That from hensforth all the elecons of the maiors of this towne shalbe solemnized, made, done & p'formed in the Court Hall of this towne, as a place more decent apt & secreat for such affaires to be done or used, Any old custome usage or decreee to the contrary notw'thstanding.[81]

Similarly, the ruling oligarchy of Winchester had grown so restrictive by the 1620s that even the members of the Twenty-Four complained that the mayor and his brethren (in this case the eleven former mayors) failed to admit them to the council chamber to partake in deliberations. And in Chester, during a time of similar duress in 1640, participation in the traditional 'calveshead breakfast' became severely restricted to a very élite few and moved behind the doors of the Guildhall which were now locked behind them, as a 'more particular priuat dynar for the Aldermen, gentlemen & Archers only *and no loose people to troble the hall*' [author's italics].[82]

---

[79] The town 'constitution' of 1562 in Bedford Town Hall documents, B 1, fo. 5ᵛ. This act was repealed in the iconoclastic enthusiasm of the Commonwealth in 1650.

[80] Hammer, 'Anatomy of an Oligarchy', 7; Stanford, *Ordinances of Bristol*, 29.

[81] Entry of 6 April 1603, Hastings Town Record Book entry as cited in J. M. Baines, *Historic Hastings* (Hastings, 1955), 55.

[82] Rosen, 'History of Winchester', 233; BL, Harleian MS 2125, fo. 133, as cited in Clopper, *REED, Chester*, 451. An early example of this may be found in the Guildhall of London, England's only true metropolis, where in 1430 a chamber was constructed to which the mayor and aldermen could retire and consider nominations put to them by the members of the Common Hall; Michael Berlin, 'Civic Ceremony in Early Modern London', *Urban History Yearbook* (1986), 17 and C. M. Barron, *The Medieval Guildhall of London* (1974), 31.

In this atmosphere we find numerous references to locks being added to town hall doors (Barnstaple in 1553–4, West Looe in 1589) or repaired when they had broken (Bridport, 1626), and evidence that the locks were not necessarily meant to work from the outside. In the attempt to quell the 1586 election dispute in Chichester, the mayor put out of the hall several noisy and angry opponents, locked the door from the *inside*, kept the key, and proceeded to conduct the parliamentary election so hotly at issue.[83]

In so far as surviving evidence allows us to discover, the furnishings and decoration of town halls also developed to reflect not just the dignity of the mayor, but of the whole structure over which he presided. Certainly the functional development of space itself, as noted in Chapter 2 above, was well under way as a reflection of the increasing specialization and complexity of conciliar and judicial responsibility. While in towns where local jurisdiction failed to evolve, as at Elstow and Titchfield, halls remained undifferentiated, the growing complexity of jurisdiction in others led to a parallel development in the use of space, and to the distinct emergence of court rooms, council chambers, 'chequers' for the payment and recording of accounts, and other rooms. Jury rooms, already apparent at the Fordwich hall in what we must assume was a particularly early example,[84] emerged later in Barking,[85] Leighton Buzzard (by 1585),[86] Kendal (by the 1590s),[87] and Barnstaple (1625)[88] as well, no doubt, as in many other towns. Buildings constructed or converted after those early examples came frequently to provide for such functional distinctions from the beginning.

Though we may assume that these furnishings were still rudimentary, we do read of the construction of permanent benches for court rooms and council rooms (in Abingdon,[89] Gloucester,[90] Barnstaple,[91] Northampton,[92] and Marlborough,[93]) and even oak seating with carved

[83] N. Devon Atheneum, MS 3972, no. 42, m. 2 (24–5 Henry VIII); Cornwall RO, MS B/W LOOE/21, mayor's summary account for Oct. 1589; Dorset RO, MS B3/M2, item 1049; PRO, STAC 5/C41/1, Answer of George Chatfield, Mayor of Chichester.

[84] C. Woodruff, *A History of the Town and Port of Fordwich*, [1895] (Canterbury, n.d.) 110–11.

[85] *VCH, Essex* v (1966), 218.

[86] Bedfordshire Co. RO, MS KK 319.

[87] Cumbria RO, Kendal, MS WMB/K8, fos. 16–17ᵛ. My thanks to the *REED* Centre in Toronto for access to its microfilm copy of these accounts, and to Dr Audrey Douglas of *REED* for her help with them.

[88] N. Devon Atheneum, MS 3972, no. 205. My thanks again to the *REED* Centre for permitting me access to the microfilm copy of these accounts.

[89] Berkshire RO, MS D/EP7/83, fo. 74, reference to 1564–5.

[90] Gloucestershire RO, MS GBR/F4/3, fo. 132ᵛ (n.d.).

[91] N. Devon Atheneum, MS 3972, no. 42, m. 2, 24–5 Henry VIII.

[92] Christopher A. Markham and Revd J. Charles Cox (eds.), *The Records of the Borough of Northampton*, 2 vols. (Northampton, 1898), ii. 172.

[93] Wiltshire Co. RO, G22/1/205/2, fo. 7.

inscriptions (of imprecise date) for the magistrates of Bromsgrove.[94]
Walls, too, received special treatment. Those which remained stone or
plaster inside were conventionally whitewashed (for example Southampton and Chard),[95] painted (Plymouth, 1565 and Oxford, 1615),[96] or
panelled: early clinker-boarding at Lavenham in the mid-fifteenth
century, more refined linenfold in Elizabethan Totnes and probably
in Kingston-upon-Thames.[97] Good examples of such panelling still
survive from Jacobean Much Wenlock (see Plate 12).[98] Wainscotting
(Shrewsbury in 1577–8 and Marlborough in 1632)[99] or moulded plaster
work (Wotton-under-Edge in 1609)[100] were also employed by the end of
our period. Floors continued to be strewn with mats or rushes as at
Rye,[101] but were also coming to be carpeted as at Marlborough by 1575,
Oxford by 1599–1600, and Plymouth by 1614.[102]

An especially instructive and still largely surviving example of such
furnishings may be seen at Much Wenlock, though one must put out of
mind the impressive Victorian additions which dominate the whole. Here,
in 1624, the larger and original hall of the two-room floor, called
alternatively the Council Chamber and 'thelection house' received a large
table and forms for the councillors, a wainscot door leading to the inner
room or 'court house', whitening on the walls and 'greening' on the 'court
post' and window frames. Such renovations cost £26. 7s. 7d.[103] In 1608–9
the Plymouth Guildhall was supplied with a 'table board, two chests,
forms and sealing', with twelve new cushions for the forms in the Council
Chamber, brought all the way from London.[104]

Even when we move beyond 'the mayor and his brethren' (for example
to councillors or aldermen) in the hierarchy of town government, we may
still observe the cultivation of deference. It should almost go without

[94] The inscription read *Fiat Justicia, Ruat Coelum* 'Let justice be done though the Heavens may
fall'. The seating and inscriptions were moved from the 'old' to the new guild-hall upon the
demolition of the former in 1832. W. G. Leadbetter, *The Story of Bromsgrove* (Bromsgrove, 1949), 86.
[95] F. J. C. and D. M. Hearnshaw (eds.), *Court Leet Records 1603–1624* (Southampton Record
Society, vol. i in 3 pts., 1905–7), i. pt. iii, 428; Somerset RO, MS DD/6/Ch, 1623 (unpag.).
[96] W. Devon RO, MS Worth 131, fo. 2ᵛ; Salter, *Oxford Council Acts, 1583–1626*, 408.
[97] DoE, 'List of Buildings of Historic Interest, District of S. Hams, Devon', notes by Michael
Laithwaite (1978), 43–4; D. M. Johnston, *A Schedule of Antiquities of the County of Surrey* (Guildford,
1913), 40; W. D. Biden, *The History and Antiquities of Kingston-upon-Thames* (Kingston, 1852), 125.
[98] Observed in visit of May 1986.
[99] Leighton, 'Early Chronicles of Shrewsbury', 281; Wiltshire Co. RO, MS G22/1/205/2, fols.
72–73ᵛ (1632).
[100] Nikolaus Pevsner and David Verey, *BoE, Gloucestershire*, 2 vols. (Harmondsworth, 1970), i.
495.
[101] E. Sussex County RO, MS 60/3, fo. 54ᵛ. I am indebted to the *REED* Centre for access to the
microfilm copies of these accounts.
[102] Wiltshire Co. RO, MS G22/1/205/2., fo. 79; Salter, *Oxford Council Acts*, 380; W. Devon RO,
MS Worth 132, fo. 177ᵛ.
[103] Much Wenlock Bor. Archives, MS B3/1/1, pp. 537–8.
[104] W. Devon RO, MS Worth 132, fos. 168 and 177ᵛ.

saying that the role of sundry lesser officials grew along with the power of town government in general at this time. Constables experienced the challenges posed by an increasingly mobile and possibly even more lawless society. Chamberlains and treasurers had to cope with the expanded fiscal authority of many communities, and also with the persistently fragile state of urban finance. Yet of the common offices, the development of the town clerk's and the recorder's offices seem especially interesting and central to our concerns.

From what has been said above about the growing importance of record keeping it should be obvious that the keepers of those records, usually town clerks, would gain in responsibility and status as well. The development of this role is demonstrated most dramatically in the borough of Boston, a town whose effective self-government may chiefly be said to date from the curtailment of ecclesiastical lordship and the subsequent incorporation of civic government in 1546. From the very beginning of this new era in Boston's history the town employed a clerk for the keeping of records, and the minutes of the Assembly began to be recorded on a regular basis. Still it seems to have taken at least a short while for officials to get used to these procedures. Some early mayors took Borough Assembly minutes home with them before they could be recorded in the town minute book,[105] and the first clerk received only £3. 6s. 8d. per annum for his (perhaps not too arduous) labours.[106] But change came rapidly, and the clerk's duties and worth grew apace. In response to pleas of underpayment his wages were augmented in 1549 by a share of market court revenues, and in 1562 by the addition of a dwelling-house free of charge. This, plus five marks in salary and more in fees were valued at £20 per annum.[107] Though the clerk's dwelling-house in Boston was a separate structure from the hall itself, such quarters were carved out of existing space in the hall at Wymondham[108] and included in the purpose-built hall at Barking in 1567,[109] while in Oxford the clerk had use of an office under the Council House during the sixteenth century.[110] This allocation of space bears vivid testimony both of the importance of the clerk's role and the manner in which the civic hall was made to accommodate that office.

[105] Bailey, *Minutes of Boston*, i. 3, 7.
[106] Ibid. 2 (1546).
[107] Ibid. 4 and 53.
[108] Norfolk and Norwich RO, ref. Neville 12.12.66/Q173 B, fos. 87–8.
[109] A. W. Clapham, 'The Court House or "Old Town Hall" at Barking', *Transactions of the Essex Archaeological Society*, NS 12(1913) 295–8.
[110] *VCH, Oxfordshire*, iv (Oxford, 1979), 149. By no means, however, did the provision of an official residence of sorts in any English town hall approximate the elaborate residential quarters provided for leading officials in many Italian halls of the same era. See Mark Girouard, *Cities and People, a Social and Architectural History* (1985), 53.

The recorder, though socially at least the equal of the town's leaders, was often a Westminster-based lawyer and not resident in the community. Yet his office was increasingly valued and handsomely rewarded. As he came more often to dwell at court than 'at home' at least one town (Leicester) provided him with a handsome dwelling chamber in the town hall in which to put up during his visits.[111] Undoubtedly he could have been lodged at a local inn in the manner of assize justices and other visiting officials, but that would have imparted far less dignity to his office, and no identification of his authority with that symbolized in the hall.

Similar points may be made for other officials. The serjeant-at-mace was a subordinate rather than a social equal to the community élite, but like the gentlemen-in-waiting or bodyguard of the king's court, he reflected the dignity and status of his employers. Understandably, in view of what has been said above, his importance and rewards grew steadily throughout this era. He came commonly to be provided with livery, as in Totnes (1554),[112] and sometimes he, too, gained dwelling space in the town hall, as in Boston again, in 1546.[113]

By these numerous devices Tudor and early Stuart urban élites attempted to inculcate the civic deference essential for effective government. In so doing, they tied the requirements of political legitimacy and effective rule to the structure, furnishings, use, and mystique of the town hall. In the process they created an intimate working relationship between architecture (in the broadest sense) on the one hand and power on the other. Yet even these gentle strategies were often insufficient in the pursuit of orderly direction or as recourse against violations of law and civic tranquillity. Inevitably, and especially in the period from c.1550 to c.1620, the translation of authority into actual power required an effort to impart the values of the urban élite to the rest of civic society; as a last resort, it required the powers of coercion. These requirements called forth a somewhat more authoritarian aspect of the relationship of political power to the built environment.

THE BUILT ENVIRONMENT AND THE POWER OF COERCION

We have already noted the way in which popular perceptions of increasing disorder, and possibly that disorder itself, grew apace during these decades, providing a climate of support for the accretion of civic (and mayoral) authority. Central to those contemporary perceptions lay an

---

[111] Pegden, *Leicester Guildhall*, 15. The room has been restored and is open to the public at the time of writing.

[112] Devon Co. RO, MS 1579A/7/3.

[113] Bailey, *Minutes of Boston*, i. 11 (1552).

augmented concern for the facilities for enforcement: for punishment, incarceration, and a combination of the two. Indeed, punitive incarceration itself, employed but not emphasized in the medieval period, became much more common in these years. The more established members of society came to recognize the value of removing serious offenders from circulation for lengthy periods of time, and sometimes, following the lead of central government, for purposes of coercion or political detention where corporal or capital punishment would have been less appropriate.[114] The emergence of the ideas that idleness was sinful, that productive labour might bear rehabilitative value, or simply (if perhaps over-optimistically) that prisoners could be made to defray the costs of their keep, were contemporary. All were also germane to the establishment of the house of correction.[115]

In addition, there are signal indications of a substantially higher conviction rate for many felonies and misdemeanours which seem connected with developments in trial procedure. The advent of effective prosecution as a component in trial proceedings, the strengthening of the magistrate's role, and—in consequence of both—changes in the function of the jury, all seem to have made conviction in felony cases more likely.[116] Finally, it may be at least suspected that many misdemeanours which had been punished by a fine were now met with imprisonment, especially in an era when offenders were less likely to have the means to defray the costs of a fine. Whether for purposes of temporary detention or punitive incarceration, all these tendencies contributed to an increase in the prison population, and hence in the civic responsibility for such facilities.

How were such pressures served by civic halls? First let us remember that prison facilities, especially the basic lock-up, cage, or single cell, had for so long been part of the urban built environment that the foremost historian of imprisonment in medieval England considered them 'a natural part of the equipment of every town'. Indeed he goes on, 'some kind of prison seems to have been tucked away in the cellar or attic of every *fifteenth* century guildhall'.[117] Town gaols were thus not only common but closely connected with the town hall even before the Tudor period.

[114] John Bellamy, *Crime and Public Order in England in the Later Middle Ages* (1973), 163; Harding *et al.*, *Imprisonment in England and Wales*, 55–6, 82.

[115] Christopher Hill, 'William Perkins and the Poor', in *Puritanism and Revolution* (1958), 215–38; A. L. Beier, 'Poor Relief in Warwickshire, 1630–1660', *P and P* 35 (1966), 77–100; Valerie Pearl, 'Puritans and Poor Relief: The London Workhouse, 1649–1660', in D. Pennington and K. Thomas (eds.), *Puritans and Revolutionaries* (Oxford, 1978), 206–32; Harding *et al.*, *Imprisonment in England and Wales*, 61, 65–73.

[116] T. A. Green, *Verdict According to Conscience, Perspectives on the English Criminal Trial Jury, 1200–1800* (Chicago, 1985), 107.

[117] R. B. Pugh, *Imprisonment in Medieval England* (Cambridge, 1968), 101.

In these years, however, there are indications that facilities for detention and incarceration became both larger and more complex, even prior to the introduction of the corrective concept. The developing use of prison space in such larger towns as Exeter and York will be familiar from Chapter 2 above. Yet even in smaller towns there seems a growing interest in such developments as the segregation of prisoners by one criterion or another: sex, normal place of residence, or duration of incarceration, with less favoured prisoners given harsher surroundings. Though these segregative tendencies are well precedented before 1500, they may be more pronounced thereafter.[118] In a fundamental sense, the important distinction which developed in Tudor social legislation between the deserving poor who were entitled to charity, and the vagrant poor who were sent to houses of correction, presented a segregation of its own, and one with obvious ramifications for physical facilities. But even within incarceratory institutions, segregation seems to have been fairly common. Neath (1542) and Lancaster (1572), for example, distinguished between strangers and freemen, permitting only the latter to be imprisoned in the town hall. Strangers went elsewhere, where the sight and smell of them were further from the more refined frequenters of the hall.[119] Hereford not only had a distinct 'freeman's prison', which survived until the present century from its construction in the reign of Henry VIII, but permitted freemen prisoners to attend religious services at St Peter's Church in the company of the keeper.[120] In Oxford freemen were imprisoned in a separate room, with 'standing beds' and curtains (!) by the mid-sixteenth century, in what is surely a surprising attestation to the growing concern for personal privacy as well as an example of segregation amongst prisoners. In circumstances still familiar in Dickens's day, freeman prisoners in Oxford supplied their own food and drink, received visitors, carried on their trades, and collected money from passers-by through their windows.[121]

Undoubtedly there would have tended to be a difference in location for many town prisons before and during our period. Earlier prisons were more likely to have been under the jurisdiction of manorial authorities and thus to have been housed in castles, castle gates, or other characteristically seigneurial edifices. Often they were built in such secure structures as gatehouses or town walls. Such edifices, along with castles, were little built or maintained after c.1500.[122]

---

[118] Pugh, *Imprisonment*, 353–7; Bateson, *Borough Customs*, i. 66.

[119] Bateson, *Borough Customs*, i. 66.

[120] Alfred Watkins, 'The Freeman's Prison at the Boothall, Hereford', *Transactions of the Woolhope Naturalists' Field Club* (1938 for 1934), 49–53 and Hereford Co. RO, MS GH 1/51–61.

[121] *VCH, Oxfordshire*, iv. 126.

[122] Pugh, *Imprisonment*, 347–8.

Though many town prisons still remained in such older structures (especially gatehouses)[123] there was a tendency and almost certainly a desire for newly autonomous towns to move prison facilities from castles or other seigneurial buildings to new, purpose-built facilities, either free-standing or physically connected to town halls. Such was the case in Banbury, for example, which moved its town prison from the lord's castle to the town hall a year after it ratified its effective independence by charter in 1555, and in Hereford, as cited above, which moved freemen prisoners to a purpose-built structure from a lock-up in Bistrete Gate during the reign of Henry VIII.[124]

Even when the prison had traditionally been in a 'neutral' location, its control often remained an important point of contention between man-orial and civic authorities. Such was certainly the case in late medieval Bury St Edmunds, where the town gaol, located in the chief market-place, proved a constant source of friction between the abbot and the townsmen. Both the burgesses and the abbot as lord seem to have used the gaol, and thus its control became a natural focal point for the larger contest over local authority.[125]

On grounds of political symbolism alone, then, we might well anticipate that civic authorities would seek to locate new prison facilities—and occasionally, as in Banbury, relocate existing facilities—in or adjacent to standing town halls. Indeed, many towns did precisely that, while still others employed parts of their halls for miscreants in times of particular strife, when ordinary facilities proved insufficient and incapable of proper supervision.[126]

Yet the close proximity of prisoners to town halls on a regular basis bore some strong disadvantages as well, and these sometimes militated against the desire for such close physical association between prisons and halls. Simply put, it is hard to imagine any environment of human habitation in the pre-industrial world more unpleasant and unhealthy than a prison or a gaol. Not only did such facilities tend to offend the increasingly refined sensibilities of the authorities who had the most frequent recourse to town halls, but they posed a genuine threat of contamination from typhus, plague, gaol fever, and from the assorted vermin which helped carry the rest and which were the invariable companions of the inmates.

In Francis Bacon's view,

---

[123] e.g. Abingdon: Berkshire Co. RO, MS D/EP7/84, fo. 4.

[124] *VCH, Oxfordshire*, x (1972), 41.

[125] R. S. Gottfried, *Bury St Edmunds and the Urban Crisis* (Princeton, NJ, 1982), 172–5.

[126] e.g. Newark: Newark Town Hall, Newark Corporation Minute Book, fo. 24ᵛ; Exeter: H. Lloyd Parry, *The History of the Exeter Guildhall and the Life Within* (Exeter, 1936), 14–16. I am indebted to the REED Project for access to its microfilm copy of the Newark Corporation Minute Book.

the most pernicious infection next the plague is the smell of the jail, when prisoners have been long and close and nastily kept [as, with the sixteenth century increase in punitive incarceration, they more commonly were] . . . Therefore it were good wisdom, that in such cases the jail were aired before they be brought forth.[127]

Though prison facilities which were located in town halls may therefore have been better maintained—a factor which would account for some towns relegating resident offenders to the hall prison and aliens elsewhere—many towns which built their main prisons in this era, including Hertford, East Dereham, Hereford, Newark, Lyme Regis, Ilchester, and Guildford, did so away from the hall.[128] These towns may still have left a lock-up for temporary detention in the hall itself.

There were additional good reasons for such a locational choice, and the chief of these was the simple availability of space. Large halls, like those in Exeter, York, or Norwich, permitted some degree of reorganization of available space through the partitioning off of a large chamber or the addition above or even below existing floors. But in most cases where new prison building needed to be undertaken such remedies were simply inadequate for the greater demands of the day. There remained little remedy but to convert some other premises to use as a prison or to build anew on open ground. This last option almost certainly meant a location well away from the central and most congested area in the town and thus away from the town hall.

Apart from the need for greater space, a whole new chapter in the development of urban incarceratory facilities opened with the house of correction. The idea that prisoners could be put to productive work probably derives as much from the desire to make their labour pay for their upkeep as from any distaste for idleness or concept of redemption through productive labour. As with a great deal of Tudor social legislation, the concept of a corrective facility in which incarceration would be combined with productive and perhaps rehabilitative labour arose through local initiative. When Mary Tudor's government chartered the former Bridewell Palace in London as a corrective facility in 1556, renaming it Bridewell Hospital, indigent offenders were put to work

[127] Bacon, 'Sylva Sylvarum or Natural History', in James Spedding (ed.), *The Works of Francis Bacon*, ii (1859), 646; Cynthia Herrup, *The Common Peace, Participation and the Criminal Law in Seventeenth Century England* (Cambridge, 1987), 89 and n. 36.

[128] Hertford: see map in BL, Add. MS 32350, fs. 24ᵛ and 25ʳ; East Dereham: PRO, E 317/ Norfolk/no. 10, fos. 3–4 and Norfolk and Norwich RO MS PD 86/181; Hereford: Watkins, 'The Freeman's Prison', 49–54; Newark Town Hall, Newark Corporation Minute Book, fo. 24ᵛ; Lyme Regis: Dorset Co. RO, MS B7/G1/4a, fo. 14: £31 paid in 1583; Ilchester: *VCH, Somerset*, iii (1974), 186 (it was noted in Ilchester that the former gaol, in the hall, was considered 'too small . . . and noisome'); Guildford: Dance, *Guildford Borough Records* 17.

milling corn with a treadmill, baking, working cloth, and making nails.[129] Other occupations followed shortly. By 1576 the experiment's success, reinforced by similar experiences abroad (especially that of Amsterdam *Rasphuis* of the same vintage)[130] moved Parliament to approve the establishment of houses of correction in each county for the punishment of rogues and vagabonds. This was implied in 14 Elizabeth, c. 5 and clearly stated in 18 Elizabeth, c. 3. That policy was restated in 1597/8 (39 Elizabeth, cc. 4 and 5) and given sharp teeth in 1610 (7 James I, c. 4) in the form of substantial fines for each JP in counties which failed to erect the proper facility.

Though the legislation requiring at least one house of correction in each shire directed its demands to JPs, who were responsible for naming trustees and governors and for the other details of implementation, its implications also rang loud and clear for town officials. By the same legislation (for example 39 Elizabeth c. 4) mayors and analogous officials gained the summary power to commit rogues and vagabonds, and this proved a potent weapon in local hands. In addition, mayors also often served as governors of houses in their own towns. Some towns erected corrective facilities or schemes of their own, both in response to the statutes and in the anticipation that the receipts of inmate labour would defray charges and even turn a profit, while solving the pressing problem of social disorder. Civic involvement in such schemes may well have been stronger after the legislation of 1609–10, but well back in the Elizabethan era such towns as Norwich, Ipswich, Hadleigh, and Worcester undertook their own initiatives along similar lines. Some counties, like Norfolk, had erected a virtual network of such houses in towns by *c.*1600.[131]

Where were such facilities located? Though town leaders may well have wished to place them near the town hall, thus linking them with the seat of local hegemony, most were simply too large. Thus, while some halls proved sufficiently spacious and flexible to accommodate houses of correction within them (for example Hadleigh converted a chamber of its guild-hall to use as a bridewell in 1574[132]), most could not. In consequence, houses of correction were most often placed in other civic-held structures converted to that use (such as Moyses Hall in Bury St Edmunds or High Cross House in Walsall), or constructed from scratch,

---

[129] E. G. O'Donoghue, *Bridewell Hospital, Palace, Prison, Schools*, 2 vols. (1923–9), i. 197–200.

[130] Harding *et al.*, *Imprisonment*, 69.

[131] John Pound, 'An Elizabethan Census of the Poor, the Treatment of Vagrancy in Norwich, 1570–1580', *Birmingham University Historical Journal*, 8 (1962), 135–51; Pound, *The Norwich Census of the Poor of 1570* (Norfolk Record Society, II, 1971); John Webb, *Poor Relief in Elizabethan Ipswich* (Suffolk Record Society, 9, 1966); W. A. B. Jones, *Hadleigh Through The Ages* (Ipswich, 1977), 33; J. Thirsk, *Economic Policy and Projects* (Oxford, 1978), 66.

[132] Jones, *Hadleigh*, 33.

as in Barnstaple in 1618 and Chesterfield by 1630.[133] Though much of this new construction or renovation would have been supported by county-wide levies, the mayor's powers to commit rogues and vagabonds, and sometimes actually to govern such facilities, became an important component of his growing authority. The increasing availability of incarcerating space, often in premises over which he himself presided, proved a natural concomitant to these powers.

CONCLUSION

The period particularly between 1500 and 1640 (and even more sharply between $c.1540$ and $c.1620$), characterized by rapid population growth, social change, and perceived threats to public order, quite logically saw a political response intended to augment powers of social control at local levels of authority. This response may be measured most clearly by the yardstick of the written record—enabling legislation or proclamations directed at officials of county and town, charters of incorporation and town by-laws—but it may also be gauged by a scrutiny of public buildings, their use, design, and development, over the period at hand.

Several points emerge from such an exercise. Town halls came more than ever before to represent the seat and symbol of civic authority: an authority which contemporary circumstances permitted to become more oligarchic than in the past. This process of adapting particular buildings to political requirements included the inculcation of deference through specifically contrived decorum, the delineation of space to reflect political and administrative requirements, and even the evolution of specific furnishings to enhance the desired effect. At its most pronounced, the ascendant role of civic government may be seen in the striking growth in authority granted particularly to the mayor. This is reflected in consequent developments both within and without the hall in the growth of civic facilities for enforcement and punishment.

---

[133] N. Devon Atheneum, MS 3972, item 191, mb. 2; payment of £45. 2s. 10d. in 1616; P. Riden and J. Blair (eds.), *History of Chesterfield*, v (Chesterfield, 1980), 246–7.

6

Civic Culture and the Doorway
to the Community

THE ROLE OF THE DOORWAY

Having at least implicitly recognized the town hall as the seat and symbol of their position, the urban leaders of the day also appear to have understood its role in sustaining a wide range of their own group interests. That is to say that, in a variety of ways, civic leaders employed the hall in the effort to encourage attitudes and activities which were compatible with their own values, and to discourage those which were not. This chapter takes up the significance of the hall in reflecting the interests both of the governing élite and of the 'middling sort' (merchants, artisans, and others with a stake in the community) from which those leaders emerged and for whom they usually spoke.

This use of the hall in both practical and symbolic terms may readily be likened metaphorically to the doorway: a regulated barrier marking crucial points of interchange, both between the urban community and the world outside, and also between the civic leaders on the one hand and the residents on the other.[1] This doorway controlled access across the threshold, permitting entry and egress only on the conscious decision by the authorities within. While physical access to the town itself remained open on a casual basis, only permission to enter the doorway enabled one to join or interact with the community. Denial of such access meant expulsion. The fact that most halls were conventionally located on or adjacent to the town's centre, rather than at its gateways, and that they were connected to the gateways by major arteries, lends strength to the metaphor.[2]

This image allows us to see that contemporary civic authorities utilized

[1] The concept is suggested implicitly by Jean Christophe Agnew, *Worlds Apart: The Market and The Theatre in Anglo-American Thought, 1550–1750* (Cambridge, 1986), especially ch. 1. Agnew applies this concept to the market and market-place.

[2] This siting pattern was especially, but not exclusively, characteristic of the type B, pillared halls, as described in Ch. 2 above. The concept of the town itself as a crossroad is interestingly developed by Robert S. Lopez, who recalled the ancient ideogram of the city as a cross within a circle, representing the arterial intersection within the fortified boundary; Robert S. Lopez, 'The Crossroads within the Wall', in Oscar Handlin and John Burchard (eds.), *The Historian and the City* (Cambridge, Mass., 1963), 27–43, especially 27–8.

the hall in a number of ways to foster their image of civic culture. Most obviously, it facilitated a regulated interchange between two overlapping but distinct social contexts. On the one hand lay the agrarian, still dominated by custom, kinship, and hierarchical ties, and by a still less highly developed sense of capitalist enterprise. On the other lay the urban, more open to social innovation and increasingly characterized by impersonal, contractual, and formalized ties of a distinctly bourgeois nature. Through its portals and by leave of its authorities came goods, services, ideas, and people. Those who came to trade were governed by local bylaws issuing from the hall's chambers or by statutory law enforced in its courts. They paid for that privilege the tolls, fees, fines, and other perquisites which went to the hall coffers: colloquially, 'to the hall'. Migrants, too, came through, to register apprenticeship indentures in the mayor's court room or to join the community by paying freemen's fines. And, under the terms of the Poor Laws promulgated during the course of the sixteenth century, those who came seeking sustenance were sorted out by officers of the hall, given relief if found deserving and punishment (often meted out in front of or even within the hall) if not.

In addition to its role in facilitating economic interchange between the town and country the hall served as a doorway between two sets of values: that of greater licence, potential disorder, and subversion on the one hand, and that of order and authority on the other.[3] Ironically, for the hall as we have seen was often situated on or in the market-place and indeed often did double duty as a market hall, the urban space most associated with disorder was that very market-place. Along with providing the actual venue for the exchange of goods and services, the market-place represented a peculiar and almost extra-territorial space (metaphorically, inside the gates, but not necessarily inside the doorway) in the medieval and Renaissance town. There occurred here not only a good deal of endemic disorder, but also almost all the popular and unofficial festivities, including carnival, misrule, and other rites and rituals of mockery and social inversion, as well, of course, as the more officially sanctioned activities of medieval religious and folk ritual.[4] Here, too, more than anywhere else, reigned the language and gesture of the colloquial, the familiar, and the 'indecent', the 'billingsgate' of popular culture. 'The marketplace of

---

[3] As applied to the market-place itself, this idea has been suggested by Agnew, *Worlds Apart*, 20–32. See also Peter Stallybrass and Allon White, *The Politics and Poetics of Transgression* (1986), 27–30.

[4] Agnew, *Worlds Apart*, 25–35; Stallybrass and White, *Poetics and Politics*, 27–8. Both derive their analysis from Mikhail Bakhtin, *Rabelais and His World* (trans. Hélène Iswolsky, Cambridge, Mass., 1968). See also Michael D. Bristol, *Carnival and Theatre: Plebeian Culture and the Structure of Authority in Renaissance England* (New York, 1985), especially pt. 1. For an 'official' acknowledgement of the tendency to use the market-place for activities of protest and disorder, see the proclamation of 1547 'Silencing Disputes on the Eucharist', P. Hughes and F. L. Larkin (eds.), *Tudor Royal Proclamations*, 3 vols. (1964–9), i. 296.

the Middle Ages and the Renaissance', as Mikhail Bakhtin described it,[5]

was a world in itself, a world which was all one; all 'performances' in this area, from loud cursing to the organized show . . . were imbued with the same atmosphere of freedom, franchise and familiarity . . . The marketplace was the center of all that is unofficial; it enjoyed a certain extraterritoriality in a world of official order and official ideology.

In juxtaposition to this area of unrestraint, like Victorian mission to Whitechapel beer hall, lay the town hall. Representative, as we have seen, of the restrained, disciplined, and bourgeois values of contemporary ruling élites, the hall looked out on the spontaneous and potentially disruptive activities of the market-place below. It stood between order and disorder, hierarchy and inversion, some forms of contemporary cultural activities accessible to all and, especially by the seventeenth century, some emerging forms of cultural activity accessible chiefly to the wealthy, literate, and more sophisticated.

Still another role of the hall as doorway lay in linking the present with the past. Not only were halls often of ancient standing, and thus existing reminders of earlier times, and not only did they often convey past associations by their very names (such as 'guild-hall', 'yeldehall', etc.), but they also provided places to display images of the town's heritage, even when such heritage may have been folkloric or mythical. We will note especially how some post-Reformation towns utilized their halls to revive folkloric and heroic traditions, celebrating the foundations of the community or to perpetuate the memory of its important citizens and benefactors. In so doing, the civic leaders of our period tried to grace their own brows with the laurels of their forebears, whether mythical or historical.

In sum, the civic authorities of the day utilized the hall as doorway to accomplish two goals. First, they established the rules for access to the community, thus seeking to regulate the flow of goods, services, people, ideas, and activities. Second, they used the hall as an integrative device, to mediate between potentially conflicting values, groups of people, ideas, and activities: between the agrarian and the urban, the traditional and the capitalist, the greenhorn and the resident, the orderly and the disorderly, the heroic virtues of past leaders and the aspirations of the living.

---

[5] Bakhtin, *Rabelais and His World*, 153–4, and see also ch. 2, 'The Language of the Marketplace in Rabelais'. Although one must not overemphasize the existence in England of carnival itself, there were numerous popular rites and festivities which performed the same functions and in a similar manner. Cf. Peter Burke, *Popular Culture in Early Modern Europe* (1978), 191–9 and Charles Phythian-Adams, *Desolation of a City, Coventry and the Urban Crisis of the Late Middle Ages* (Cambridge, 1979), 178.

These functions of regulation and mediation were by no means novel in the sixteenth century, but for a variety of reasons they assumed greater importance at that time. First, some of the mediatory functions which had been carried out between town and country by ecclesiastical institutions, especially the religious fraternities and parish guilds of the town, had been swept away or transformed in the Reformation, leaving considerable tensions in their wake.[6] Second, many of the officially sanctioned ritual-istic activities associated with the same religious institutions, including the socially important liturgical play cycles and similar procession-centred rites, went by the board in the decades thereafter. Unlike the un-sanctioned and often spontaneous rites of misrule, these activities had been controlled by local authorities. They were intended, *inter alia*, both to release social tensions and to reaffirm rather than to subvert the structure of the community. They had played crucial mediatory roles between town and country, and amongst the different occupational and social groupings which comprised the fabric of urban society.[7]

In addition, the increase in total population, especially throughout most of the sixteenth century, and the net population movement from country-side to town, greatly increased the frequency of personal interaction and potential for social conflict.[8] Finally, the more rapid development of capitalist organization, both in scale and sophistication, sharpened the contrast between the traditional and contemporary. As Christopher Hill, Keith Wrightson, William Hunt, and others have shown, social polarization—fuelled by widening gaps in literacy, personal wealth, economic and legal sophistication, and religious persuasion—moved on steadily in these years.[9] And, though these were not gaps between urban

[6] Rodney Hilton, *The English Peasantry in the Later Middle Ages* (Oxford, 1975), ch. 5. and esp. 91–4. For the manner in which pre-Reformation religious observance promoted social harmony in general terms, see Susan Brigden, 'Religion and Social Obligation in Early Sixteenth Century London'. For the function of parish guilds and fraternities in pre-Reformation society, see Barbara Hanawalt, 'Keepers of the Lights: Late Medieval English Parish Gilds', *Journal of Medieval and Renaissance Studies*, 14/1 (1984), 21–38; Phythian-Adams, *Desolation of a City*, 118–25; and J. J. Scarisbrick, *The Reformation and the English People* (Oxford, 1984), 19–39.

[7] Burke, *Popular Culture in Early Modern Europe*, 199–204 *et passim*; Bakhtin, *Rabelais and His World*, 9–10; Charles Phythian-Adams, 'Ceremony and the Citizen: the Communal Year at Coventry, 1450–1550', in Peter Clark and Paul Slack (eds.), *Crisis and Order in English Towns, 1500–1700* (1972), 57–85; Mervyn James, 'Ritual, Drama and Social Body in the Late Medieval English Town', *P and P* 98 (1983), 3–29; David H. Sacks, 'The Demise of the Martyrs: the Feasts of St Clement and St Katherine in Bristol, 1400–1600', *Social History*, 11 (1986), 141–69; V. A. Kolve, *The Play Called Corpus Christi* (Stanford, Calif., 1966); Alan H. Nelson, *The Medieval English Stage, Corpus Christi Pageants* (Chicago, 1974).

[8] E. A. Wrigley and R. S. Scholfield, *The Population History of England, 1541–1871, a Reconstruction* (1981), *passim*; A. L. Beier, *Masterless Men, the Vagrancy Problem in England* (1985), 19–22; Clark and Slack, *Crisis and Order*, 17–18.

[9] Christopher Hill, *Society and Puritanism in Pre-Revolutionary England* (1964), esp. ch. 4; K. Wrightson, *English Society, 1580–1680* (1982), *passim*; K. Wrightson and D. Levine, *Poverty and Piety in an English Village, Terling, 1525–1700* (New York, 1979), *passim*; Wrightson, 'Aspects of

and rural society as much as between social and income groups, they seem likely to have been more pronounced in the urban than in the rural milieu.

It is in consequence of these factors that the town hall came more than ever to represent a strategic doorway to the urban community and to the values which came to prevail in that milieu. Here more than anywhere else therein were located those facilities for representing and inculcating the values of the town and of its bourgeois leadership, both in regard to outsiders and to townsmen themselves.

The ensuing discussion will consider three applications of the hall's doorway role: 1. the regulation of the commercial exchange, 2. the regulation of cultural expression (and of its underlying attitudes) using the example of theatrical performance, and 3. the legitimization of contemporary leadership through the display of historical imagery.

COMMERCE AND THE HALL

It seems incontrovertible that economic exchange of one form or another was the most basic function of almost every English town at this time. In the end, the development and perpetuation of that activity almost certainly loomed larger in the minds of most residents—especially those with a material stake in the community—than almost any other issue. In this context, the hall almost always took a prominent place, and even more so in those most frequent instances where it housed marketing as well as administrative facilities.

These buildings, especially the open-sided, type B halls, conventionally held such paraphernalia of marketing regulation as scales, weighing beams, standard weights and measures, and similar devices. Some of them were designed to facilitate visual surveillance of the surrounding market area. Regardless of hall type, it had long been the custom in some towns for substantial covenants between buyer and seller to be acknowledged and even recorded before a bailiff or similar official in the hall.[10] In addition, the hall's conventionally central and market-oriented location made it an ideal place for the display of clocks and the hanging of bells. As we shall see, these mechanical devices were integral to the inculcation of

Social Differentiation in Rural England, c.1580–1660', Journal of Peasant Studies, 5 (1977), 33–47; William Hunt, The Puritan Moment: The Coming of Revolution in an English County (Cambridge, Mass., 1983), passim and ch. 6. See also David Cressy, Literacy and the Social Order, Reading and Writing in Tudor and Stuart England (Cambridge, 1980); Martin Ingram, 'The Reform of Popular Culture? Sex and Marriage in Early Modern England', in B. Reay (ed.), Popular Culture in Seventeenth Century England (1985), ch. 4; W. G. Hoskins, The Age of Plunder, the England of Henry VIII, 1500–1547 (1976), chs. 2–4 and esp. 96–100; and P. Clark; '"The Ramoth-Gilead of the Good", Urban Change and Political Radicalism at Gloucester, 1540–1640', in Clark, A. G. R. Smith, and N. Tyacke (eds.), The English Commonwealth, 1547–1640 (Leicester, 1979), 173–7.

[10] Mary Bateson, Borough Customs, 2 vols. (Selden Society, 1904 and 1906), ii. 173–4.

the merchant's sense of time and work discipline upon the citizenry at large.

The right to maintain and utilize the regulatory devices of marketing cited above was amongst the oldest and most essential rights of any marketing community, and the obligation to maintain proper measures remained amongst the most honoured of administrative imperatives.[11] Goods sold in the market were expected to be weighed by these standard measures, and chartered market towns exacted tolls for such measurement which comprised an important share of local revenue. This was the job of the town toll gatherer who, along with sweepers, scavengers, market-lookers, bellmen, ale conners, leather searchers, wool aulnagers (inspectors), bread-tasters, common warehouse keepers, and the like, formed the foot soldiery of local market administration. In their activity both the marketing and the administrative functions of the hall (at least where a single hall served for both) found expression, while the building itself provided their base of operations.[12]

A further effort to ensure fair practice came with the time-honoured injunction that marketing must be carried out openly in the market-place rather than outside the boundaries of the town or elsewhere in its midst. This most common of local by-laws, to which there were also numerous exceptions, rested on foundations of proclamation and statute.[13] It was chiefly intended first to discourage and then to stem the tide of private marketing, and thus to prevent unfair dealing, the sundry forms of hoarding, and the likelihood of conflict or violence amongst the practitioners. Enforcement of such regulations may often be seen in surviving market court records, but there is also evidence that the obligation to trade only in the open market-place, and more generally to keep the peace, became a consideration in the design as well as in the location. Hence we have what appear to be surveillance galleries built on to some halls so that the constables or other market officials could keep an eye on

[11] M. Beresford, *New Towns of the Middle Ages* (1967), 85, 215–17, 240–1; Susan Reynolds, *An Introduction to the History of English Medieval Towns* (Oxford, 1977), 125–8; R. H. Britnell, 'The Proliferation of Markets in England, 1200–1349', *Ec HR* 34/2 (1981), 209–21; P. Hughes and J. F. Larkin (eds.), *Stuart Royal Proclamations*, i: *Proclamations of King James I, 1603–1625* (Oxford, 1973), 12; J. H. Thomas, *Town Government in the Sixteenth Century* (1933), 68–9; G. H. Tupling, 'Lancashire Markets in the Sixteenth and Seventeenth Centuries, I', *Transactions of the Lancashire and Cheshire Antiquarian Society*, 58 (1947 for 1945–6), 25–34.

[12] Alan Everitt, 'The Marketing of Agricultural Produce', in J. Thirsk (ed.), *The Agrarian History of England and Wales*, iv, *1500–1640* (Cambridge, 1967), 482–3, 486–7; Agnew, *Worlds Apart*, 30; Tupling, 'Lancashire Markets, I', 20–5.

[13] 3 Henry VIII, c. 10 (re: leather); 3 and 4 Edward VI, c. 19 (re: cattle); 3 and 4 Edward VI, c. 21 (re: butter and cheese); 5 and 6 Edward VI, c. 14 (re: regrators, forestallers, and engrossers); 5 and 6 Edward VI, c. 15 (re: leather); 2 and 3 Philip and Mary, c. 7 (re: horses); Everitt, 'The Marketing of Agricultural Produce', 488, 581; Hughes and Larkin, *Tudor Royal Proclamations* i, no. 242; Thomas, *Town Government*, 69; Tupling, 'Lancashire Markets, II', *Transactions of the Lancashire and Cheshire Antiquarian Society*, 59 (1948 for 1947), 2–6.

the market-place before them, and also so that such officials could be seen doing so by market-goers below.

Both in Titchfield and Thaxted evidence for these galleries remains more or less visible today. This is literally visible in the Titchfield hall, which has recently been restored to its original condition by the authorities of the Weald and Downland Open Air Museum to which the structure has been moved. The existence of a surveillance gallery in Thaxted has been worked out from structural evidence of the building as it exists, twice 'restored' at least, today. In both instances we have an open first-floor gallery, flush with the façade of the whole building, and facing the main market-place on one or more sides. In Thaxted, whose central street plan is perfectly preserved, the field of vision for the 'market watcher' extended not only to the marketing area on three sides, but also far up the main artery into the town from which that market-place opens out. Yet another surveillance gallery appeared on the fifteenth-century town hall of Wigan; it is depicted on the 1695 seal of the borough.[14]

One of the most important regulatory functions of the hall, illustrative as well of its function in both administration and marketing, lay in the conduct and registration of a myriad of financial and legal transactions, especially those between townsmen and outsiders. These are extremely important services: much more important than we might guess on the basis of the scant research and publication which has been devoted to them. Here were carried out the posting of bonds for the delivery of goods and services and for the payment of debts. Here we find licences issued for the transport of scarce commodities, common market tolls paid and recorded, and market stalls and booths let to traders. Here, too, the apprenticeship of the recent migrant was recorded along with that of the townsman, here the new freeman took his oath and paid his fine, and here the violators of either apprenticeship or the privileges of freemanry were brought, tried, and punished, often by expulsion.

In the indigenous market court, however it may have been known in specific towns, the rules and regulations of the market, founded in the economic interests principally of the middling and leading sort, found

---

[14] The open gallery at Titchfield has been restored in the restoration of the whole building, and may be seen at the Weald and Downland Museum: cf. R. Harris, *Weald and Downland Open Air Museum Guidebook* (Worthing, 1982), 28–9. Such a gallery no longer exists at Thaxted but has been established by Mr James Boutwood, Assistant County Architect of Essex, from the discovery of shutter grooves running vertically outside the first-storey arches. Such grooves show that those arches, six on each of the three sides of the building which face the marketing area, were initially open. I am indebted to Mr Boutwood's communication of July 1985, to this effect. Cf. M. Arman and James Boutwood, 'Thaxted Guildhall, the Story of a Building in Use for almost Six Centuries' (Essex County Council research report no. TL611 310, n.d.). For Wigan, see Tupling, 'Lancashire Markets, I', 6, and Henry Taylor, 'The Ancient Crosses of Lancashire', *Transactions of the Lancashire and Cheshire Antiquarian Society*, 19 (1901), 229.

frequent promulgation and prompt enforcement. The conduct of these activities formed the docket of the court's proceedings, filled the pages of its minute book, and bore the reputation of the market. The mayor himself, usually sitting as judge in the market court, brought to bear in those proceedings the force of local and royal authority.

The role of these halls in the regulation of marketing activities and in the mediation between contrasting interests was often considerably augmented by two other features which began to appear in our era: clocks and bells.

After the labours of Carlo Cipolla, Jacques LeGoff, E. P. Thompson, and David Landes, it is no longer startling to note that Englishmen of a certain economic and social outlook became increasingly conscious of the importance of time, and the precision of its measurement, in this era.[15] By the opening decades of the sixteenth century, townsmen, to a greater degree than their country cousins, conceived of time in regular, measurable units. In the laconic phrasing of the anonymous contemporary tract *Dives et Pauper*, 'In cities and townes men ruled theym by the clocke.'[16]

Though this shift from time told by the light of day to 'merchants'' time measured by the hour was gradual and by no means either geographically or chronologically uniform throught the realm, we should not overlook its fundamental importance. We have here nothing less than the establishment of a modern, capitalist, and bourgeois outlook, the emergence of Weber's 'Homo Economicus', amongst those townsmen with the greater stake in the local economy. These are the men (and occasionally women) who had recognized and adapted to contemporary market forces and who had begun to internalize a modern sense of time and work discipline. Characteristically, they dated indentures and other contracts by the calendar day rather than by the saint's day, and they told time by the clock.[17] In addition, they expected their apprentices, servants, and workers—subordinates who had their own characteristic sense of time—to do the same. These were also the people whom we have seen work

[15] J. LeGoff, 'Au moyen âge: Temps de l'église au temps du marchand', *Annales, SEC* 15/3 (1960), 417–33 and 'Le temps du travail dans la "crise du XIVᶜ s.": du temps médiéval au temps moderne', *Le Moyen Age*, 69 (1963), 597–615; S. De Grazia, *Of Time, Work and Leisure* (New York, 1962); K. Thomas, 'Work and Leisure in Pre-Industrial Society', *P and P* 29 (1964), 50–62; E. P. Thompson, 'Time, Work-Discipline and Industrial Capitalism', *P and P* 38 (1967), 56–98; Carlo Cipolla, *Clocks and Culture, 1300–1700* (1967); and David S. Landes, *Revolution in Time, Clocks and the Making of the Modern World* (Cambridge, Mass., 1983).

[16] Anon., *Dives et Pauper* (1536 edn.), fo. 30ᵛ, as cited in Keith Thomas, *Religion and the Decline of Magic* (Harmondsworth, 1973), 744. My thanks to Mr Michael Berlin for bringing this to my attention.

[17] For an interesting continental parallel cf. Gerald Moran, 'Conception of Time in Early Modern France: An Approach to the History of Collective Mentalities', *Sixteenth Century Journal*, 12/4 (1981), 3–19.

towards civic autonomy from seigneurial control and who spearheaded the move toward oligarchy in urban government and society.

One test of the assertion of the mature sense of time and work discipline amongst this ruling element is the frequency with which town leaders most instrumental in the design and acquisition of town halls provided for the placement of clocks. Though clocks, of course, considerably pre-date the period of our discussion—the oldest working clock in England today has been ticking away in Salisbury Cathedral since the mid-fourteenth century—the vast majority of the earlier examples were constructed in church buildings. These structures were far less likely to be sited in the central areas of the town, relatively rarely on or in the market, and their clocks were thus not often visible from the high street or market-place. It cannot thus be said that church clocks played much part in the consciousness or daily routines of most medieval townsmen and women.

Outside London and apart from churches, clocks were still far from common even in the Tudor age. David Palliser notes that nearly a century and a half passed between the admission of the first and second clock maker in even as large a city as York.[18] Yet he is correct to remind us that time seems more often to be expressed 'by the clock' from this age forward. The point seems amply borne out in the language of parliamentary statute, town by-law, and apprenticeship indenture, all three of which were expressions of the dominant social groups of that age.

Lest we assume that the addition of clocks to civic halls in this period was somehow peripheral to the emerging bourgeois outlook of urban leaders, it would be well to note how they were to be employed in that milieu. The 1620 town ordinances of Godalming in Surrey prove particularly instructive:[19]

That forasmuch as *the use of a clock in the said town is very necessary for the inhabitants thereof for the keeping of fit hours for their apprentices, servants and workmen,* That the Warden and assistants . . . may as occasion requireth from time to time make assessments for the keeping, amending and maintaining of the said clock, to be taxed upon all Inhabitants which are housekeepers in the said town according to their ability.

The bailiffs of Shrewsbury seem to have been thinking along the same lines in 1591 when they had constructed a clock with three faces: one visible from the interior of the guild-hall, one 'to serve the highe streete market and passers by and the inhabytants there, and the oder towards the corne markett'. The two outside faces also showed the phases of the

---

[18] David Palliser, 'Civic Mentality and the Environment in Tudor York', *Northern History*, 18 (1982), 79.

[19] Surrey RO, MS 2253/1/1. (Italics are my own; the spelling has been modernized.)

moon, which, with obvious local pride, a literate inhabitant described as 'verey artificiall and comodius to the beholders'.[20]

In view of the very low survival rate of public buildings from the sixteenth and early seventeenth centuries to begin with and the obvious likelihood that clocks on surviving halls may have been added at any time since construction, it is obviously impossible to say how many of our structures were built with clocks. Yet despite these difficulties, archival sources have yielded up more than a score of towns which most assuredly did put clocks on the face of their town hall prior to the year 1640.[21] This suggests that a great many other towns may have followed suit, and the thought that this had grown to common practice is certainly supported by the increasingly frequent written references to time told 'by the clock' in these and other communities.

Bells, too, initially pertained to the church, where they rang at predetermined times to denote the angelus or regular devotional exercises. Yet they did not, as a rule, ring to tell the hour, much less quarterly divisions of the same. This use seems to have begun as a matter of course chiefly when bells moved to secular buildings, when we begin to find them used more frequently for the opening and closing of the market or the announcement of curfew. Maidstone's market hall had a 'fish bell', rung when fish had been brought for sale to the market, while in Abingdon no grain, wool, or other commodities were to be sold on market days before the ringing of the market bell, a very common regulation in market towns of this era.[22] There were other uses, too. By the time of Elizabeth's reign the bell on the town hall in Northleach, Gloucestershire, rang to summon members to meetings of the council, while Carlisle and other communities had 'watch' bells. In the Shropshire town of Oswestry no one could open the town chest to examine the town's charters and seals without first ringing the bell to summon witnesses to the event.[23] The ringing of bells to commemorate victories, such as over the Armada, or such famous days as the anniversaries of royal accessions, also became common, and may well have played a major role in the efforts of the ruling élites to encourage

[20] Revd W. A. Leighton, 'Early Chronicles of Shrewsbury, 1372–1603, *Transactions of the Shropshire Archaeological and Natural History Society*, 3 (1880), 325.

[21] Aylesbury, Bridgwater, Bromley, Carlisle, Chard, Godalming, Grampound, Guildford, Hedon, Helston, Hereford, Launceston, Leominster, Liskeard, Maidstone, Much Wenlock, Oswestry, Plymouth, Royston, Shrewsbury, Tewkesbury, Thame, Thornbury, Truro, Wendover, and Weymouth–Melcombe Regis.

[22] Edward Hasted, *The History . . . of the County of Kent*, 12 vols. (1797–1801), iv. 264; Berkshire RO, MS D/EP7/84, fo. 13d (1585).

[23] Revd David Royce, 'The Northleach Court-Book', *Transactions of the Bristol and Gloucestershire Archaeological Society*, 7 (1882–3), 94–5; Cumbria RO, Carlisle, MS CA/4/2, unpag., but *passim*. My thanks to the *REED* project and Dr Audrey Douglas for making films of these accounts available. For Oswestry, see case of *Lloyd* v. *Morrys*, 7 James I, PRO, STAC 8/198/27, answer of Hugh Morrys.

in others a sense of deference to authority.[24] But chief amongst all these functions was still the ringing of the hour, so that the townsman's life and labour could be regulated by precisely measured units of time.

Bells and clocks were thus closely linked, and for all the other occasional uses noted above, they seem to have been a part of the contemporary effort by the merchant-élite of urban society to inculcate a sense of time and work discipline upon the community at large. This appears clearly in the petition of a group of merchants to the mayor and council of Hereford in the year 1566. The petitioners wanted a bell to be rung every quarter of an hour in the morning during the short, dark days between Michaelmas and Lent, because 'there also is not waytes to Ryse the people at the houre they shuld rise to goo there which is agrete dutye Amongste the poore'.[25]

If we are not quite at the stage perceived by Michel Foucault, at which 'time permeates the body, and with it all the meticulous controls of power', the evidence of clocks and bells on the civic halls of this era does seem to point in that direction.[26] The common appearance of these additions to the hall marked a milestone in the transition from a traditional, agrarian-based, and early capitalist era to one more commonly dominated by commercial considerations and more mature bourgeois values.

PLAYERS IN THE HALL

When we turn to the more narrowly 'cultural' implications of the hall's doorway function at this time, two closely interrelated factors come to the fore. One of these was the venue provided by the hall for a wide variety of cultural activities, including ceremony and theatre. The second, consequentially, was the opportunity for civic authorities to regulate such activities and to place their own stamp upon them as a means of shaping the cultural tenor of urban society. The following pages examine the means by which civic leaders of the day employed the physical space of the hall to obtain these objectives.

Though we still have a great deal to learn of the circumstances of dramatic performance, especially outside London, the theatre presents an especially valuable example of the use of the hall as a doorway to the

[24] J. E. Neale, 'November 17th', in *Essays in Elizabethan History* (1958), 9–20. See also David Cressy, *Bonfires and Bells* . . . (1989) which appeared too late for consideration here.
[25] Hereford Co. RO, Hereford Law Day Session, 1566, item no. 10, uncatalogued. I am indebted to Miss Susan Hubbard, Archivist, for locating this item for me.
[26] Michel Foucault, *Discipline and Punish: the Birth of the Modern Prison*, trans. Alan Sheridan (New York, 1977), 152. My thanks to my Concordia colleague Michael Mason for this reference. It is interesting to note the distance which remains between Foucault's concept and that expressed in the passage cited above from *Dives et Pauper*, which goes on to note that 'properly to speake, the clocke reuleth not them [i.e. men], but a man ruleth the Clocke', anon., *Dives et Pauper*, fo. 30ᵛ.

community. Visiting players and entertainers of every art and skill were certainly prominent amongst those from the outside who came to the community to fulfil their occupational calling. Such entertainers, of course, dealt in emotions, fantasies, and ideas rather than in the more common coin of the market. Though they were by no means as numerous as tradesmen, the nature of their calling brought them even more swiftly and surely to the attention of local authorities. Whether they were residents whose theatrical calling placed them outside the normal social and occupational structure or, as was ever more commonly the case, strangers to begin with, travelling from place to place, they rarely fitted into the urban community on a permanent basis.[27] Often grouped with rogues, vagabonds, and other 'masterless men' (as in the Elizabethan Poor Law of 1597, 39 Elizabeth, c. 4), the players' occupation lent itself more than most to scrutiny and regulation at the threshold of the community.

The years following the Reformation saw a number of developments which closely relate to that scrutiny and regulation. The full spectrum of street theatre from pre-Reformation days, running from, for example, formal cycle plays at one extreme to bear-baiting and juggling at the other, narrowed substantially. At the same time, performers became more professional and freer from the rigid constraints of medieval religious drama. In these and other ways, the formal conventions of dramatic performance matured considerably. Such developments were encouraged by a variety of factors, including the advent of religious change, the greater concern for civic order, the increase in royal, aristocratic, and civic patronage, and even the growing bifurcation between popular and a more distinctly élitist cultural ethos. And, if dramatic performances and performers still represented a threat to civic authority—indeed, perhaps a more intensely perceived threat than ever before—that authority at sundry levels was probably more vigilant in their regard.

In the context of civic authority, one of the more significant developments in theatrical performance of this period was the shift in the venue of performance from outdoors to indoors. This meant that by about the last third of the sixteenth century the most favoured site in the countryside became the banqueting hall of the aristocratic household; in the town, the inn and civic hall.[28]

---

[27] Agnew, *Worlds Apart*, 103; Muriel Bradbrook, *The Rise of the Common Player, a Study of the Actor and Society in Shakespeare's England* (1962), 40, 188; and Beier, *Masterless Men*, 96–9.

[28] G. Wickham, *Early English Stages, 1300–1600*, 3 vols. (1959–81), ii, pt. I, pp. 153–86, especially 177–9; Nelson, *Medieval English Stage*, 136, 191; Gloucester RO, MS GBR F4/3, fos. 78, 79, 107, as cited in Audrey Douglas and Peter Greenfield (eds.), *REED, Cumberland, Westmorland and Gloucester* (Toronto, 1986), 253; Sally-Beth MacLean, 'Players on Tour, New Evidence from the Records of Early English Drama', unpublished typescript (*c.* 1988), 3; Bailey, *Minutes of Boston*, i. 75. I am indebted to Dr MacLean for providing me with a copy of her typescript.

There were many reasons for this shift. From the performers' perspective, the interior space of the hall provided protection from the elements as well as from the noise and distractions of the outdoors.[29] Security was also more manageable indoors. The walls and doors of the building served as natural barriers to casual or mischievous access, while costumes and props could be locked up safely between performances. Further, players seem to have found it easier to gather a large paying audience in such central, comfortable, and commodious places.[30] We know that playgoers in town halls were at least sometimes seated, and, given the known dimensions of several halls used as playing sites, some simple arithmetic tells us that audiences of several hundred at a time— large gatherings in the small towns of the day—were entirely possible.

In addition, the indoor venue may also be seen in the context of the changing nature of dramatic performance. Indoor sites, where the same stage could be constructed from town to town and in which the players were now physically separated from their audience in a similarly standardized spatial setting, permitted the actors themselves to control their playing space as never before. This, in turn, facilitated the development of their art to new levels of sophistication and helped transform the nature of performance itself.[31] It has even been argued that this new juxtaposition of players and audience, in which the former activity of players in the midst of their audience gave way to their physical separation (by distance or elevation or both) permitted theatre to reflect society from without, and thus to develop as a potentially more critical, iconoclastic, and even subversive force.[32]

[29] One is reminded here of Wickham's report of the distractions inherent in the recreating of a Shakespearean play in the courtyard of the New Inn in Gloucester, a project which had to be abandoned because of the frustrations involved in such a noisy and heavily trafficked venue, Wickham, *Early English Stages*, ii. pt. I, p. 188.

[30] Wickham, *Early English Stages*, ii, pt. I, pp. 153–71, 176–9, 183–6. Cf. also Andrew Gurr, 'The Elizabethan Stage and Acting' in Boris Ford (ed.), *The Age of Shakespeare*, rev. edn. (1982), ii. 246 and John Wasson (ed.), *REED, Devon* (Toronto, 1986), pp. xxv–xxvi. In the same passage Wasson notes a distinction between the preferred playing place of local and amateur players on the one hand and the travelling professional on the other. The former preferred the parish church; 'first choice' for the latter was the guild-hall.

[31] Agnew, *Worlds Apart*, 59–63, 103–6; Bradbrook, *Rise of the Common Player*, 18, 23–9, 32–4, 47–8, 100, 127–30, 283; Wickham, *Early English Stages*, ii, pt. I, pp. 100–6; Bristol, *Carnival and Theatre*, 112–14; F. P. Wilson, *The English Drama, 1485–1585*, (Oxford, 1969), 37–41 and 50–2; Don E. Wayne, 'Drama and Society in the Age of Jonson, an Alternative View', *Renaissance Drama*, 13 (1982), 106–7; Roy Strong, *Splendour at Court, Renaissance Spectacle and Illusion* (London, 1973), 73.

[32] M. D. Bristol discusses the scholarly traditions which have portrayed the theatre first as harmony-inducing or at least benign and, later on, the theatre as potentially subversive, in *Carnival and Theatre*, 13–25, 112–18. See also L. C. Knight's classic, *Drama and Society in the Age of Jonson* (1937); Agnew, *Worlds Apart*, 109–14; Wilson, *English Drama*, 37–41; Margot Heinemann, *Puritanism and Theatre, Thomas Middleton and Opposition Drama under the Early Stuarts* (Cambridge, 1980), 16 and chs. 12–13; David Bevington, *Tudor Drama and Politics* (Cambridge, Mass., 1968); Stallybrass and White, *Poetics and Politics, passim*; and Bradbrook, *Rise of the Common Player*, 23–9, 62–4.

From the perspective of civic authorities, the use of the hall was equally desirable. In view of the widespread social unrest of the 1530s and 1540s, the new-found freedom and associated subversive potential of this theatre and the gathering together of large audiences (considered at least by many contemporaries to be idle and prone to mischief) gave authorities at every level deep pause for thought. Even without reference to plot or 'message', which could obviously be unsettling to figures in authority, plays were feared as the common occasion for tumults, riots, and other breaches of the peace.[33] Far from reinforcing the hierarchical structure of contemporary society as the dramatic activities associated with Corpus Christi (for example) were at least supposed to have done,[34] the performance of a particular play in 1549 was even considered by some contemporaries to have led to Kett's Rising.[35] The initial response to this subversive potential, as we will observe, seems to have been for civic authorities, and indeed the central government as well, greatly to encourage players to move into the more easily supervised playing space of the hall, where entrances could be watched and where the size of audiences could be controlled.

One important milestone along this regulatory route was in the proclamation of 16 May 1559, for 'Prohibiting Unlicensed Interludes and Plays', which gave mayors and similar officials the responsibility for scrutinizing theatrical and other cultural activities in their communities.[36] Another such turning point came in the 1570s. This decade not only saw the opening of the first public theatre in London by James Burbage, but also the royal prohibition of all performing companies save those few which the Queen either took under her own wing or entrusted to the patronage and supervision of favoured peers or courtiers. In a similar manner she restricted the permissible playing sites. Though the reign of James may have seen some degree of moderation in censorship, the licence it did permit always lay within strictly defined boundaries.[37] From 1603 the Master of the Revels received responsibility for the players,

---

[33] Bradbrook, *Rise of the Common Player*, ch. 4. Cf. also the proclamation as early as 1544, 'Limiting Performances of Interludes and Plays', in Hughes and Larkin, *Tudor Royal Proclamations*, i, no. 240. For an introduction to the complex subject of the government's increasingly censorious tendencies, see G. R. Elton, *Policy and Police, The Enforcement of the Reformation in the Age of Thomas Cromwell* (Cambridge, 1972) and David Loades, 'The Theory and Practice of Censorship in Sixteenth Century England', *TRHS* 5th ser. 24 (1974), 141–57.

[34] Phythian-Adams, 'Ceremony and the Citizen'; James, 'Ritual, Drama and Social Body', 3–30; Bristol, *Carnival and Theatre*, especially chs. 2–4.

[35] Agnew, *Worlds Apart*, 40. See also Wickham, *Early English Stages*, ii, pt. i, pp. 66–7; Barret L. Beer, *Rebellion and Riot, Popular Disorder During the Reign of Edward VI* (Kent, Ohio, 1982), 83.

[36] Hughes and Larkin, *Tudor Royal Proclamations*, ii, no. 458.

[37] See e.g. Leah S. Marcus, *The Politics of Mirth, Jonson, Herrick, Milton, Marvell and the Defense of Old Holiday Pastimes* (Chicago, 1986), *passim*, 5, 9; and Annabel Patterson, *Censorship and Interpretation, the Conditions of Writing and Reading in Early Modern England* (Madison, Wis., 1984).

playwrights, and theatres, and through his offices an even more exclusive royal control ensued thereafter. In consequence, and while neither provincial nor polemical theatre had by any means disappeared by the turn of the seventeenth century, all theatre certainly came under very stringent controls as defined by statute, proclamation, and royal licence.[38]

Local officials shared most of the concerns which lay behind this royal policy, but their own attitudes could also be complicated by factors tied more closely to their own needs than to those of the Crown. On the one hand the enforcement of this unfolding national policy fell inescapably on the shoulders of England's mayors and aldermen. It was precisely the desire for such agents of enforcement which had led the Tudors to invest local officials with more power to begin with. Yet if such officials had to answer to the Crown at the risk of official displeasure, and indeed if they had their own good reasons for wishing so to comply, they had also to contend with popular sentiment in their own communities. Especially before the middle of Elizabeth's reign and the entrenchment of widespread puritanical attitudes, this still seems largely to have favoured the players and their craft.[39]

In most communities a solution came to be worked out by the middle of the sixteenth century which considerably supported the desire of local officials to move theatrical performances indoors into such controlled playing sites as the town hall. It gained further impetus from the royal proclamation of 1559. Under this arrangement visiting players came first to the mayor, presented their licence to perform, and awaited his pleasure in granting them permission to proceed. Approved players were then conventionally required to give their first performance at the mayor's command and at an indoor playing site which was frequently the town hall:[40] often the most secure of all town sites. The format of this command performance, following the presentation of credentials and the grant of permission, promised something for everyone. It demonstrated the mayor's authority, while his presence on opening night lent dignity both to himself and to the occasion. It provided the players with the official

[38] Bradbrook, *Rise of the Common Player*, 17–18, 37–8, 40, *et passim*; Wickham, *Early English Stages*, ii, pt. I, pp. xiii, 75–90; Heinemann, *Puritanism and Theatre*, 36–47; Martin Butler, *Theatre and Crisis, 1632–1642* (Cambridge, 1984), chs. 7–9.

[39] Wickham, *Early English Stages*, ii, pt. I, p. 145. See the contemporary account of such practice by Ralph Willis, writing of Gloucester in 1639, reprinted in Wilson, *The English Drama*, 76–7. On the dilemma of local officials trying simultaneously to enforce royal policy and live on good terms with their neighbours, see K. Wrightson, 'Two Concepts of Order, Justices, Constables and Jurymen in Seventeenth Century England', in J. Brewer and J. Styles (eds.), *An Ungovernable People?* (New Brunswick, NJ, 1980), 21–46, and Joan Kent, *The English Village Constable, 1500–1642* (Oxford, 1986), chs. 7, 8.

[40] Hughes and Larkin, *Tudor Royal Proclamations*, ii, no. 115; Wickham, *Early English Stages*, i. 269—70, ii, pt. I, pp. 178–9; Bradbrook, *Rise of the Common Player*, 115; Douglas and Greenfield, *REED, Cumberland, Westmorland and Gloucestershire*, 253.

endorsement of the mayor and perhaps some immunity from local harassment. It created the aura of proper decorum appropriate to performance in the town's seat of government, while at the same time relegating the players' activities to that civic space most able to be supervised and controlled. Finally, it allowed town officials to scrutinize the content of the performance, and presumably to forbid 'unseemly' ideas from wider expression. The willingness, indeed sometimes the insistence, on the part of local authorities to have plays moved to the secure indoor space of the hall must be considered as one of a piece with the desire of the leaders of Hastings to move mayoral elections, or the authorities of the city of Chester to move their annual 'calveshead breakfast', behind the doors of their respective halls at about the same time.[41] Those, too, had come to be viewed as potential occasions of public disorder.

Under these circumstances most town officials were initially content to permit entertainment which would draw spectators from both within and without the community to a space suitable for the occasion. In that place they would witness a performance which presumed emotional involvement and which, especially under less controlled circumstances, still held considerable potential for disorder. This strategy was closely related to that developed by the Crown. The mayor's approval and presence at the first performance served the same function as the royal presence, and the approved use of the town hall resembled the court's sanctioned use of the royal palace, aristocratic house, or licensed public theatre.

It is also clear that civic authorities often went to a lot of trouble to insure safe and successful performances in the hall. Use of the hall as a theatre frequently meant permission to clear out or rearrange the usual furniture, to construct a scaffold of planks across one end of the largest chamber to serve as a stage, and often to provide seating for at least some of the audience.[42] A mid-sixteenth-century Norwich account describes wide 'popill' (presumably poplar) planks raised on barrels in this manner.[43] In Gloucester at roughly the same time the audience sat on benches, which may not have been part of the regular furnishings of the hall, while the players strode a raised platform built by a local carpenter.[44] Stafford players erected stages in a covered area of the Shirehall throughout the first four decades of the seventeenth century.[45] Similar

[41] Cf. Ch. 5 above, p. 118.

[42] Richard Southern, *The Staging of Plays Before Shakespeare* (1973), 332–41.

[43] Nelson, *The Medieval English Stage*, 136; Southern, *The Staging of Plays*, 333; Wickham, *Early English Stages*, ii, pt. 1, 184.

[44] Douglas and Greenfield, *REED, Cumberland, Westmorland and Gloucestershire*, 253, 298. Gloucestershire RO, MS GBR F/4, fos. 78, 79, 107.

[45] K. R. Adey, 'Aspects of the History of the Town of Stafford, 1590–1710' (Keele Univ. MA thesis 1971), p. xiii.

references derive from Maidstone (1568) and Exeter (1604),[46] and these could probably be matched in a good many of the towns where halls were used for the performance of plays. Some towns were even willing to foot the bill for carpenters' work in building the stage. The city of Gloucester paid the local carpenter John Battye 4*d*. to make a scaffold in the Booth Hall for the Queen's Players in 1559–60, and Shrewsbury placed a very generous £5 limit on the town's expenses for erecting a stage for players.[47]

There were other concessions as well. The mayor of Cambridge, in granting permission for Iohannis Duke and Thomas Greene to put on a performance in the Town Hall in 1606, 'did also give them the key of the Towne Hall', presumably to lock their effects in between performances.[48] Norwich authorities employed the services of a doorkeeper during performances,[49] and even risked the lighting of candles and charcoal fires inside the hall, both to provide warmth and to illuminate evening performances. (This was a most surprising indulgence in view of the devastating Norwich fire of 1507: that conflagration destroyed 718 homes and left burned and void ground near the city centre on into the 1530s, and its memory must long have lingered.[50])

In addition, it was common (though not novel) in this mid-century period for the mayor to bestow gifts on the companies of players sponsored by the Crown or notables at court. Payment of players by the mayors of Exeter is recorded even back into the fifteenth century[51] and was probably not new even then. Similar payments issued forth from the chamberlains of Plymouth in the 1530s and 1540s,[52] the mayors of Norwich throughout the 1540s and 1550s,[53] the mayors of Bristol throughout most of the century,[54] the chamberlains of York as late as the 1580s and 1590s with a final payment in 1606,[55] the chamberlains of Bath during the same decade,[56] and the mayors of Gloucester throughout the sixteenth century.[57]

---

[46] Wickham, *Early English Stages*, ii, pt. 1, pp. 183–4; John Wasson, *REED, Devon*, p. xxvi.

[47] For Gloucester, see n. 67 above; Southern, *The Staging of Plays*, 338–9.

[48] Alan H. Nelson, *REED, Cambridge*, 2 vols. (Toronto, 1989), i. 403.

[49] Southern, *The Staging of Plays*, 338.

[50] Wickham, *Early English Stages*, ii, pt. 1, p. 184; 26 Henry VIII, c. 8, 'An Act for the Reedifying of Void Grounds in the City of Norwich'; E. L. Jones, S. Porter, and M. Turner, *A Gazetteer of English Urban Fire Disasters, 1500–1900* (Historical Geography Research Series, 13, 1984), table 3.

[51] Wasson, *REED, Devon*, 92, 111, 115, 116, 146, 148, 150, 157.

[52] Wasson, *REED, Devon*, 227, 228, 229 258.

[53] D. Galloway, *REED, Norwich, 1540–1642* (Toronto, 1984), 7, 31.

[54] Information provided by Dr Mark Pilkinton, editor of the *REED* volume for Bristol, in preparation. I am indebted to Dr Pilkinton for this note.

[55] Alexandra Johnston and Margaret Rogerson (eds.), *REED, York*, 2 vols. (Toronto, 1979), i. 409, 419, 430, 435, 436, 441, 442, 471, 476, 488, 491, 501, 521.

[56] Information provided from the Bath Chamberlains' Accounts by Dr Robert Alexander, editor of the forthcoming *REED* volume on Bath. I am indebted to Dr Alexander for his help.

[57] Douglas and Greenfield, *REED, Cumberland, Westmorland and Gloucestershire*, 253, 298–9.

Yet this openness and receptivity was neither an unexcepted nor a permanent attitude amongst authorities of Tudor and early Stuart towns. Just as royal favour for the production of plays diminished considerably during our period, so did the favour of leading townsmen. In addition, though mayors and their brethren were, as we have seen, obligated to follow the lead of central government and were in any event largely in accord with central government policy, they also came to have their own motives for removing their support. Amongst these concerns the fear of 'idleness' and the civil disorder which it was considered likely to induce figured prominently, as did the related concern for the repair and dignity of the hall itself.

This latter issue, concern for the repair and dignity of the hall, emerges as a central (though not widely recognized) theme particularly in the last decades of the sixteenth century. Well might it have done so, for simple wear and tear and more serious damage were constant problems for those who sponsored theatrical performances. Five years after opening the Rose Theatre in London in 1587, Philip Henslowe had to pay £108 to repair it.[58] Save for the frequency of its use as a full-time theatre and hence the scale of damage, the story was little different in the halls of particular towns. Norwich, Gloucester, and Bristol are among the towns whose authorities removed civic furnishings for the duration of theatrical performances, while in Cambridge players were required to remove the glass window panes of the Town Hall prior to performing.[59] In what was then the small town of Liverpool efforts were made in the 1570s to limit the holding of 'wedyng diners or pleyes of dawnsyng therein to the damagyng, decayng, or falling of the floor of the same' through the imposition of costly licences for such events.[60]

Towns accounts and other records provide numerous examples of the sort of damage which could occur despite such precautions. The town of Barnstaple paid for the repair of the Guildhall ceiling broken by the 'Enterlude Players'.[61] The bailiff of Peterborough charged players for repair of the hall stairs during their performance in 1621.[62] The Earl of Pembroke's Players broke into the armoury of the Bath Guildhall and broke some weapons in the fiscal year 1592–3.[63] In York the doors, locks,

[58] Bradbrook, *Rise of the Common Player*, 113.

[59] Nelson, *Medieval English Stage*, 136; Southern, *Staging of Plays*, 338, 241.

[60] R. J. Broadbent, *Annals of the Liverpool Stage* (Liverpool, 1908), 6. This reference was kindly provided by Dr David F. George, to whom I am greatly indebted. Cf. J. A. Twemlow, *Liverpool Town Books*, 2 vols. (Liverpool, 1918 and 1935) ii. 10, 72, 74–5.

[61] Wasson, *REED, Devon*, 46.

[62] W. T. Mellows (ed.), *Peterborough Local Administration, 1541–1689*, 2 vols. (Northamptonshire Record Society, 10, 1937–9), ii. 30.

[63] Information provided by Dr Robert Alexander from Bath Chamberlains' Accounts, as in n. 56 above.

keys, windows, boards, benches, and other furnishings of the Common Hall were found in 1591 to be 'greatly impaired and hurte, and diverse of the same broken, shaken loose and riven up by people repairing there to see and hear plays'.[64] Similar repairs have been cited for Bristol, Leicester, and Canterbury,[65] and were almost certainly widespread elsewhere.

The dangers inherent in the business of setting up the stage, or in the press of an excited audience entering, exiting, or merely watching the play in the highly participatory manner of the time, should have been no greater in the second half of the century than before. Yet town authorities seem to have become less tolerant of such behaviour and more willing to anticipate its likelihood as we approach the end of the century.

Some of the explanation for this apparent hardening may lie in the better keeping of records, but also very likely in the increasingly elaborate and valuable civic furnishings of the hall and the augmented efforts to dignify the environment of that building, which we know to have been characteristic of the same period.[66] As the relatively empty and un-adorned shell of earlier halls filled up with wall panelling, carved coats of arms, mayors' chairs, jurats' benches, magistrates' tables, document chests, wooden railings, and the like, the rough work of erecting scaffolding and the large (and perhaps also rough) crowds which clamoured to witness performances could only have seemed more dangerous.[67] In addition, some of the more highly specialized and larger of these furnishings may have come to be built in or affixed to the floor, making them impossible to move for performances as had been the earlier practice. Above all, in the words of an Assembly Minute Book of the city of Chester, to which we will momentarily return, any activity which disrupted the aura of 'the solempne meetinge and Concourse of this howse' by converting it to 'a Stage for Plaiers and a Receptacle for idle persons' increasingly became unacceptable to those who ruled.[68]

[64] Johnston and Rogerson, *REED, York*, i. 449.

[65] Wickham, *Early English Stages*, ii, pt. I, pp. 184–5.

[66] See Ch. 5 above.

[67] The social composition of the Elizabethan theatrical audience is still too hotly debated to permit definitive conclusions, especially regarding performances outside London. Yet we may note in passing that Ann J. Cook's revisionist view that playgoers were more likely to be more affluent and privileged than the apprentices and journeymen traditionally identified in Elizabethan audiences is based entirely on the London scene. While provincial and urban theatres undoubtedly drew upon reasonably affluent townsmen and even nearby shire gentry, both the substantial playing capacity of most town halls and the evidence of concern for rowdiness suggests a socially mixed clientele away from London. In addition, of course, affluence has never been a guarantee of gentility. See Alfred Harbage, *Shakespeare's Audience* (New York, 1941); Ann J. Cook, *The Privileged Playgoers of Shakespeare's London, 1576–1642* (Princeton, NJ, 1981); and Butler, *Theatre and Crisis*. My thanks to my Concordia colleague Dr Ed Pechter for bringing to my attention the last named.

[68] City Assembly Books, Chester City Archives, MS AB/1, fol. 331ᵛ, cited in L. M. Clopper (ed.), *REED, Chester* (Toronto, 1979), 292–3, minutes of 20 October 1615.

We may thus take this concern for 'idleness' as an extension of the earlier recognition of the plays' subversive potential and of the disorder which was considered likely to ensure from their performance before large audiences. Yet we find in the second half of our period not only fear of subversion of a civil or political nature, such as might lead to violence or to physical damage to the hall, but fear of economic and moral subversion as well.

To traditional historians of the English drama, this meant that Puritanism had taken hold.[69] While there may be some truth to this, and while many ardent opponents of the theatre from Philip Stubbes and William Prynne on down were indeed Puritans in most uses of that battered term,[70] this equation between the proponents of a theological tradition so-labelled and the behavioural characteristics attributed to them is no longer so simple. The examples of Stubbes or Prynne notwithstanding, the definition of Puritan doctrine has become less and less precise as we learn more about it.[71] In the same vein, while some recent scholarship has shown that Puritanism could well even favour some forms of theatre, there are also a great many indications that even Roman Catholic societies in Europe were undergoing a similar crackdown on aspects of popular cultural expression at the same time.[72] A more accurate assessment may be that an ascetic, literate, bourgeois, somewhat authoritarian, and recognizably 'polite' culture, such as Hill, Wrightson and Levine, Hunt, and others have observed, took hold in many English communities at this time. To men and women of such inclinations, some of whom might be labelled Puritans and some not, the disruptive potential of dramatic texts, performances, and audiences had become too risky even to be assayed in the town hall. In addition, we must remember that the economically stressful decade of the 1590s and much of the first four decades of the seventeenth century, the period of this greater regulation of theatre, contributed to an increasing concern for

[69] On Puritan opposition to the stage generally, see Jonas Barish, *The Antitheatrical Prejudice* (Berkeley, Calif., 1981), ch. 4, and bibliography on the subject provided in notes, 82; Wickham, *Early English Stages*, ii, pt. 1, pp. 78–9, 83–4, 109–10, 112–13, 120–1, and 133–4; Bradbrook, *Rise of the Common Player*, especially chs. 3 and 4; M. M. Knappen, *Tudor Puritanism*, a chapter in the History of Puritanism (Chicago, 1939), 439–41, and Heinemann, *Puritanism and Theatre*, 18–21.

[70] Philip Stubbes, *Anatomy of Abuses* [1583] ed. F. J. Furnival (1877–9); William Prynne, *Histrio-mastix* [1633] repr. 2 vols. (New York, 1972).

[71] Christopher Hill, 'The Definition of a Puritan', in *Society and Puritanism in Pre-Revolutionary England* (1964), 13–30; Patrick Collinson, *The Religion of Protestants* (Oxford, 1982); Peter Lake, *Moderate Puritans and the Elizabethan Church* (Cambridge, 1982); Margaret Spufford, 'Puritanism and Social Control?', in A. Fletcher and J. Stevenson (eds.), *Order and Disorder in Early Modern England* (Cambridge, 1985), 41–57; Heinemann, *Puritanism and Theatre*; M. C. Bradbrook, *John Webster, Citizen and Dramatist* (1970), and S. Shepherd, *Amazons and Warrior Women, Varieties of Feminism in Seventeenth Century Drama* (Brighton, 1980).

[72] Butler, *Theatre and Crisis*, chs. 5–6; Heinemann, *Puritanism and Theatre*, 27; Burke, *Popular Culture in Early Modern Europe*, 207–33.

public order throughout the realm. This, too, as we have seen, gave rise to more authoritarian (and often more oligarchic) rule in many cities and towns.[73]

In consequence, where for a half century or so urban authorities seemed willing and even anxious to move players out of the market-place and into the town hall as one of the most secure of all playing sites, by the latter years of the sixteenth and on into the opening decades of the seventeenth century even that site seemed too risky. By that time, players often came to be barred altogether from performing within in town limits. Such prohibitions seem even more frequent in the worst years of economic distress.[74]

These attitudes were abundantly expressed in Norwich from 1589 when the City Assembly passed an ordinance forbidding any freeman from attending plays. Norwich authorities considered that plays profaned the Sabbath and led to vice and sin, but also that they resulted in brawling and other forms of unrest. This particular ordinance was undoubtedly provoked by a specific incident of which we now have no inkling, and it does not seem to have been enforced for some years to come. But by 1624, a time when the central government itself was concerned that attendance at plays would keep people away from their work, the mayor wrote to the Privy Council to reinforce that conclusion. He pointed out that 'the maintenance of the Inhabitants here doth consist of worke & makinge of manufactures', which activities were threatened by workers and apprentices who spent their time at plays.[75]

Players were forbidden to perform in the Guildhall of Great Yarmouth after 1595,[76] though they had long done so, while in 1608 the mayor and aldermen of Durham prohibited any performances in the Tolbooth except at the mayor's pleasure.[77] In 1614 the City Council of Chester banned plays in the Common Hall and other places in its jurisdiction after six o'clock p.m. Its rationale, embracing a host of concerns for morality, economic activity, and the dignity both of the city and its Hall, must be read *in extenso* to be fully appreciated:[78]

Moreover at the same Assemblie Consideracion was had of the Comon Brute and Scandall which this Citie hath of late incurred and sustained by admittinge of

[73] Clark, 'Ramoth-Gilead of the Good', 162–89; J. M. Martin, 'A Warwickshire Town in Adversity: Stratford-upon-Avon in the Sixteenth and Seventeenth Centuries', *Midland History*, 7 (1982), 26–41.

[74] Heinemann, *Puritanism and Theatre*, 31–6.

[75] Galloway, *REED, Norwich*, p. xxxiii.   [76] Nelson, *Medieval English Stage*, 191.

[77] 'The Order Book of the City of Durham' (no ref. no.), Durham Co. Records Office, 24. I am indebted to Professor Tom Craik, editor of the forthcoming *REED* volume on Durham, for this reference.

[78] Chester Assembly Books, Chester City Archives MS AB/1, fo. 331v., as cited in Clopper, *REED, Chester*, 292–3.

Stage Plaiers to Acte their obscene and vnlawful Plaies or tragedies in the Comon Hall of this Citie thereby Convertinge the same, beinge appointed and ordained for the Iudiciall hearinge and determininge of Criminall offences, and for the solempne meetinge and Concourse of this howse, into a Stage for Plaiers and a Receptacle for idle persons. And consideringe likewise the many disorders which by reason of Plaies acted in the night time doe often times happen and fall out to the discredit of the government of this Citie and to the greate disturbance of quiet and well disposed People, and beinge further informed that mens servantes and apprentices neglectinge their Masters busines doe Resorte to Innehouses to behold such Plaies there manie times wastfullie spende thar Masters goodes ffor avoidinge of all which inconveniences It is ordered that from hensforth noe Stage Plaiers vpon anie pretence or color Whatsoever shalbe admitted to set vp anye Stage in the said Comon Hall or to acte anie tragedie or Commedie or anie other Plaie by what name soever they shall terme hit, in the said Hall or [in] anie other Place within this Citie or the Liberties therof in the night time or after vi^c of the Clocke in the eveninge.

Not surprisingly, recorded expenditures for feasting visiting players also became infrequent in these years. In their place we begin to find payments given to persuade players *not* to perform, by which means town officials gracefully urged performers to move elsewhere without hard feelings.[79] With this turnabout, local attitudes towards the performance of plays in many towns reached that stern ascetic stance which would be confirmed by the national prohibition of 1642.

This last point may perhaps belong more to the history of drama than of urban society. Yet the evolving policy of urban leaders towards the theatre demonstrates the manner in which they employed the town hall to control a potentially subversive activity, as a doorway to regulate the flow of ideas and people, both players and audience, from outside. When the increasingly puritanical, if not necessarily Puritan, civic leaders of many early seventeenth-century towns found the risks of theatrical performance too great even for such a controlled space as the hall, they shut the doorway altogether, anticipating the national prohibition of theatre to come.

THE CIVIC HERITAGE

This much, then, is in the end a negative story. It describes the way in which civic authorities first encouraged a particular cultural activity to relocate in the civic hall for what they saw as purposes of containment and regulation. Subsequently, as the intellectual climate grew less tolerant, it

---

[79] Bradbrook, *The Rise of the Common Player*, 115; Galloway, *REED, Norwich*, p. xxxiv; Wasson, *REED, Devon*, 258; Wickham, *Early English Stages*, ii, pt. 1, 146–7; HMC, *Tenth Report* (1984), ('Report on the MSS of Plymouth Corporation'), App., pt. iv, p. 540.

shows that many of them then proscribed it altogether from even that controlled space and thus from the town. Yet before we conclude this discussion, it is important to point out that in cultural as well as economic terms, civic authorities also found positive ways to employ the hall in their efforts to inculcate an outlook compatible with their own.

This brings us to the third doorway function of the hall: its role in the effort of the contemporary leadership to legitimize itself through historical (or pseudo-historical) association. The celebration of civic office by the ceremonial feasting which one perhaps more readily associates with the earlier period has already been noted in passing, though the costs of such banquets may have begun to bring them into disrepute. In addition, the use of interior design and furnishing towards the end of civic legitimation were discussed in Chapter 4. But a less familiar activity may be equally supportive of the point. This is the enduring and perhaps growing interest in local history and historical mythology (not that contemporaries drew a firm line between the two) and including the idea that folkloric heroes were involved in civic foundations or in otherwise serving particular communities. As Keith Thomas has reminded us, the historical vision of the sixteenth and seventeenth centuries was essentially didactic, with the choice of epoch or episode determined by the requirements of the present.[80] And, while many students of the role of folklore in social and political behaviour have dwelt on the manner in which popular figures like Robin Hood[81] or myths such as the Norman Yoke[82] could be harnessed to subvert authority, other subjects could as easily be employed in support of such authority.

Here Thomas concluded that 'the most common reason for invoking the past was to legitimize the prevailing distribution of power'.[83] We have already seen how acutely the newly empowered civic leadership needed such legitimation. We must extend that point to their use of the past as well as their use of the present. While the use of the past could extend to the forging of charters[84] or the common appeal to authority exercised 'from time out of mind', it also extended to the perpetuation or revival of interest in myths of foundation or other heroic deeds and to the visual promulgation of those myths before a wide and largely illiterate public.

---

[80] Keith Thomas, 'The Perception of the Past in Early Modern England', Creighton Lecture (London University, 1983), especially 2–4. I am indebted to Dr Daniel Woolf for bringing this important essay to my attention.

[81] Scholarship both old and new is summarized in John G. Bellamy, *Robin Hood, an Historical Enquiry* (Bloomington, Ind. 1985).

[82] Christopher Hill, 'The Norman Yoke', published as ch. 3 of *Puritanism and Revolution* (1985).

[83] Thomas, 'The Perception of the Past', 2.

[84] Susan Reynolds, 'The Forged Charters of Barnstaple', *English Historical Review*, 84 (1969), 699–720.

Bevis of Hampton, Guy of Warwick, Godiva of Coventry, and even the obscure Hikifricke of the equally obscure village of Tilney Smeath in the Norfolk fens, were all mythological figures who were by no means élitist creations but who sprang from the popular culture of an earlier period; they were dusted off and put on display, as much by the authorities as by anyone else, in this era.[85] More often than not, such figures were also associated with the town hall in a logical linking of symbols for historical legitimacy on the one hand and contemporary civic authority on the other.

Although these efforts were not without precedent from earlier periods, episodes such as the evocation of King Ebrauk of York when Henry VII visited that city in 1486, or the removal of Ebrauk's statue, the image of the city's founding father, to the Common Hall in 1501,[86] seem to have become more common and to have occurred in smaller and more remote communities as we come to the latter decades of our period. Thus, for example, Bath's new Town Hall of 1625 included statues of both King Edgar and King Coel.[87]

The point is particularly well illustrated by Coventry, a larger provincial centre with a long and rich civic history, and by Bridport, a very much smaller town in Dorset, whose traditions were far less ancient or extensive. In Coventry, the essential civic myth concerned Lady Godiva, that pre-Norman, quasi-historical figure who sacrificed her modesty so that the citizens of Coventry could gain tax relief from her husband Leofric, the ruling lord.

The story seems to have been revived in the 1490s, in a context which had led townsmen to reflect on the sanctity of their ancient liberties. Here, in a poem posted on the church door at a time of Lammastide hedge-breaking in 1495, and in a second posting of verses a year later, the evocation came as an assertion of perceived entitlement against the action of contemporary authorities. But in the next round of 'Godiva-quotation', her image had been co-opted by the authorities of the town: presumably in the effort to rally townsmen to civic pride but also of course to link the ruling élite with a popular image of legitimacy. We find in the year 1580 a reference to Godiva worked into the inscriptions of the newly rebuilt market hall, and, in 1586, the purchase of her portrait to be hung in St Mary's Hall, the functioning town hall. By 1609, in a remarkable

---

[85] Thomas, 'The Perception of the Past', 2–3. In the view of Professor Sir Geoffrey Elton, those whose duties at court isolated them from some aspects of popular culture liked to think that their fellow countrymen were above such superstitious beliefs, but in the event, that optimism proved unfounded; Elton, *Policy and Police*, 196.

[86] A. Raine (ed.), *York Civic Records, Yorkshire Archaeological Society Record Series*, 8 vols. (1939–53), i. 156 and ii. 171.

[87] Revd John Collinson, *History and Antiquities of the County of Somerset*, 3 vols. (Bath, 1791), i. 31–2; Bryan Little, *The Buildings of Bath* (1947), 54 and plate 22.

apotheosis of civic imagery, her statue had replaced a figure of Jesus in the same building.[88]

For perhaps the most interesting example of folkloric beliefs associated with a town hall and supporting the objectives of a particular town— interesting because of its modest size and presumed typicality—we must turn to the remarkably well-documented Dorset town of Bridport. Here the fewer than a thousand inhabitants of the 1590s hoped to establish their community as a marketing centre after the silting up of its harbour. The Town Chamberlains' Accounts record with particular thoroughness the festivities surrounding the completion of the new town and market hall of 1593. Here we find evidence of lavish feasting, marked by the purchase of three dozen trenchers on which to bear trays of food, attendance of dignitaries from nearby communities and the surrounding countryside, and the services 'from Wednesday to Saturday' of several musicians who were liveried, fed, and sheltered at the town's expense. Indeed, this conjures up a scene from Bruegel the Elder as easily as from a Lord Mayor's Show in London, but the best is yet to come. We also find recorded here an expenditure for the construction of a King Lud, apparently to be carried through the high street in some form of procession, much as the effigy of a saint or the host itself might have been carried in pre-Reformation times.[89]

Lud had no particular association with Bridport itself. Both in the ancient Welsh legend in which he first appeared and in the derivative account of Geoffrey of Monmouth, Lud was the English king responsible for the founding of London: Geoffrey even derived the name London from 'Lud's Town'.[90] Bridport's townsmen, obviously familiar with this legend, were borrowing that image most appropriately to celebrate the opening of the new civic hall which, they hoped, would help revive their own community and thus bring credit to its leaders.

The objective of legitimizing civic leadership by deliberate reference to historical imagery in the town hall was also assayed through the development of civic portraiture, and by the display of such portraits in the civic hall. The purchase and display of a Godiva portrait in St Mary's Hall, Coventry, already suggests this practice with reference to long deceased and quasi-mythical figures, but there are numerous examples of less mythical and more recently deceased figures as well. Most of the subjects

[88] I. N. Brewer, *A Topographical Historical Description of the County of Warwick* (1820), 139; R. W. Ingram, *REED, Coventry* (Toronto, 1981), 577; Edwin S. Hartland, *The Science of Fairy Tales* (1891), 74; F. Bliss Burbidge, *Old Coventry and Lady Godiva* (Birmingham, n.d.), 51–3; Joan C. Lancaster, *Godiva of Coventry* (1967), 50–1.

[89] Dorset Co. RO, 'Accounts . . . for the buyldinge of the MarKett House', Bridport Bor. Archives, MS B3/M15, unpag.

[90] See Lady Charlotte Guest (ed.), *The Mabinogian* (1906), 89–94 and Geoffrey of Monmouth, *Historia Regum Brittaniae*, ed. Acton Griscom (New York, 1929), 103–4.

for this sort of display were mayors, and most of those portraits which survive, or of which records survive, derive, as one would suspect, from the larger towns and cities.

The Norwich Guildhall, for example, came to display in our period portraits of Robert Jannys, mayor in 1517 (painted after his death in 1530) (see Plate 13) and John Marsham, mayor in 1518, the famous Augustine Steward (thrice mayor between 1534 and 1557 and probably the most distinguished Norfolk citizen of his time), and several other sixteenth-century mayors.[91] Exeter, too, displayed several Tudor and early Stuart mayoral portraits in its Guildhall. Leicester hung at least one in its Guildhall in the early seventeenth century. The smaller and much less politically mature town of Bury St Edmunds purchased a portrait of the important citizen and townsmen of the late fifteenth century, Jankyn Smith, for its hall in 1616, just a decade after gaining its long awaited incorporation. Gloucester acquired the portrait of John Falkner, cap-maker and mayor, at about the same time.[92]

There are several relevant observations one might make regarding these portraits. First, the practice of displaying full oil portraits in civic halls seems to supersede two earlier practices. In the pre-Reformation period it was common for former mayors to be buried in a prominent part of the parish church, and for a funerary brass to be commissioned showing them in mayoral robes. Second, it was also common during the same period to use the stained glass of the church windows to display the initials or the arms of deceased mayors.[93] In both cases, of course, the action seems to have been initiated by the individual himself as part of the arrangements for death and burial, and the church served as the venue of display. The depiction of mayoral garb seems intended to add the lustre of office and town to the reputation of the deceased.

When we turn to the mayoral portraits displayed in the town hall, some apparent distinctions appear. For example, there is strong indication that mayoral portraits of that age were commissioned by and almost certainly possessed by the town itself rather than by the individual. An examination of the wills of all the Norwich mayoral sitters, for example, turns up no mention of any portrait in any will. This implies either that they were painted during the subject's life and were not part of the estate at death or that they were painted after death but not by order of the sitter's will. In both cases the role of the town officials seems likely. (In Norwich, where

[91] B. Cozens-Hardy and E. A. Kent (eds.), *The Mayors of Norwich, 1403–1835* (Norwich, 1938), opp. 48, 49, 90.

[92] H. Lloyd Parry, *The History of Exeter Guildhall and the Life Within* (Exeter, 1936), 150–5; Henry Hartopp (ed.), *The Roll of the Mayors of the Borough of Leicester* (Leicester, c. 1935), 76–7; M. Statham, *Jankyn Smith and the Guildhall Feoffees, 1481–1981* (Bury St Edmunds, 1981), 3; Joan Johnson, *Tudor Gloucestershire* (Gloucester, 1985), 4.

[93] e.g. Cozens-Hardy and Kent, *Mayors of Norwich, passim*.

all the surviving sixteenth-century portraits show the death's head, indicating a posthumous portrayal, it is obviously the latter case which applies, but this appears not necessarily to have been so elsewhere.) In nearly all contemporary mayoral portraits, whatever the venue, sitters pose in mayoral gowns, and sometimes with other symbols of office: Robert Jannys, for example, is shown with the skeletal figure of death wresting away his mace of office. All these observations point to one conclusion. Not only has the venue of display shifted from the parish church to the town hall, but the objective of such display has shifted as well. It was now employed to add the image of the mayor—symbolic of public service—to the lustre of the town.

Examples such as these, which can only become more numerous as research on local customs proceeds, remind us that to the civic leadership of the day and to many others in the urban community, the town hall could well be employed to cultivate a sense of tradition. Here we see civic leaders opening the doorway to admit the imagery of local heritage, to inculcate a sense of civic pride and to legitimize themselves through that legacy.

CONCLUSION

If we watch carefully what goods, services, people, and ideas were permitted to pass through the doorways of English towns, and how that permissible traffic changed over time, we gain some strong impressions of what mattered to civic leaders of the day. It is no revelation to note that trade mattered first and foremost, for the effectiveness with which commercial activity was conducted and regulated could determine the livelihood of the whole community. To obtain a favourable reputation through its hinterland, a town had to provide appropriate facilities for marketing, attentive administration, and enforcement of local rules and by-laws that were seen to be both practical and just. Failure to do this could easily cause the discretionary trader to take his business elsewhere, as when Channel Islanders habitually chose to trade in Poole, rather than in Southampton, whose merchants they saw as inhospitable.[94] In this light the existence of a town hall geared for marketing, the facilities it provided, and the administrative activities carried out in its midst, constituted elements of extreme economic importance.

The operation of this doorway also mattered greatly in transmitting economic and cultural values from the merchant element which dominated the provincial town to those others, both resident and non-resident, who still shared a more traditional outlook. As we have seen, the hall bore

[94] Robert Tittler, 'The Vitality of an Elizabethan Port: the Economy of Poole, c.1550–1600', *Southern History*, 7 (1985), 104.

the additional burden of conveying, through its clocks, bells, marketing by-laws, and even portraits of merchant-mayors, the values of a bourgeois society to those still attuned to an agrarian milieu. Here, too, the hall served to mediate between one interest and another.

Save for the intensification of some of these characteristics, the role of the hall as a doorway to the *economic* life of the urban community, and to all which is implied therein, changed little between the beginning of the sixteeth century and the outbreak of the Civil War. The image of the hall as a doorway to other aspects of urban culture is altogether more mutable and complex. Here we must view the hall as a device by which urban leaders sought to regulate the transfer of ideas and mentalities as well as the transfer of commodities or people. And, as such ephemeral and intangible phenomena changed a great deal over the era in question, so did the use made of this entrance-way in their regard.

The first great milestone in this story came with the Reformation, and with the decline and transformation of medieval forms of dramatic expression in its wake. These vast changes in traditional forms of cultural activity also coincided with the changes taking place in civic politics and government described in Chapters 4 and 5 above. They led the urban leaders after *c*.1540 to pick their way carefully amongst the sundry forms of medieval civic culture, to co-opt and encourage what they found useful, to regulate what seemed manageable, and to prohibit what seemed dangerous.

In this business of picking and choosing, the hall came to be used as the preferred performing space for permissible theatrical activity. Yet as civic authorities began to take the dignity of their symbolic edifice more seriously and simultaneously became more moralistic, as increasing social pressures made them more mindful of security, and as the halls them-selves became more elaborately furnished, official tolerance of such theatrical activities, even in such controlled spaces as the town hall, diminished rapidly in the sixteenth and early seventeenth centuries. In the decades prior to 1642 we see many civic authorities turning players from the door as they had earlier with other interests, and bidding them go elsewhere. On a more positive note, the hall also came into use as the show-place for civic traditions, mythological or historical, which could legitimize the urban leadership and dignify its position.

Epilogue

This study will no doubt have different significance for different readers. It is, however, chiefly intended as a contribution to our knowledge of English urban communities, and especially to our understanding of the political culture which came to predominate in those communities between *c.* 1500 and 1640. Of course the word 'culture' has many meanings. It has already been employed in Chapter 6 to denote the broad intellectual and creative expressions of Tudor and early Stuart society. The classic study by Kroeber and Kluckhohn identified no fewer than 164 meanings.[1] The term 'political culture' employed here should be taken to denote the political outlook of the townsmen of this era, and the means by which they sought to obtain their civic goals. It embraces the requirements, aspirations, expectations, fears, and convictions which people had in relation to concerns which we normally describe as political: power, authority, legitimacy, administrative relationships, and so forth.

Thanks to those who have developed the concept of *mentalités collectives*, or related notions of 'popular culture', it is no longer appropriate to think of political culture as including only participants in formal political processes. And, certainly, within the wide range of those involved in the total political culture of the Early Modern English urban community, the town hall also meant different things to different people. Yet in contrast to most 'material objects' which have received scholarly attention, the hall is justifiably associated most directly with the ruling element rather than with the community as a whole. These were the men with the greater material stake in the community, whose careers had become most thoroughly enmeshed in the fabric of local society, and whose passage, at least in most cases, through a well understood career cycle had brought them to positions of authority over their fellows.

We must exercise considerable caution in discussing such élites in the period at hand, for the very task of description invites the risk of overemphasizing the homogeneity or number of their members, or even their importance. Still, as several historians have proposed a social and 'cultural' bifurcation in agrarian society during at least the latter half of our period, so does there appear to be a similar divergence in the town.[2]

---

[1] A. L. Kroeber and Clyde Kluckhohn, *Culture* (Cambridge. Mass., 1952).

[2] Keith Wrightson and David Levine, *Poverty and Piety in an English Village, Terling, 1525–1700* (New York, 1979), esp. ch. 7; Wrightson, *English Society, 1580–1680* (1982), esp. chs. 1 and 2; Margaret Spufford, *Contrasting Communities, English Villages in the Sixteenth and Seventeenth Centuries* (Cambridge, 1974); William Hunt, *The Puritan Moment: The Coming of Revolution in an English County* (Cambridge, Mass., 1983).

Our task has not so much been to establish the identity of that civic élite,
for that has been done well enough by others,[3] but rather to learn what we
can about the participation of its members in the political culture of their
immediate milieu. We have tried to do this by employing the town hall, the
natural working environment of those leading citizens, as a point of focus.

We were able to take up this task to begin with only because this
appeared (and eventually proved) to be an especially concentrated period
for the acquisition or rebuilding of town halls, and only because, in turn,
of the peculiar political conditions which brought about that phenomenon. The recognition of the relationship between hall acquisition and
political change, facilitated by the simple technique of counting such halls
and correlating them at least in a representative way with political change
in individual towns, uncovered some important milestones in the long
history of English towns and their governing structures. This era proves
nothing less than a watershed in the establishment of civic autonomy, in
the rise of indigenous ruling oligarchies, and in the emergence of several
related factors as well, all of which form the underpinnings for the rapid
growth in civic halls. Like the halls themselves, these are phenomena
which could be found in some towns of an earlier period, but which
became much more prevalent and even characteristic of towns in general
during the years at hand.

In these circumstances, the resurgence of the civic hall followed
logically and easily. We can now little doubt that it played a vivid and
revealing role in the emerging political culture of English towns at this
time. The hall's very existence often stemmed from a new-found civic
pride: pride of the sort which a new owner takes in a home which he has
long inhabited as a mere tenant. It often stemmed from a need for greater
office space in an expanding civic administration. Above all, it often
stemmed from the requirement of the ruling element for both a seat and
symbol of newly acquired or newly augmented governing authority.

The hall served these roles well. The response to civic pride may be
seen in the display area it provided for material reminders of the civic
heritage and for the paraphernalia of contemporary authority. As a source
of office space, it catered to the ever more specific spatial needs of an
increasingly authoritative and specialized administration. And in its role
as the seat and symbol of civic authority it received a wide range of
furnishings and other material objects, which served to legitimize and
dignify the town's officers and its institutions.

[3] Peter Clark and Paul Slack, *English Towns in Transition, 1500–1700* (Oxford, 1976), esp. chs. 8
and 9; Charles Phythian-Adams, *Desolation of a City, Coventry and the Urban Crisis of the Late Middle
Ages* (Cambridge, 1979), esp. ch. 10; John T. Evans, *Seventeenth Century Norwich: Politics, Religion and
Government, 1620–1690* (Oxford, 1979), esp. chs. 1 and 2; Susan M. Battley, 'Elite and Community,
the Mayors of Sixteenth Century King's Lynn' (State U. of N.Y., Stony Brook, Ph.D. thesis 1981).

To the civic élite, the hall provided the place in which the business of government and the exercise of power proceeded, and through which appropriate attitudes, values, and ideas could be encouraged. To the community at large it represented the civic heritage on the one hand and the power and legitimate authority of contemporary administration on the other. And to the world outside it meant the point of access to the community: in modern parlance the visa office, the immigration desk, the ticket window, the labour exchange, the customs booth, and certainly the seat of government. It did, indeed, 'mark the center as [the] center', reminding us once more that civic authority, like majesty, is 'made, not born'.[4]

---

[4] Clifford Geertz, 'Centers, Kings and Charisma: Reflections on the Symbolics of Power', in Joseph Ben-David and Terry Nichols Clark (eds.), *Culture and its Creators, Essays in Honour of Edward Shils* (Chicago, 1977), 160.

Appendix

Census of Town Halls Acquired in England, 1500–1640

Note: Though it was initially intended to compile a comprehensive list of all English town halls built, converted, or substantially reconstructed in the period at hand, it cannot now be said that this has been accomplished or, perhaps, is possible to accomplish. Suffice it to say that this is as complete a list as could be drawn from surviving sources, both published and unpublished.

Undoubtedly there will be omissions, and the author will respond gratefully to news of additions and corrections. But the reader should bear in mind that some *apparent* omissions have been intentional. Many buildings known to fall within this era could not be verified as having served as town halls as defined in the text. Dartford's market hall and schoolroom or the simple market halls of Beaconsfield, Winster, Witney, or Chipping Campden fit this category. Other buildings which undoubtedly did serve in the appropriate manner (including the familiar and important Thaxted Guildhall) could not be shown to have been built or converted during the appropriate era. Still others may have served as halls of a sort and derive from the proper period, but not in communities which could be considered 'towns' rather than 'villages' at the time: Barkway in Hertfordshire, and both Ashden and Steeple Bumpstead in Essex come to mind here. Alan Everitt's list of markets published in the fourth volume of the *Agrarian History of England and Wales* (Joan Thirsk (ed.), Cambridge, 1967, 468–75) has been an invaluable, if not entirely infallible, guide in making such decisions.

Finally, it should be said that the very interdisciplinary nature of the study has itself created some measure of difficulty: what may be a town hall to an architectural historian or a post-medieval archaeologist may not so qualify in the mind of an expert on local government, a student of economic institutions, or a specialist in local ceremony and customs. Though indebted beyond the expression of gratitude to practitioners in these and other fields, the author remains an historian both by training and inclination, and can only apologize should the criteria applied in constructing this list seem to others either arbitrary or frivolous.

Town Hall List, 1500–1640

KEY TO SYMBOLS:
- (v)   Visual evidence, in the form of a drawing or photograph, still exists, but the edifice itself does not.
- (*)   The building survives to the present.
- (**) Part of the building survives, or survives in much altered form.

Town halls by county, 1500–1640.
(Numbers correspond to the Town Hall List.)

Descriptive labels are taken from contemporary usage where possible and should by no means always be taken in a technical or literal sense. County designations are historical rather than modern.

Bedfordshire
1. Ampthill (v)   Moothall, 16th C.
2. Elstow (*)   Moothall, late 15th–early 16th C., but *c.*1600 additions
3. Toddington (v)   Town House/Sessions House, 16th C.

Berkshire
4. Abingdon   Guildhall converted from chapel *c.*1563
5. Maidenhead   Town Hall, mid–1580s
6. Newbury   Guildhall, 1611
7. Reading   'New Guildhall' converted from part of church 1540s
8. Wokingham (v)   Town Hall, *c.*1585

Buckinghamshire
9. Aylesbury   Guildhall/Market House, *c.*1530
10. High Wycombe   Market Hall/Assize Hall, 1604
11. Ivinghoe (**)   Town Hall, 16th C.
12. Olney   Town House/Hall, 1556
13. Wendover (v)   Town House/Market House converted church house 1524; enlarged 1613

Cambridgeshire and Ely
14. Linton (v **)   Guildhall, *c.*1500

Cheshire
15. Chester (**)   Common Hall converted from chapel 1545
16. Macclesfield (v)   Guildhall/Moothall, late 16th C.

Cornwall
17. Falmouth   Market House, 16th C.
18. Fowey   Town Hall converted from chapel at Dissolution
19. Helston   Market House with guild-hall, corn chamber, and clock, 1576
20. Penryn (*)   Market House, *c.*1549
21. Penzance   Market House/Guildhall, 1615
22. Truro   Market Hall/Town Hall, with clock, 1615
23. West Looe (**)   Town Hall converted from chapel after Dissolution

Cumberland
24. Keswick   Moot Hall, 1571

Derbyshire
25. Alfreton   Moothall, 16th C.
26. Bakewell (*)   Town Hall with market hall and hospital, 1602

27. Chesterfield   'Guildhall' with prison, *c.*1617–30; 'New
                                House', 'Council House'

Devon
28. Ashburton   School/Town Hall converted from chapel
                                16th C.
29. Axminster   Guildhall, 1560
30. Barnstaple (v)   Guildhall, 1532
                                Banking Hall, *c.*1620
31. Bideford   'Meeting Place or Hall' converted from
                                chapel 1575
32. Crediton   Common Hall acquired by patent 1547
33. Exeter (*)   Guildhall, extensive rebuilding 1590s
34. Plymouth (v)   Guildhall, 1565;
                                New Guildhall, 1606
35. Tiverton   Guildhall, *c.*1615
36. Totnes (*)   Guildhall, *c.*1553; renovated 1624

Dorset
37. Beaminster   Market Hall/Sessions House, *temp.*
                                James I
38. Blandford Forum   'Yelde Hall', 1593
39. Bridport   Market House/School, 1593
40. Lyme Regis   Town Hall, 1612
41. Poole   Guildhall, *c.*1568–70
42. Shaftesbury (v)   Guildhall/Townhouse/Market Hall,
                                *c.*1568/9
43. Wareham   Town Hall/School converted from church
                                at Dissolution
44. Weymouth (**)   Town Hall, *c.*1571

Durham
45. Durham   Toll Booth/Town House, *c.*1555
46. Hartlepool   'Town House'/Guildhall, *c.*1600

Essex
47. Barking   Court House/Town Hall, 1567–8
48. Great Dunmow (**)   'Yieldhouse'/'Town House', *c.*1578
49. Horndon-on-the-Hill (*)   Market Hall/Town Hall, 16th C.
50. Maldon (**)   'New Moot Hall' acquired in 1576
51. Saffron Walden   Moothall converted from Holy Trinity
                                Guildhall after Dissolution

Gloucestershire
52. Bristol   Council House/Tolzey, 1551
53. Chipping Sodbury   Town Hall/Alms House bought and
                                converted 1558
54. Cirencester (*)   Town Hall/Church Porch built *temp.*
                                Henry VIII
55. Gloucester (v)   Tolsey, 1602; Booth Hall, 1606

56. Leonard Stanley — Market House rebuilt 1620
57. Newent (*) — Market House, late 16th or early 17th C.
58. Painswick (v) — Court House, late 16th C.
Town Hall with blind house and school, 1628
59. Stroud (v) — Market House with 'Town Hall' room, 1590
60. Tewkesbury — Tolsey converted 1576; Boothall, 1585
61. Wotton-under-Edge (*) — Court House, by 1609

Hampshire and Isle of Wight
62. Andover — Town Hall/Market Hall bought or built, c.1575
63. Portsmouth — Guildhall/'Town House', 1530s
64. Romsey (**) — Town Hall purchased early 17th C.
65. Titchfield (*) — Market Hall/Town Hall, late 16th C.

Herefordshire
66. Hereford (v) — Town Hall built by Abel (?) late 16th C.
67. Leominster (**) — Town Hall, 1633–4

Hertfordshire
68. Berkhamsted (v) — Market House, Elizabethan
69. Hemel Hempstead (v) — Market House with 'court loft', between 1571 and 1619
70. Hertford — Assize/Town/Market Hall, c.1610
71. St Albans (**) — Town Hall converted from Charnel House 1548–53

Huntingdonshire
72. Godmanchester — Court House, 1508

Kent
73. Ashford — Market/Court hall with cage, built c.1512–28
Market/Court hall 50 yards west, c.1602
74. Dover — Town Hall, 1605–6 ('A market crosse to be built for a guildhall')
75. Faversham (**) — Market Hall, c.1575
76. Fordwich (*?) — Town Hall, c.1540s (?)
77. Gravesend — Town Hall purchased or built 1573
78. Maidstone (v) — Court House/Corn Market, 1608
79. Sandwich (v**?) — 'Courthall', c.1578
80. Sevenoaks (v) — Town House, early 16th C.

Lancashire
81. Ashton-under-Lyne — 'Market House'/'Court House', 1638
82. Clitheroe — Moot Hall, first decade of 17th C.
83. Liverpool — 'Lady House'/Town Hall bequeathed 1515

Leicestershire
84. Leicester (*) — 'Old Guildhall' purchased 1564 or 1563

Lincolnshire
85. Boston (*?)   Guildhall of St Mary, transferred to town
                                   16th C.
86. Bourne   Town Hall, 16th C.
87. Lincoln (*)   Guildhall, 1520, over gate
88. Louth   Blessed Virgin Mary Guildhall converted at
                                   Dissolution
                                   Town House/Market Hall, *c.*1580–95
89. Stamford   Town Hall over bridge, 1558
Norfolk
90. Diss   Guildhall built *temp.* Henry VIII; acquired
                                   by town 1584
91. East Dereham   Toll House converted from sessions house
                                   *c.*1559, rebuilt 1600 and reconverted to
                                   sessions house
92. Great Yarmouth   Market Cross rebuilt in 1509 and 1604;
                                   Guildhall rebuilt 1546
93. King's Lynn (*)   Guildhall acquired after Reformation
94. Norwich (*)   Extensive additions, including Council
                                   Chamber, 1535
95. Swaffham   Market 'Cross'/House, 1575
96. Thetford   Conversion of 1337 Guildhall to Common
                                   Hall, 1573
97. Wymondham (*)   'Market Cross', *c.*1617
Northamptonshire
98. Brackley   Court Hall, between 1585 and 1616
99. Kettering   Sessions House, 1629
100. Oundle   Guildhall, *c.*1565
                                   Market Cross with penthouse, 1591
101. Peterborough (*)   New 'Mote' Hall, *c.*1618
                                   Guildhall, transferred to town 1572
102. Rothwell (*)   Market House built by Thomas Tresham
                                   1587

Nottinghamshire
103. Newark-on-Trent   Sessions Hall given to town by James I
Oxfordshire
104. Banbury (v)   Town Hall, 1556, renovated 1590
                                   Town Hall/Market Hall, *c.*1633–6
105. Bicester   Town House, by 1599
106. Burford (*)   Tolsey/Court House, by 1561
107. Chipping Norton (*)   Guildhall, 16th C.
108. Deddington (*)   Town Hall, shortly before 1611
109. Henley   'New Hall', mid-16th C.
110. Oxford   Lower Guildhall acquired 1562
                                   Council House rebuilt 1616
111. Thame (v)   Market Hall, 16th C.

Rutland

Shropshire
112. Church Stretton (v)   Market Hall/Town Hall, 1617
113. Much Wenlock (*)   Guildhall, *c*.1557
114. Newport   Guildhall, 1615
115. Shrewsbury   Guildhall rebuilt 1512

Somerset
116. Bath   Town Hall and Market House, 1625
117. Bruton   Market House, *c*.1620
118. Castle-Cary   Market House, 1616
119. Chard   Town House converted from chapel after
                               Dissolution
                               'New Hall' (Assize and Town Hall), early
                               17th C.
                               'Court Hall', 16th C.
120. Dunster (*)   Yarn Market, 1589, rebuilt as Town Hall
                               1635
121. Glastonbury   Market House/Town Hall, between 1509
                               and 1524
122. Langport   Building converted to Town Hall 16th C.
123. Wells   Market cross/public hall, 1542

Staffordshire
124. Stafford   Assize/Town Hall, 1580s
125. Tamworth   Town Hall, just before 1603
126. Uttoxeter   Common Hall and Town Oven, *temp.*
                               James I
127. Walsall   Town Hall converted from St John's
                               Guildhall at Dissolution
                               High Cross House/Market House built
                               1589

Suffolk
128. Aldeburgh (*)   Moothall, *c*.1520–1540
129. Beccles   Tollhouse/Sessions House rebuilt entirely
                               1574
130. Bury St Edmunds   Building converted to Guildhall 1569
131. Debenham (**)   Guildhall built *c*.1500
132. Hadleigh (*)   Guildhall acquired by town in 1573
133. Lavenham (*)   Guildhall built 1529, converted and taken
                               by town at Dissolution
134. Stoke-by-Nayland (*)   Guildhall, 16th C.
135. Woodbridge   Shire Hall/Market Hall 'given' in 1575

Surrey
136. Croydon (v)   Market/Town Hall, 1566 or 1609
137. Dorking (v)   Market House/Assize hall, 16th C.
138. Farnham (v)   Market House/Town House, *c*.1566

139. Guildford (**)	Guildhall, partly 16th and partly 17th C.
140. Kingston upon Thames (v)	Town Hall, Elizabethan
141. Southwark	Court House/Compter converted from church c.1550

Sussex

142. Brighton	Town Hall, c.1580s
143. East Grinstead	Sessions House/Town Hall by 1618
144. Horsham	Town Hall, early 17th C.
145. Lewes	Sessions House/Town Hall, 1565
146. Midhurst	Market Hall, 16th C., second Market Hall, 1552
147. Rye	Court Hall, between 1529 and 1619

Warwickshire

148. Alcester	Town Hall, 1618
149. Coventry (*)	St Mary's Hall converted after Dissolution; 'Mayour's Parlour', 1574
150. Henley-in-Arden	Market Hall/Town Hall, 1596
151. Sutton Coldfield	Mooth Hall, *temp.* Henry VIII
152. Warwick	'Great Hall of St Mary' obtained after Dissolution; exchanged for Shire Hall with Earl of Leicester, 1571

Westmorland

153. Appleby (*)	Moothall, c.1596
154. Kendal	Moot Hall, 1592

Wiltshire

155. Calne	Church House/Guildhall, *temp.* Elizabeth I
156. Chippenham	'Old Yelde Hall'/Town Hall, 16th C.
157. Cricklade	Market House, 1569
158. Devizes	Guildhall, early 16th C.; Tolsey added 1563
159. Malmesbury	Guildhall, 16th C.
160. Marlborough	Town Hall/Market Hall, 1631–3 Guildhall, pre-1572
161. Salisbury (v)	Council House rebuilt 1580–4

Worcestershire

162. Bromsgrove (v)	Town Hall/Market Hall, Elizabethan
163. Droitwich	'Chequer House', 1581; Market House, 1628
164. Evesham (*)	Boothall or 'Roundhouse', 16th C.; Town Hall, c.1580

Yorkshire

165. Barnsley	Moothall by 1622
166. Beverley	Town buys house for guild-hall c.1500
167. Bradford	Hall of Pleas by 1570 Court House by 1632

168. Doncaster   Town Hall conversion 1557
169. Halifax   Court House, 1567
170. Howden   Toll Booth, 1547
171. Hull   Council House, 1633
172. Knaresborough   Court House, 1515
                        Toll Booth, 1592
173. Leeds   Moothall/Common Oven, 1598
                        Moot Hall, 1615
174. Ripon   Toll Booth, by 1599
                        New Town House, 1611
175. Rotherham   Town Hall, by 1584
                        Toll Booth, by 1627
176. Sheffield   Court House/Assembly Hall, by 1571
                        Town Hall, by 1638
177. Wakefield   Moothall, *temp.* Henry VIII
178. Whitby   Toll Booth, 1640

TOTAL TOWNS: 178   TOTAL BUILDINGS: 202

NOTES

(NB: Notes are numbered to correspond with the numbers of the towns as listed.)

1. *VCH, Bedfordshire*, iii (1923), 268; James Dugdale, *The British Traveller*, 4 vols. (1819), i. 10–11; PRO, E 317/Bedford/9 (survey of the Town), fos. 7 and 17; E 315/338, fo. 53; BL, Add. MS 36356, fo. 10A (Buckler drawing, 1835).
2. Pevsner, *BoE, Bedfordshire and the County of Huntingdon and Peterborough* (Harmondsworth, 1968), 87; DoE, Bedford Rural District, ref. 1913/11/A (1960).
3. J. H. Blundell, *Toddington, its Annals and its People* (Toddington, 1925), 179, 181, and map opp. 24.
4. *VCH, Berkshire*, iv (1924), 433; Berkshire Co. RO, MS D/EP7/83 *passim* and D/EP7/84; A. C. Baker, *Historic Abingdon* (Abingdon, 1963), 28, 46–7; Dugdale, *British Traveller*, i. 64.
5. *VCH, Berkshire*, iii (1923), 96; Berkshire RO, MS M/TI/1–26 (deeds referring to the building).
6. *VCH, Berkshire*, i (1924), 131; Berkshire RO, MS D/P 89/5/1, fo. 2ᵛ.
7. G. Astill, *Historic Towns in Berkshire, an Archeological Appraisal* (Reading, 1978), 78; Dugdale, *British Traveller*, i. 89; *VCH, Berkshire*, iii. 344–9, 355.
8. *VCH, Berkshire*, iii. 226–7; PRO, E 134/Hi1/39 Eliz., no. 4; BL, Add. MS 36356, fo. 215b (Buckler drawing); Dugdale, *British Traveller*, i. 124.
9. Robert Gibbs, *A History of Aylesbury* (Aylesbury, 1885), 402; Leland, *Itinerary*, ii. 111.
10. John Parker, *The Early History and Antiquities of Wycombe* (Wycombe, 1878), 32; *VCH, Buckinghamshire*, iii (1925), 114; R. W. Greaves (ed.), *The First Letter Book of High Wycombe* (Buckinghamshire Record Society, ii, 1956 for 1947), 129–30; Thomas Langley, *History and Antiquities of Desborough and the Deanery of Wycombe* (1797), 33.
11. Royal Commission on Historical Monuments, *Buildings of England, Bucks.* (1960), 179; *VCH, Buckinghamshire*, iii. 379.
12. *VCH, Buckinghamshire*, iv (1924), 430–1; PRO, C 93/9/21, m. 3.
13. George Lipscomb, *History and Antiquities of the County of Buckingham*, 4 vols. (1847), ii. 301; T. P. Smith, 'The Early Schoolhouse of Dartford Grammar School', *Dartford Historical and Antiquarian Society Newsletter* (1977), 19; F. W. Reader, 'Discovery of a Drawing of the Wendover Market House', *Records of Buckinghamshire*, 13 (1934), 69–76; BL, Add. MS 36356, fo. 93a (Buckler drawing).
14. Hilda Nockolds, *Linton* (Royston, 1954), 12.
15. BL, Add. MS 29780, fo. 127 and 139; BL, Harleian MS, 1944, fo. 61; George Ormerod, *The History of the County Palatine and City of Chester*, 2nd edn., 3 vols. (1852), i, pt. I, p. 234; Dugdale, *British Traveller*, i. 310.

16. Ormerod, *History of Chester*, iii, pt. II, p. 741; C. S. Davies (ed.), *A History of Macclesfield* (Manchester, 1968), frontispiece.

17. H. M. Jeffery, 'The Early Topography of Falmouth', *Journal of the Royal Institute of Cornwall*, 9 (1886–7), 157.

18. C. G. Henderson, *Essays in Cornish History* (Oxford, 1935), 35.

19. H. S. Toy, *The History of Helston* (1936), 166; C. S. Gilbert, *An Historical and Topographical Survey of the County of Cornwall*, 2 vols. (Plymouth, 1819–20), ii. 766.

20. R. J. Roddis, *Penryn, the History of an Ancient Cornish Borough* (Truro, 1964), 30, 98–9; DoE, 'List of Buildings, Borough of Penryn' (1971), unpag.

21. Joseph Polsue, *A Complete Parochial History of the County of Cornwall*, 4 vols. (Truro, 1867–72), 236; P. A. S. Pool, *A History of the Town and Parish of Penzance* (Penzance, 1974), 30–2, 135, 220–3.

22. Gilbert, *Survey of Cornwall*, ii. 501, 817, 786.

23. Ibid. ii. 923; Charter of 16 Eliz., Cornwall RO, MS B/W Looe/21, 16 Eliz, p. 6.

24. DoE list of Buildings, 'District of Allerdale' (1971), 7.

25. William Stevenson, 'The Old Court House at Alfreton', *Journal of the Derbyshire Archaeological and Natural History Society*, 38 (1916), 127–30.

26. Pevsner, *BoE, Derbyshire*, 2nd edn. (1978), 75; Revd Daniel and Samuel Lysons, *Magna Brittania*, 9 vols. (1813–22), v. 23–9.

27. P. Riden and J. Blair (eds.), *History of Chesterfield*, v (Chesterfield, 1980), 246–7; D. F. Botham, 'A History of the Chesterfield Marketplace' (thesis presented to the Royal Institute of British Architects, 1974), 13.

28. Dugdale, *British Traveller*, ii. 105.

29. James Davidson, 'Collections for Axminster and District' (unpublished MS of *c.*1830), pp. 368, 379, 998; Devon Co. RO, MS 123M/E34.

30. C. Wills, *A Short Historical Sketch of the Town of Barnstaple* (Barnstaple, 1855), 13–4, 21; B. W. Oliver, 'The Long Bridge at Barnstaple', *Transactions of the Devonshire Association*, 78 (1946), 191.

31. J. Watkins, *An Essay Towards the History of Bideford* (Exeter, 1792), 26.

32. *Calendar of Patent Rolls*, Edward VI, i. 44; Devon Co. RO, MS 252B/APF/75.

33. H. Lloyd Parry, *The History of the Exeter Guildhall and the Life Within* (Exeter, 1936), ch. 2.

34. Edwin Welch (ed.), *Plymouth Building Accounts of the Sixteenth and Seventeenth Centuries* (Devon and Cornwall Record Society, NS. 12, 1967).

35. W. Harding, *A History of Tiverton*, 2 vols. (Tiverton, 1845–7), i. 147; Devon Co. RO, MS R4/1/C/93, nos. 1 and 2.

36. Devon Co. RO, MS 1579/1/5 (charter), 1579/1/10, 1579A/7/106a; DoE, 'List of Buildings, District of S. Hams, Devon' (1978), 43–4.

37. *The History and Antiquities of the County of Dorset*, 3rd edn., corrected by John Hutchins, W. Shipp, and J. W. Hodson, 4 vols. (1861–73), ii. 118, 274.

38. Dorset Co. RO, Blandford Forum Chamberlains' Accounts, 1564–1750', B5 fo. 1.

39. Dorset RO, MS B3/M15, unpag.

40. Dorset RO, MS B7/G1/4a, fo. 27.
41. Poole Borough Archives MS 108(63), fo. 100; H. P. Smith, *The History of the Borough and County of the Town of Poole*, 2 vols. (Poole, 1949–51), ii. 95; Dugdale, *British Traveller*, ii. 240.
42. C. H. Mayo, 'Shaftesbury', *Proceedings of the Dorset Natural History and Antiquarian Field Club*, 15 (1894), 47; BL, Add. MS 36361, fo. 165 (Buckler drawing); PRO, E 134/James I/H.22.
43. Dorset Co. RO, MS P5/MA3, fo. 8ᵛ; Hutchins, *History of Dorset*, i. 109.
44. 'Letter Book of Robert Gregory', Harvard University Widener Library, MS fMs/Eng./757, fos. 1–2; V. L. Oliver, 'Tudor Building in Weymouth', *Proceedings of the Dorset Natural History and Antiquarian Society*, 62 (1941 for 1940), 61; Hutchins, *History of Dorset*, ii. 454, 725; Weymouth Town Museum, Minute Book 'C' (1617–1700), pp. 1, 3, 23, 74, 80, 84.
45. *VCH, Durham*, iii (1928), 34; Dugdale, *British Traveller*, ii. 299.
46. Cuthbert Sharpe, *A History of Hartlepool* (Hartlepool, 1851), 105; Robert Surtees, *History and Antiquities of the County Palatine of Durham* 4 vols. (1816–40), iii. 105.
47. A. W. Clapham, 'The Court House or "Old Town Hall" at Barking', *Transactions of the Essex Archaeological Society*, NS 12 (1913), 295–8; G. Biddell, 'The Court House, Barking', ibid. NS 16 (1923), 133–6; *VCH, Essex*, v (1966), 217–18, 235.
48. Essex Co. RO, MS D/B1/2; Royal Commission on Historical Monuments, *Inventory of the Historic Monuments of Essex*, i (1916), 122; DoE, 'Survey of Dunmow Local District' (1952), 24.
49. Royal Commission, *Inventory of Essex*, 76; J. R. Armstrong, *Traditional Buildings Accessible to the Public* (Wakefield, 1979), 116.
50. W. J. Petchey, 'The Borough of Maldon, Essex, 1500–1688' (Univ. of Leicester Ph.D. thesis 1972), 6; DoE, 'List of Buildings, the Borough of Maldon' (1971), 23.
51. Wendy Walker, *Essex Markets and Fairs* (Chelmsford, 1981), 11–12.
52. Elizabeth Ralph (ed.) *Guide to the Bristol Archives Office* (Bristol, 1971), p. ix.
53. F. J. Fox, 'On the Gilds of Sodbury and Dyrham', *Transactions of the Bristol and Gloucestershire Archaeological Society*, 13 (1888–9), 8; Gloucestershire RO, MS D 2071/E11 and D 2071/L8.
54. Anon., *The History and Antiquities of the Town of Cirencester* (n. p. 1863), 65; BL, Add. MS 36362, fo. 176.
55. M. D. Lobel (ed.), *Historic Towns, Maps and Plans of Towns and Cities in the British Isles* (Baltimore, n.d.), i. 13.
56. Revd Charles Swynnerton, 'Stanley St. Leonards', *Transactions of the Bristol and Gloucestershire Archaeological Society* 44 (1922), 256–7.
57. Nikolaus Pevsner and David Verey, *BoE, Gloucestershire*, 2 vols., ii (Harmondsworth, 1970), 304; Joan Johnson, *Tudor Gloucestershire* (Gloucester, 1985), 90.
58. *VCH, Gloucestershire*, xi (1976), 59, 60 79; F. A. Hyett, *Glimpses of the History of Painswick* (Gloucester, 1928) 77.
59. Paul Hawkins Fisher, *Notes and Recollections of Stroud, Gloucestershire* [1871, 1891] (1989) 60–4; Pevsner and Verey, *BoE, Gloucestershire* i, 431.

60. Gloucestershire, Co. RO MS TBR/AI/I, fo. 11, 12R^V. 14^v, 16^{r-v}; *VCH, Gloucestershire*, viii (1968), 118, 141.
61. Pevsner and Verey, *BoE, Gloucestershire*, 495–7.
62. Andover Borough Library, MS 6/mk/1.
63. R. East (ed.), *Extracts from the Records of Portsmouth* (Portsmouth, 1891), 806–7.
64. P. Berrow, B. Burbidge, and P. Genge, *The Story of Romsey* (Newbury, 1984), 284.
65. Anon., *Titchfield, a History* (Titchfield, 1982), 53; letter from Ms. Marjorie Hallam, Hon. Librarian, Weald and Downland Open Air Museum.
66. Hereford Co. RO, MS GH 1/51–61; Norman Drinkwater, 'The Old Market Hall, Hereford', *Transactions of the Woolhope Naturalists' Field Club*, 33 (1949), 1–13; John Duncomb, *Collections towards the History and Antiquities of the County of Hereford*, 3 vols. (Hereford, 1804–66), i. 416; John Clayton, *A Collection of the Ancient Timbered Edifices of England* (1846), unpag.
67. George F. Townshend, *The Town and Borough of Leominster* (Leominster, 1863), 327–9; Alec Clifton-Taylor, *The Pattern of English Building* (1972), 316.
68. *VCH, Hertfordshire*, ii (1908), 164 n. 21; BL, Add. MS 36365, fo. 12a (Buckler drawing); J. W. Cobb, *Two Lectures on the History and Antiquities of Berkhampsted [sic]* (1888), 94–5; PRO, E 315/366, fos. 3, 72, 73^v–74, and E 315/365 *passim*.
69. BL, Harleian MS 427, fols. 97–106, especially fo. 98; Susan Yaxley (ed.), *History of Hemel Hempstead* (Hemel Hempstead, 1973), 173.
70. Hertfordshire Co. RO, Hertford Bor. Records, vol. 33, no 4; *VCH, Hertfordshire*, iii (1912), 490, 494, 500; BL, Add. MS 32350, fols. 24^v–25 (map) and 43.
71. St Albans Bor. Records, MS 32, fos. 3, 17; *VCH, Hertfordshire*, ii (1908), 471–2, 480–1; BL, Add. MS 32351, fo. 10^r.
72. *VCH, Hunts.*, ii (1932), 287 n. 29.
73. W. R. Briscall, 'The Ashford Cage', *Archaeologia Cantiana*, 101 (1985 for 1984), 57–68.
74. S. P. H. Statham, *History of the Castle, Town and Port of Dover* (1899), 127; Kent Archives Office, Maidstone, 'Dover Corporation Record Book, 1603–1673', uncatalogued, fos. 10 and 58–90.
75. E. Jacob, *The History of the Town and Port of Faversham in Kent* (1774), 131–4; Sidney Wilson, *A Saunter Round Faversham* (Faversham, 1936), 13; Pevsner, *BoE, North East and East Kent*, 2edn. (1976), 314.
76. C. E. Woodruff, *A History of the Town and Port of Fordwich* [1895] (Canterbury, n.d.), 110–11, 113; S. E. Rigold, 'Two Types of Court Hall', *Archaeologia Cantiana*, 83 (1968), 1–22; Canterbury Cathedral Library, MS U 4/bundle 8/27.
77. Kent Archives Office, Maidstone, MS GR/AC 1, fo. 15.
78. Edward Hasted, *The History and Topographical Survey of the County of Kent*, 2nd edn., 12 vols. (1797–1801), iv. 264; BL, Add. MS 32367, fo. 128 (Buckler drawing).

79. William Boys, *Collections for the History of Sandwich in Kent*, 2 vols. [1792] (Canterbury, n.d.), 695.

80. S. E. Rigold, 'Two Types of Court Hall', 2; Sir John Dunlop, *The Pleasant Town of Sevenoaks* (Sevenoaks, 1964), 86.

81. W. S. Weeks, *Clitheroe in the Seventeenth Century* (Clitheroe, n.d.), 98, 306–7; G. H. Tupling, 'Lancashire Fairs and Markets in the Sixteenth and Seventeenth Centuries', 1, *Transactions of the Lancashire and Cheshire Antiquarian Society*, 58 (1947 for 1945–6), 25–34.

82. William Bowman, *England in Ashton-under-Lyne* (Altrincham, 1960), 294–5.

83. J. A. Twemlow (ed.), *Liverpool Town Books*, 2 vols. (Liverpool, 1918 and 1935), i. 353 n. 3.

84. *VCH, Leicestershire*, iv (1958), 361; T. H. Fosbrooke and S. H. Skillington, 'The Old Town Hall of Leicester', *Transactions of the Leicestershire Archaeological Society* 13 (1923–4), 38–9, 71–2; N. A. Pegden, *Leicester Guildhall, a Short History and Guide* (Leicester, 1981).

85. M. R. Lambert and R. Walker, *Boston, Tattershall and Croyland* (Oxford, 1930), 117–18; Bailey, *Minutes of Boston*, 3 vols. (1981–3), i. 9–11; Pishey Thompson, *The History and Antiquities of Boston* (Boston, 1856), 234–5.

86. Thomas Allen, *The History of the County of Lincoln*, 2 vols. (1834), ii. 278–9; William Marrat, *The History of Lincolnshire*, 3 vols. (Boston, 1814–16), iii. 77.

87. HMC, *Various Collections, Fourteenth Report* (1895), viii. 27; Lincoln Co. RO, 'Registers of the Accounts of the Corporation', ii. 1511–42, fo. 109b.

88. J. E. Swaby, *A History of Louth* (1951), 161; R. W. Goulding, *Louth, Old Corporation Records* (Louth, 1891), 156–8; Lincolnshire Co. RO, MS LGS B/III/1, fos., 187–9, 194, 213ᵛ, 278ᵛ.

89. Marrat, *History of Lincolnshire*, ii. 321, 325, 350.

90. S. W. Rix, 'An Account of the Guildhall at Diss', *Norfolk Archaeology* 2 (1849), 11; Francis Blomefield and C. Parkin, *An Essay Towards a Topographical History of Norfolk*, 11 vol. (1805–10), i. 33.

91. G. A. Carthew, *The Town We Live In* (Norwich, 1849), 103; DoE, 'List of Buildings, Urban District of E. Dereham' (n.d.), 31; Norfolk RO, MS PD 86/181.

92. Henry Manship, *The History of Great Yarmouth*, 2 vols. (Great Yarmouth, 1854–6), i. 176–7, 281; R. F. E. Ferrier, 'The Toll House at Great Yarmouth', *Journal of the British Archaeological Association*, NS (1925), 100–6.

93. Pevsner, *BoE, North-west and South Norfolk* (Harmondsworth, 1962), 230.

94. Pevsner, *BoE, North-east Norfolk and Norwich* (Harmondsworth, 1962), 259.

95. 'W. H. K.', *An Account of Swaffham Markets and Fairs* (Swaffham, c.1832), 8.

96. W. G. Clarke, *A Short Historical Guide to Thetford* (Thetford, 1908), 35–6.

97. Pevsner, *BoE, North-west and South Norfolk*, 396; C. J. W. Messant, 'The Market Crosses of Norfolk', *East Anglian Magazine* 2/1 (1936), 29–32; Norfolk and Norwich RO, MS Neville 12–12–66/Q173 B, *passim*.

98. Northamptonshire RO, MSS E(B) 512, fo. 1a; E(B) 523, fo. 1a; E(B) 562; E(B) 278.

99. *VCH, Northamptonshire*, iii (1930), 218–19; Northamptonshire RO, photocopy no. 1374.

100. W. Smalley, *Oundle's Storey* (Oundle, n.d.), 35.

101. W. T. Mellows (ed.), *Peterborough Local Administration, 1541–1689*, 2 vols. (Northamptonshire Record Society, 9 and 10, 1937–9), i. 146 *et passim*; ii. 193–6.

102. N. Pevsner, *BoE, Northamptonshire*, 2nd edn., rev. B. Cherry (Harmondsworth, 1973), 393; Northamptonshire RO, MS ZA 4211.

103. J. Brown, *History of Newark-on-Trent*, 2 vols. (Newark, 1904–7), i. 256–7; Newark Town Hall, Newark Corporation Minute Book, fo. 24^v.

104. *VCH, Oxfordshire*, x (1972), 24, 82; William Potts, *A History of Banbury* (Banbury, 1958), 106, 143–4, 175; Alfred Beesley, *History of Banbury* (1841), 252, 257.

105. *VCH, Oxfordshire*, vi (1959), 17; John Dunkin, *History and Antiquities of Bicester* (1816), 18.

106. R. H. Gretton, *Burford Records* (Oxford, 1920), 187; correspondence with Revd A. Moody and Mr Michael Laithwaite.

107. J. Sherwood and N. Pevsner, *BoE, Oxfordshire* (Harmondsworth, 1974), 539; PRO, STAC 8/162/7.

108. H. M. Colvin, *A History of Deddington, Oxfordshire* (1963), 6; *VCH, Oxfordshire*, xi (1983), 119; National Commission on Hist. Monuments, photo file, 1944 photo.

109. Oxfordshire RO, MS C.I. 10, fo. 2$^{r–v}$.

110. *VCH, Oxfordshire*, iv (Oxford, 1979), 331–3; H. E. Salter (ed.), *Oxford Council Acts, 1583–1626* (Oxford Historical Society, 1928), lvii, 410–11.

111. *VCH, Oxfordshire* vii (1962), 181, 166.

112. C. W. Campbell Hyslop and E. S. Cobbold, *Church Stretton*, 2 vols. (Shrewsbury, 1904), ii. 173, and plate opp. 173.

113. Much Wenlock Bor. Archives, MS B3/1/1, pp. 139–44, 450; W. F. Mumford, *Wenlock in the Middle Ages* (Shrewsbury, 1977), 99–145; Pevsner, *BoE, Shropshire* (Harmondsworth, 1958), 213.

114. Pevsner, *BoE, Shropshire*, 219.

115. Ibid. 273; Mary C. Hill, *The History of Shropshire's Many Shire Halls* (Shrewsbury, 1963), 1.

116. Bryan Little, *The Buildings of Bath, 47–1947* (1947), 54; Revd John Collinson, *History and Antiquities of the County of Somerset*, 3 vols. (Bath, 1791), i. pt. XII, pp. 6–13, 31–2; A. J. King and B. H. Wells (eds.), *The Municipal Records of Bath, 1189–1604* (n.d.), 58; E. Holland, 'The Earliest Bath Guildhall', *Bath History*, ii (1988), 163–79.

117. Revd W. Phelps (ed.), *The History and Antiquities of Somersetshire*, 2 vols. (1836), i. 228, 242.

118. Collinson, *History and Antiquities of Somerset*, ii. 56.

119. Ibid. ii. 471; Somerset RO MS DD/6/Ch, references for 1613; Pevsner, *BoE, South and West Somerset* (Harmondworth, 1958), 118–19.

120. Somerset RO, Dunster Records, Box 15, item 30; BL, Add. MS 36381, fo. 167 (Buckler drawing); Fred Crossley, *Timbered Buildings in England* (1951), 157; M. L. Turner, *Somerset* (1949), 155, 158, 206.
121. Phelps, *History and Antiquities of Somersetshire*, i. 497, 531.
122. *VCH, Somerset*, iii (1974), 27–31; PRO, E 134/42 and 43 Eliz., m. 27, deposition of Alexander Gent.
123. Collinson, *History and Antiquities of Somerset*, iii. 337.
124. *VCH, Staffordshire*, iv (1979), 201–2, plate opp. 161; William Salt Library, MS D (W) 1721/1/4 and D(W)/1744/33.
125. Charles F. Palmer, *The History of the Town and Castle of Tamworth*, (Tamworth, 1844), 483–4.
126. Francis Redfern, *History and Antiquities of Uttoxeter*, 2nd edn. (1886), 295–6, 370–1; PRO, D L 44.551; Staffordshire, Co. RO MS D3891/8/1–2, p. 56.
127. *VCH, Staffordshire*, xvii (Oxford, 1976), 187, 218; E. J. Homeshaw, *The Corporation of the Borough and Foreign of Walsall* (Walsall, 1960), 10–11; PRO, E 133/1/61.
128. N. Pevsner and E. Radcliffe, *BoE, Suffolk*, 2nd edn. (1975), 72; DoE, 'List of Special Buildings, District of Suffolk Coastal' (1974), 11; discussions with Mr Michael Gooch, restoration architect.
129. Nesta Evans, *Beccles Rediscovered* (Beccles, 1984), 5–7.
130. Margaret Statham, 'The Guildhall, Bury St Edmunds', *Proceedings of the Suffolk Institute of Archaeology*, 31 (1970), 117–57; H. J. M. Evans, 'The Town Hall and the Guildhall, Bury St Edmunds', *Archaeological Journal*, 108 (1952 for 1951), 167.
131. Pevsner and Radcliffe, *BoE, Suffolk*, 186–7.
132. W. A. B. Jones, *Hadleigh Through the Ages* (Ipswich, 1977); Revd Hugh Pigot, *Hadleigh* (Lowestoft, 1860), 19.
133. Pevsner and Radcliffe, *BoE, Suffolk*, 327; J. S. Corder, 'The Guildhall . . . Lavenham', *Proceedings of the Suffolk Institute of Archaeology*, 7 (1891) 113–8; W. H. Godfrey, 'The Lavenham Guildhall', *Archaeological Journal*, 108 (1952 for 1951), 193–4.
134. Pevsner and Radcliffe, *BoE, Suffolk*, 440.
135. Ibid. 449; J. Arnott, 'Town Hall, Woodbridge', *Proceedings of the Suffolk Institute of Archaeology*, 9 (1897), 334.
136. *VCH, Surrey*, iv (1967), 218; Ronald Bannerman, *Forgotten Croydon* (Croydon, 1933), 22.
137. *VCH, Surrey*, iii (1911), 142; J. S. Bright, *History of Dorking* (Dorking, 1884), 13.
138. *VCH, Surrey*, ii (1905), 586–9; M. O'Connell, *Historic Towns in Surrey* (Guildford, 1977), 19.
139. Enid M. Dance (ed.), *Guildford Borough Records, 1514–1546* (Surrey Record Society, 24, 1958), 42–3; M. O'Connell, *Historic Towns in Surrey*, q.v.; E. R. Chamberlain, *Guildford, a Biography* (1970), 69, 82–3, 95.
140. *VCH, Surrey*, iii, 490; Surrey RO MS KD/5/1/1, *passim*.
141. D. J. Johnson, *Southwark and the City* (Oxford, 1969), 97, 130–2, 222–3.
142. *VCH, Sussex*, vii (1940), 251.

143. P. D. Wood, 'Topography of East Grinstead', *Sussex Archaeological Collections* 106 (1968), 60.
144. E. D. Hurst, *History and Antiquities of Horsham* 2nd edn. (1889), 106.
145. *VCH, Sussex*, vii. 16.
146. Ibid. iv (1953), 74; Nikolaus Pevsner, *BoE, Sussex* (Harmondsworth, 1965), 272–3.
147. A. F. de P. Worsfield, 'The Court Hall, Rye', *Sussex Archaeological Collections*, 66 (1925), 208.
148. *VCH, Warwickshire*, iii (1945, repr. 1965), 9–10.
149. Ibid. viii (1969), 141–3.
150. William Cooper, *Henley-in-Arden, an Ancient Market Town* (Birmingham, 1946), 75.
151. *VCH, Warwickshire*, iv (1947), 234 and n. 61.
152. Ibid. ii (1908), 306 and viii, 421; Warwickshire Co. RO MS CR 1618/W4/4, item i.
153. David Lloyd, *The Making of English Towns* (1984), 69; Arthur Oswald, 'A Market Town with a Norman Plan, Appleby, Westmorland, II', *Country Life* (13 Oct 1966), 910–13.
154. DoE, HLG 42665, list no. 2 (1969), 17; Cumbria RO Kendal, MS WMB/K8/ and K9.
155. H. E. W. Marsh, *A History of the Borough and Town of Calne* (Calne, n.d.), unpag.; Wiltshire Co. RO MS G/18/1/1, fos. 71–2.
156. Arnold Platts, *The History of Chippenham, 853–1946* (1948), 23–5.
157. T. R. Thompson, *Materials for the History of Cricklade* (Cricklade, 1958–61), 76.
158. *VCH, Wiltshire*, x (1975), 277 and ii (1955), 590.
159. Bernulf Hodge, *A History of Malmesbury*, 2nd edn. (Minety, Wilts., 1969), 27; information from Dr Jane Freeman, VCH, to whom I am thankful.
160. A. R. Stedman, *Marlborough and the Upper Kennet Country* (Marlborough, 1960), 118–20; F. A. Carrington, 'The Old Market House and the Great Fire at Marlborough', *Wiltshire Archaeological and Natural History Magazine* 3 (1857), 106–14; Wiltshire Co. RO MS G 22/1/205/2, fos. 63–71.
161. Hugh Shortt (ed.), *The City of Salisbury* (Salisbury, 1957), 37–8, 58; *VCH, Wiltshire*, vi (1962), 87; Wiltshire Co. RO MS G 23/1/3, fos. 61–2.
162. W. G. Leadbetter, *The Story of Bromsgrove* (Bromsgrove, 1949), 86.
163. *VCH, Worcestershire*, iii (1913), 80–1.
164. Ibid. ii (1906), 393.
165. Grady, Thesis, 311.
166. A. F. Leach (ed.), *Beverley Town Documents* (Selden Society, 14, 1900), 63; *VCH, Yorkshire, East Riding*, vi (Oxford, 1989), 190.
167. Grady, Thesis, 317.
168. Ibid., 331.
169. Ibid., 344.
170. 'Book of Ralph Dalton', Hull University Library, Archives Dept. MS DDJ/10/110.
171. Rosemary Horrox (ed.), *Selected Rentals and Accounts of Medieval Hull, 1293–1528* (Yorkshire Archaeological Society, Record Series, 141, 1983

for 1981), 11, 124, 176, 192; Edward Gillett and Kenneth MacMahon, *A History of Hull* (Oxford, 1980), 107–8.
172. Grady, Thesis, 368.
173. Ibid., 375.
174. Ibid., 419.
175. Ibid., 428–9.
176. Ibid., 437, 456.
177. Ibid., 464.
178. *VCH, Yorkshire, North Riding*, ii (1923), 510.

Bibliography

Manuscript Sources

Andover Borough Library
  Andover Borough Records: 6/mk/1
Bedfordshire County Record Office, Bedford
  Leighton Buzzard, Lease: KK319
  Elstow, Charter, 1553: X435/1
Bedford Town Hall
  Bedford, 'Black Book of Bedford': B1
Berkshire County Record Office, Reading
  Abingdon Borough Chamberlains' Accounts, 1557–88: D/EP7/83
  Abingdon Borough Corporation Minute Book, 1557 ff.: D/EP7/84
  Newport Record: D/P 89/5/1
  Abingdon Deeds: M/T1/1–26
  Windsor 'Gild Aule Accounts', 1514–1560: W1/FAC 1
Bodleian Library, Oxford
  Rawlinson MS Manor of Barking, Accounts: A 195, Part C B 323
British Library
  Additional MSS
    Chester MS: 11335
    Indentures for Newport Buildings: 24789
    'Breviary of Chester', c. 1643–5: 29780
    Drawings for Clutterbuck's Hertfordshire: 32348-52
    Drawings for Hasted's Kent: 32353–32375
    Buckler Drawing Collection: 36356–36397
    Buckler drawings: 39378
  Harleian MSS
    1621 Survey of Hemel Hempstead: 427
    'Ecclesiastical Census' of 1563: 595
    Re: City of Chester: 1944
    Chester Annals: 2125
Canterbury Cathedral Library
  Hatch Suit Papers
Cornwall Record Office, Truro
  Liskeard Borough Archives: B/Liskeard
  W. Looe, Mayor's Summary Accounts: B/W Looe/21
Cumbria Record Office, Carlisle
  Carlisle Chamberlains' Audit Book, II, 1613–44: CA/4/2
Cumbria Record Office, Kendal
  Kendal Borough Chamberlains' Accounts: WMB/K5–22

Devon County Record Office, Exeter
  Tiverton document: R4/1/C/93
  Crediton patent: 252B/APF/75
  Totnes Borough Accounts, 1555–1641: 1579A/7/3/106a
  Totnes Borough Charter: 1579/1/5
  'Collection for Axminster and District', James Davidson, unpublished MS of
    c.1830
Dorset County Record Office, Dorchester
  Blandford Forum Chamberlains' Accounts, 1564–1750 (uncatalogued at time
    of consultation): B5
  Bridport Borough Court Book: B3/C83
  Bridport Leet Court: B3/E2
  Bridport Bailiffs' Accounts, 1558, 1578, 1610–45: B3/M2
  Bridport Accounts for Collecting and Building the Market House and School,
    1593: B3/M15
  Bridport Charter, 36 Elizabeth: B3/O3
  Lyme Regis Borough Archives: B7/G1/4a
  Wareham documents: P5/MA3
East Suffolk Record Office, Ipswich
  Aldeburgh Borough Records: EE1
  Aldeburgh Charter, 22 November 1554: EE1/B1/3
  'Order Book A', 1564: EE1/E1/1
East Sussex County Record Office, Lewes
  Rye Corporation Chamberlains' Accounts: 60/3
Essex County Record Office, Chelmsford
  Great Dunmow document: D/B1/2
  Maldon Borough Accounts: D/B3
  Thaxted documents: D/DMg M117
Gloucestershire Record Office, Gloucester
  Newent Surveys: D 2071/E11/and L/7
  Gloucester City Chamberlains' Accounts: GBR/F4
  Tewkesbury Borough Minutes, i, 1575–1624: TBR/A1/1
Harvard University, Widener Library
  'Letter Book of Robert Gregory: fMS/Eng./757
Hereford County Record Office, Hereford
  Hereford Borough Archives: GH 1
  Hereford Law Day Session, 1566 (uncatalogued)
Hertfordshire County Record Office, Hertford
  Hertford Borough Records, vols. 20 and 33
Hull University Library, Archives Department
  'Book of Ralph Dalton': DDJ/10/110
Humberside County Record Office, Beverley
  Beverley, 'Small Order Book': BC/II/4
  Hedon Town Council Minute Book: DDHE/26
Kent County Archive Office, Canterbury
  Fordwich Borough Archives: U4
Kent County Archives Office, Maidstone

Faversham Wardmote Book (Accounts): FA/FAc 9
Gravesend Corporation Minutes, 1571–1640: GR/AC 1
Dover Corporation Record Book, 1603–1673: (uncatalogued)
Leicestershire County Record Office, Leicester
  Leicester Chamberlains' Accounts: BR III/2/31
Lincoln County Record Office
  Louth documents: LGS B/III/1
  Registers of the Accounts of the Corporation [of Lincoln], II, 1511–42
Much Wenlock Borough Archives, Corn Exchange, Much Wenlock
  Much Wenlock Borough Minute Book: B3/1/1
Newark Town Hall
  Newark Corporation Minute Book
Norfolk and Norwich Record Office, Norwich
  Wymondham Town Book: Neville 12.12.66/Q173 B
  East Dereham, Decree of 1614: PD 86/181
North Devon Atheneum
  Barnstaple Records: 3972
Northamptonshire Record Office
  Ellesmere (Brackley) MSS: E(B) 512
                             E(B)523
                             E(B)562
                             E(B)278
  Kettering documents, photocopy no. 1374
Oxford County Record Office
  Henley documents: C.I. 10
Poole Borough Archives, Civic Centre, Poole, Dorset
  'Old Record Book no. 1': 23(1)
  'Old Record Book no. 3': 25(3)
  'Old Record Book, 1568–78': 'The Great Book': 26(4)
  'A Benevolence Granted by the Inhabitants', 1568: 63(18)
  'The Answer of Christopher Ffarwell': 108(63)
  Correspondence: TDW/5
Public Record Office, Chancery Lane
  Chancery
    Early Chancery Proceedings: C1
    Chancery Proceedings, series II, Elizabeth: C3
    Patent Rolls: C66
    Proceedings, Commissioners for Charitable Uses: C93
  Duchy of Lancaster
    Rentals and Surveys: DL43
    Special Commissions and Returns: DL44
  Exchequer
    Entry Book, Decrees and Orders: E123
    Baron's Depositions: E133
    Depositions by Commission: E134
    Port Books: E190
    Exchequer, Miscellaneous Books: E315

Parliamentary Surveys, Commonwealth Period: E317
Requests
  Proceedings: Req. 2
Star Chamber
  Proceedings, Henry VIII: STAC 2
  Proceedings, Edward VI: STAC 3
  Proceedings, Mary: STAC 4
  Proceedings, Elizabeth: STAC 5
  Proceedings, James I: STAC 8
State Papers
  State Papers Domestic, James I: SP 14
Shropshire Record Office, Shrewsbury
  Shrewsbury Correspondence: 3365/2621
Somerset Record Office, Taunton
  Chard Portreeve Accounts: DD/6/Ch
  Dunster Records, Box 15, item 30 (uncatalogued)
St Albans Borough Records, St Albans (Herts.) Public Library
  Mayor's Court Book, 1586–1633: 32
  Mayor's Accounts, 1609–1610: 152
Staffordshire County Record Office, Stafford
  Stafford Borough Papers: D 1323/EI
  Survey of Uttoxeter: D 3891/8/1–2
Surrey Record Office, Guildford
  Godalming, Ordinances of 1620: 2253/1/1
  Kingston Borough Minutes: KD/5/1/1
Walsall Borough Archives, Walsall Central Library
  Walsall Lease, 1589: 276/133
  Walsall Town Chest document: 277/119
  Walsall Town Chest document: 277/251
Warwickshire County Record Office
  Warwick Borough documents: CR 1618/w4/4
West Devon Record Office, Plymouth
  Plymouth Receivers' Accounts to 1570: Worth 131
  Plymouth Receivers' Accounts, 1570–1658: Worth 132
  Plymouth, 'Accounts for the Guildhall': Worth 137
West Suffolk Record Office, Bury St Edmunds
  Bury St Edmunds, Feoffees Accounts: H2/3/1.1
  Bury St Edmunds, Feoffees Minute Book: H2/6.2
Weymouth Town Museum
  Minute Book 'C' (1617–1700)
William Salt Library, Stafford
  Stafford Borough Manuscript Book, Bagot Collection: D(W) 1721/1/4, D(W) 1744/3
Wiltshire County Record Office, Trowbridge
  Calne Gild Steward's Book, 1561–1814: G 18/1/1
  Marlborough Borough Chamberlains' Accounts, 1572–1640: G 22/1/205/2
  Salisbury, Ledger Book, 1571–1640: G 23/1/3

Theses, Dissertations, and Other Unpublished Sources

ADEY, KENNETH RAYMOND, 'Aspects of the History of the Town of Stafford, 1590–1710' (Keele Univ. MA thesis 1971).

AIRS, MALCOLM, 'Some Social and Economic Aspects of Country House Building in England, 1500–1640' (Oxford Univ. D.Phil. thesis 1972).

ARMAN, M. and JAMES BOUTWOOD, 'Thaxted Guildhall, the Story of a Building in Use for Almost Six Centuries' (Essex County Council research report no. TL611, 310, n.d.).

BATTLEY, SUSAN M., 'Elite and Community, the Mayors of Sixteenth Century King's Lynn', (SUNY, Stony Brook, Ph.D. thesis 1981).

BORSAY, PETER NIGEL, 'The English Urban Renaissance: Landscape and Leisure in the Provincial Town, c.1660–1770' (Lancashire Univ. Ph.D. thesis 1981).

BOTHAM, D. F., 'A History of Chesterfield Market Place' (thesis presented to the Royal Institute of British Architects, April 1974).

BOUTWOOD, JAMES, 'Thaxted and its Guildhalls', paper read to Vernacular Architecture Group Conference, 1984.

DEAN, DAVID MALCOLM, 'Bills and Acts, 1584–1601' (Cambridge Univ. Ph.D. thesis 1985).

DE BIÈVRE, ELIZABETH, 'The Decoration of Town Halls in the United Provinces, a Study in Style and Iconography' (Courtauld Institute, London Univ. Ph.D. thesis 1986).

DEPARTMENT OF THE ENVIRONMENT (DoE), Royal Commission on the Historical Monuments of England, National Monuments Register, 'Survey of Dunmow Local District' (1952).

—— 'Bedford Rural District' (Report 1913/11/A, Jan. 1960).

—— 'Much Wenlock' (Interim Report of 16 Feb. 1970).

—— 'List of Buildings, the Borough of Maldon' (1971).

—— 'List of Buildings, Borough of Penryn' (1971).

—— 'List of Buildings, District of Allerdale' (1971).

—— 'List of Special Buildings, District of Suffolk Coastal' (1974).

—— 'List of Buildings, District of S. Hams, Devon', notes by Michael Laithwaite (1978).

—— 'List of Buildings, Urban District of E. Dereham' (n.d.).

—— National Commission on Historical Monuments, photograph file.

—— HLG 42665, list no. 2 (1969).

GRADY, KEVIN, 'The Provision of Public Buildings in the West Riding of Yorkshire, 1600–1840' (Leeds Univ. Ph.D. thesis, 1980).

HOUSEZ, JANIS C., 'The Property Market in Bury St. Edmunds, 1540–1600' (Concordia Univ. MA essay, 1988).

MacLEAN, SALLY–BETH, 'Players on Tour, New Evidence from the Records of Early English Drama', unpublished typescript (c.1988).

MANTERFIELD, JOHN BERNARD, 'The Topographical Development of the Pre-Industrial Town of Grantham, Lincolnshire, 1535–1835' (Exeter Univ. Ph.D. thesis, 1981).

McINTOSH, MARJORIE K., 'Financing Poor Relief in Tudor England' (paper delivered at North American Conference on British Studies, Toronto, October 1984).

PETCHEY, WILLIAM JOHN, 'The Borough of Maldon, Essex, 1500–1688' (Leicester Univ. Ph.D. thesis 1972).

POCKLEY, DOROTHY, 'The Origins and Early History of the Melton Mowbray Town Estate' (Leicester Univ. Ph.D. thesis 1964).

ROSEN, ADRIENNE, 'Economic and Social Aspects of the History of Winchester, 1520–1670' (Oxford Univ. D.Phil. thesis 1975).

THOMAS, DAVID L., 'The Administration of Crown Lands in Lincolnshire under Elizabeth I (London Univ. Ph.D. thesis 1979).

Published Works

Place of publication is London unless otherwise indicated.

AGNEW, JEAN-CHRISTOPHE, *Worlds Apart: The Market and the Theatre in Anglo-American Thought, 1550–1750* (Cambridge, 1986).

AGIUS, PAULINE, 'Late Sixteenth and Seventeenth Century Furniture at Oxford', *Furniture History*, 7 (1971).

AIRS, MALCOLM, *The Making of the English Country House, 1500–1640* (1975).

——*The Buildings of Britain, Tudor and Jacobean, a Guide and Gazetteer* (1982).

ALLEN, THOMAS, *The History of the County of Lincoln*, 2 vols. (1834).

AMPHLETT, J. (ed.), *A Survey of Worcestershire by Thomas Habington*, 2 vols. (Worcestershire Historical Society, 1895 and 1899).

Anon., *Dives et Pauper* (1536).

Anon., *The History and Antiquities of the Town of Cirencester* (no place of publication, 1863).

Anon., *Titchfield, a History* (Titchfield, 1982).

APPLEBY, ANDREW, 'Agrarian Capitalism or Seigneurial Reaction? the Northwest of England, 1500–1700', *American Historical Review*, 80/3 (1975), 574–94.

——*Famine in Tudor and Stuart England* (Stanford, Calif., 1978).

ARMSTRONG, J. R., *Traditional Buildings Accessible to the Public* (Wakefield, 1979).

ARNOTT, J., 'Town Hall, Woodbridge', *Proceedings of the Suffolk Institute of Archaeology*, 9 (1897).

ASHFORD, L. J., *A History of the Borough of High Wycombe from its Origins to 1880* (1960).

ASTILL, G., *Historic Towns in Berkshire, an Archaeological Appraisal*, Berks. Archaeological Committee Publication no. 2 (Reading, 1978).

ATKINSON, TOM, *Elizabethan Winchester* (1963).

BAILEY, JOHN F. (ed.), *Transcription of the Minutes of the Corporation of Boston*, 3 vols. (Boston, 1980–3).

BAILYN, BERNARD, *The New England Merchants of the Seventeenth Century* (Cambridge, Mass., 1955).

BAINES, J. M., *Historic Hastings* (Hastings, 1955).

BAIROCH, P., 'Population urbaine et taille des villes en Europe de 1600 à 1970', *Démographie urbaine, XVᵉ–XXᵉ siècle* (Lyons, 1977).

BAKER, AGNES C., *Historic Abingdon* (Abingdon, 1963).

BAKHTIN, MIKHAIL, *Rabelais and His World*, translated by Hélène Iswolsky (Cambridge, Mass., 1968).

BALLARD, A. (ed.), *British Borough Charters, 1042–1216* (Cambridge, 1913).

BALLARD, A. and J. TAIT (eds.), *British Borough Charters, 1216–1307* (Cambridge, 1923).

BANNERMAN, R., *Forgotten Croydon* (Croydon, 1933).

BARISH, JONAS, *The Antitheatrical Prejudice* (Berkeley, Calif., 1981).

BARLEY, MAURICE, *Houses and History* (1986).

BARRON, CAROLINE M., *The Medieval Guildhall of London* (1974).

BATESON, MARY (ed.), *Borough Customs*, 2 vols. (Selden Society, 1904 and 1906).

——*Records of the Borough of Leicester*, iii (Cambridge, 1905).

BAYLE, J. R., *Early History . . . of Hedon . . .* (Hull, 1895).

BEECHAM, K. J., *History of Cirencester and the Roman City Corinium* (1887).

BEER, BARRET L., *Rebellion and Riot, Popular Disorder during the Reign of Edward VI* (Kent, Ohio, 1982).

BEESLEY, ALFRED, *History of Banbury* (1841).

BEIER, A. L., 'Poor Relief in Warwickshire, 1630–1660', *P and P* 35 (1966), 77–100.

——*Masterless Men, the Vagrancy Problem in England, 1560–1640* (1985).

BELLAMY, JOHN, *Crime and Public Order in England in the Later Middle Ages* (1973).

——*Criminal Law and Society in Late Medieval and Tudor England* (Gloucester, 1984).

——*Robin Hood, an Historical Enquiry* (Bloomington, Ind. 1985).

BENHAM, GURNEY (ed.), *The Red Paper Book of Colchester* (Colchester, 1902).

BERESFORD, MAURICE, *New Towns of the Middle Ages* (1967).

BERLIN, MICHAEL, 'Civic Ceremony in Early Modern London', *Urban History Yearbook* (1986), 15–27.

BERROW, P., B. BURBIDGE, and P. GENGE, *The Story of Romsey* (Newbury, 1984).

BEVINGTON, DAVID, *Tudor Drama and Politics, a Critical Approach to Topical Meanings* (Cambridge, Mass., 1968).

BIDDELL, G., 'The Court House, Barking', *Transactions of the Essex Archaeological Society*, NS 16 (1923), 133–6.

BIDEN, W. D., *The History and Antiquities of Kingston-upon-Thames* (Kingston, 1852).

BINDOFF, S. T. (ed.), *The House of Commons, 1509–1558*, 3 vols. (1982).

BLANCHARD, IAN, 'Population Change, Enclosure and the Early Tudor Economy', *Ec. HR* 2nd ser. 23/3 (1970), 427–45.

BLOMEFIELD, FRANCIS and C. PARKIN, *An Essay Towards a Topographical History of Norfolk*, 11 vols. (1805–10).

BLUNDELL, J. H., *Toddington, its Annals and its People* (Toddington, 1925).

BORSAY, PETER N., 'The English Urban Renaissance: The Development of Provincial Urban Culture, c.1680–1760', *Social History*, 5 (1977), 581–603.

——'The Rise of the Promenade', *British Journal for Eighteenth Century Studies*, 9 (1986), 125–40.

——*The English Urban Renaissance: Culture and Society in the Provincial Town, 1660–1770* (Oxford, 1989).

BOSWORTH, J. and T. N. TOLLER, *An Anglo-Saxon Dictionary*, with supplement by T. N. Toller, 3 vols. (Oxford, 1882–1922) and *Enlarged Addenda and Corrigenda to the Supplement*, ed. Alistair Campbell (1972).

BOWMAN, WILLIAM, *England in Ashton-under-Lyne* (Altrincham, 1960).

BOYS, WILLIAM, *Collections for the History of Sandwich in Kent*, 2 vols. (Canterbury, 1792).

BOURNE, JOHN,*The History of Newcastle-upon-Tyne* (Newcastle, 1736).

BOWDEN, PETER, 'Agricultural Prices, Farm Profits and Rents', in Joan Thirsk (ed.), *The Agrarian History of England and Wales*, iv *1500–1640* (Cambridge, 1967), 593–695.

BRADBROOK, M. C., *The Rise of the Common Player, a Study of Actor and Society in Shakespeare's England* (1962).

——*John Webster, Citzen and Dramatist* (1970).

BRAUNFELS, WOLFGANG, *Urban Design in Western Architecture, Regime and Architecture, 900–1900* (Chicago, 1988).

BREWER, I. N., *A Topographical Historical Description of the County of Warwick* (1820).

BREWER, J. S., GAIRDNER, JAMES, and BRODIE, R. H. (eds.), *Letters and Papers, Foreign and Domestic, of the Reign of Henry VIII, 1509–47*, 21 vols. 1862–1910).

BRIGDEN, SUSAN, 'Religion and Social Obligation in Early Sixteenth-Century London', *P and P* 103 (1984), 67–112.

BRIGHT, J. S., *History of Dorking* (Dorking, 1844).

BRISCALL, W. R., 'The Ashford Cage', *Archaeologia Cantiana*, 101 (1985 for 1984), 57–68.

BRISTOL, MICHAEL D., *Carnival and Theatre: Plebeian Culture and the Structure of Authority in Renaissance England* (New York, 1985).

British Record Society, *Index of Wills Proved in the Prerogative Court of Canterbury, 1605–1619*, 43 and *1620–1629*, 48 (1912).

BRITNELL, R. H., 'The Proliferation of Markets in England, 1200–1349', *Ec. HR* 34/2 (1981), 209–21.

BROADBENT, R. J., *Annals of the Liverpool Stage* (Liverpool, 1908).

BROWN, J., *History of Newark-on-Trent*, 2 vols. (Newark, 1904–7).

BROWN, MARTYN C., 'Blandford in Elizabethan and Early Stuart Times', *Notes and Queries for Somerset and Dorset*, 30 (1975), 118–22.

BRUNSKILL, R. W., *Illustrated Handbook of Vernacular Architecture* (1971, 2nd edn, 1978).

——*Traditional Buildings of Britain, an Introduction to Vernacular Architecture* (1981).

BURBIDGE, F. BLISS, *Old Coventry and Lady Godiva* (Birmingham, n.d.).

BURKE, PETER, *Popular Culture in Early Modern Europe* (New York, 1978).

BUTCHER, A. F., 'The Origins of Romney Freemen, 1433–1523', *Ec. HR* 2nd ser. 27/1 (1974), 16–27.

——'Rent, Population and Economic Change in Late-Medieval Newcastle', *Northern History*, 14 (1978), 67–77.

——'Rent and the Urban Economy: Oxford and Canterbury in the Late Middle Ages', *Southern History*, 1 (1979), 11–43.

BUTLER, MARTIN, *Theatre and Crisis, 1632–1642* (Cambridge, 1984).

Calendar of Patent Rolls, Elizabeth (1939).

Calendar of Patent Rolls, Philip and Mary, 4 vols. (1936–9).

CARRINGTON, F. A., 'The Old Markethouse and the Great Fire at Marl-borough', *Wiltshire Archaeological and Natural History Magazine*, 3 (1857), 106–14.

CARTHEW, G. A., *The Town We Live In* (Norwich, 1849).

CESCINSKY, HERBERT, 'An Oak Chair at St Mary's Hall, Coventry', *Burlington Magazine*, 39/223 (1921), 170–7.

——*English Furniture from Gothic to Sheraton* (Garden City, 1937).

——and E. R. GRIBBLE, *Early English Furniture and Woodwork*, 2 vols. (1922).

CHALKLIN, CHRISTOPHER, *The Provincial Towns of Georgian England, a Study of the Building Process, 1740–1820* (1974).

——'The Financing of Church Building in the Provincial Towns of Eighteenth Century England', in Peter Clark (ed.), *The Transformation of English Provincial Towns, 1600–1800* (1984).

CHALLONER, B., *Selections from the Municipal Charters of Abingdon* (Abingdon, 1898).

CHAMBERLAIN, E. R., *Guildford, a Biography* (1970).

CHINNERY, VICTOR, *Oak Furniture, the British Tradition, a History of Early Furniture in the British Isles and New England* (1979).

CIPOLLA, CARLO, *Clocks and Culture, 1300–1700* (1967).

CLAPHAM, A. W., 'The Court House, or "Old Town Hall" at Barking', *Transactions of the Essex Archaeological Society*, NS 12 (1913), 295–8.

CLARK, PETER, 'The Migrant in Kentish Towns, 1580–1640', in Peter Clark and Paul Slack (eds.), *Crisis and Order in English Towns, 1500–1700* (1972), 117–63.

——'"The Ramoth-Gilead of the Good", Urban Change and Political Radical-ism at Gloucester, 1540–1640', in P. Clark, A. G. R. Smith, and N. Tyacke (eds.), *The English Commonwealth, 1547–1640* (Leicester, 1979), 167–88.

——*The English Alehouse, a Social History, 1200–1830* (1983).

——(ed.), *The Transformation of English Provincial Towns, 1600–1800* (1984).

——*The European Crisis of the 1590s, Essays in Comparative History* (1985).

——and SLACK, PAUL (eds.), *Crisis and Order in English Towns, 1500–1700* (1972).

—— ——*English Towns in Transition, 1500–1700* (Oxford, 1976).

CLARKE, W. G., *A Short Historical Guide to Thetford* (Thetford, 1908).

CLAYTON, JOHN, *A Collection of the Ancient Timbered Edifices of England* (1846).

CLIFTON-TAYLOR, ALEC, *The Pattern of English Building*, 2nd edn. (1972).

——*Six English Towns* (1985).

——*Six More English Towns* (1986).

CLODD, H. P., *Aldeburgh, the History of an Ancient Borough* (Ipswich, 1959).

CLOPPER, LAWRENCE M. (ed.), *REED, Chester* (Toronto, 1979).

COBB, J. W., *Two Lectures on the History and Antiquities of Berkhampsted (sic)* (1888).

COCKBURN, J. S., 'The Nature and Incidence of Crime in England, 1559–1625, a Preliminary Survey', in Cockburn (ed.), *Crime in England, 1550–1800* (1977), 49–71.

COLLINSON, Revd JOHN, *History and Antiquities of the County of Somerset*, 3 vols. (Bath, 1791).

COLLINSON, PATRICK, *The Religion of Protestants* (Oxford, 1982).

COLVIN, H. M., 'The Restoration of Abbey Dore Church in 1633–34', *Transactions of the Woolhope Naturalists' Field Club*, 32 (1984), 235–7.

——*A History of Deddington, Oxfordshire* (1963).

——*A Biographical Dictionary of British Architects, 1600–1840* (1978).

——D. R. RANSOME, and JOHN SUMMERSON (eds.), *The History of the King's Works*, 6 vols. (1963–82).

COOK, ANN J., *The Privileged Playgoers of Shakespeare's London, 1576–1642* (Princeton, NJ, 1981).

COOPER, J. W. (ed.), *Annals of Cambridge*, 5 vols. (Cambridge, 1842–1908).

COOPER, WILLIAM, *Henley-in-Arden, an Ancient Market Town and its Surroundings* (Birmingham, 1946).

CORDER, J. S., 'The Guildhall . . . Lavenham', *Proceedings of the Suffolk Institute of Archaeology*, 7 (1891), 113–18.

CORFIELD, PENELOPE, 'Economic Growth and Change in Seventeenth Century English Towns', in C. Phythian-Adams *et al.* (eds.), *The Traditional Community under Stress* (1979).

COZENS-HARDY, BASIL and KENT, E. A. (eds.), *The Mayors of Norwich, 1403–1835* (Norwich, 1938).

CRESSY, DAVID, *Literacy and the Social Order, Reading and Writing in Tudor and Stuart England* (Cambridge, 1980).

CROSS, CLAIRE, *Urban Magistrates and Ministers, Religion in Hull and Leeds from the Reformation to the Civil War* (Univ. of York, Borthwick Papers, 67, 1985).

CROSSLEY, FRED, *Timbered Buildings in England* (1957).

CUNNINGHAM, COLIN, *Victorian and Edwardian Town Halls* (1981).

DANCE, ENID M. (ed.), *Guildford Borough Records, 1514–1546* (Surrey Record Society, 24, 1958).

DAVIES, C. S. (ed.), *A History of Macclesfield* (Manchester, 1968).

DE GRAZIA, S., *Of Time, Work and Leisure* (New York, 1962).

DENNETT, J. (ed.), *Beverley Borough Records, 1575–1821*, Yorkshire Archaeological Society Record Series, 84 (1933 for 1932).

DIETZ, BRIAN, 'Overseas Trade and Metropolitan Growth', in A. L. Beier and R. Finlay (eds.), *London 1500–1700, the Making of the Metropolis* (New York, 1986), 115–40.

DOBSON, R. B., 'Urban Decline in Late Medieval England', *TRHS* 5th ser. (1977), 1–22.

DOLBEY, GEORGE W., *The Architectural Expression of Methodism* (1964).

DOUGLAS, AUDREY and GREENFIELD, PETER (eds.), *REED, Cumberland, Westmorland and Gloucestershire* (Toronto, 1986).

DRINKWATER, NORMAN, 'The Old Market Hall, Hereford', *Transactions of the Woolhope Naturalists' Field Club*, 33 (1949), 1–13.

DUGDALE, JAMES, *The British Traveller*, 4 vols. (1819).

DUNCOMB, JOHN, *Collections Towards the History and Antiquities of the County of Hereford*, 3 vols. (Hereford, 1804–66).

DUNKIN, JOHN, *History and Antiquities of Bicester* (1816).

DUNLOP, SIR JOHN, *The Pleasant Town of Sevenoaks* (Sevenoaks, 1964).

DYER, ALAN, *The City of Worcester in the Sixteenth Century* (Leicester, 1973).

——'Warwickshire Towns under the Tudors and Stuarts', *Warwickshire History*, 3/4 (1976–7), 122–34.

——'The Market Towns of Southern England, 1500–1700', *Southern History*, 1 (1979), 123–34.

——'Growth and Decay in English Towns, 1500–1700', *Urban History Year-book*, 6 (1979), 60–72.

EAMES, PENELOPE, *Furniture in England, France and the Netherlands from the Twelfth to the Fifteenth Century* (1977).

EAST, R. (ed.), *Extracts from the Records of Portsmouth* (Portsmouth, 1891).

ELTON, G. R., *The Tudor Revolution in Government: Administrative Change in the Reign of Henry VIII* (Cambridge, 1953).

——*Policy and Police, the Enforcement of the Reformation in the Age of Thomas Cromwell* (Cambridge, 1972).

EUSTACE, G. W., *Arundel: Borough and Castle* (1922).

EVANS, H. J. M., 'The Town Hall and the Guildhall, Bury St Edmunds', *Archeological Journal*, 108 (1952 for 1951).

EVANS, JOHN T., *Seventeenth Century Norwich: Politics, Religion and Government, 1620–1690* (Oxford, 1979).

EVANS, NESTA, *Beccles Rediscovered* (Beccles, 1984).

EVANS, ROBIN, *The Fabrication of Virtue, English Prison Architecture, 1750–1840* (Cambridge, 1982).

EVERITT, ALAN, 'The Marketing of Agricultural Produce', in Joan Thirsk (ed.), *The Agrarian History of England and Wales*, iv *1500–1640* (Cambridge, 1967), 466–589.

——*Change in the Provinces, the Seventeenth Century* (Leicester, 1972).

FASTNEDGE, RALPH, *Furniture Styles, 1500–1830* (1955, repr. 1969).

FERGUSON, R. S. (ed.), *A Boke off Recorde . . . Concerning the Corporation . . . of Kirkbiekendall . . . 1575* (Kendal, 1982).

FERRIER, R. F. E., 'The Toll House at Great Yarmouth', *Journal of the British Archaeological Association*, NS (1925), 100–6.

FIRTH, RAYMOND, *Symbols Public and Private* (Ithaca, NY, 1973).

FISHER, PAUL HAWKINS, *Notes and Recollections of Stroud, Gloucestershire* (Stroud, 1871 and 1891, repr. London, 1989).

FLETCHER, ANTHONY, *A County Community in Peace and War: Sussex, 1600–1660* (1975).

——'Honour, Reputation and Local Office-holding in Elizabethan and Stuart England', in A. Fletcher and J. Stevenson (eds.), *Order and Disorder in Early Modern England* (Cambridge, 1985), 92–115.

FOSBROOKE, T. H. and S. H. SKILLINGTON, 'The Old Town Hall of Leicester', *Transactions of the Leicestershire Archaeological Society*, 13 (1923–4), 1–72.

FOUCAULT, MICHEL, *Discipline and Punish, the Birth of the Modern Prison*, trans. Alan Sheridan (New York, 1977).

FOX, F. J., 'On the Gilds of Sodbury and Dyrham', *Transactions of the Bristol and Gloucestershire Archaeological Society*, 13 (1888–9).

FREMANTLE, KATHERINE, *The Baroque Town Hall of Amsterdam* (Utrecht, 1959).

GALLOWAY, DAVID (ed.), *REED, Norwich, 1540–1642* (Toronto, 1984).

GARROW, DAVID WILLIAM, *The History and Antiquities of Croydon* (Croydon, 1818).

GEERTZ, CLIFFORD, *The Interpretation of Cultures* (New York, 1973).

——'Centers, Kings and Charisma: Reflections on the Symbolics of Power', in Joseph Ben-David and Terry Nichols Clark (eds.), *Culture and its Creators, Essays in Honour of Edward Shils* (Chicago, 1977), 150–71.

GEOFFREY OF MONMOUTH, *Historia Regum Britanniae*, ed. Acton Griscom (New York, 1929).

GIBBS, ROBERT, *A History of Aylesbury* (Aylesbury, 1885).

GIEDION, SIGFRIED, *Space, Time and Architecture, the Growth of a New Tradition*, 5th edn. (Cambridge, Mass., 1967).

GILBERT, C. S., *An Historical and Topographical Survey of the County of Cornwall*, 2 vols. (Plymouth, 1819–20).

GILL, CRISPIN, *Plymouth, a New History: Ice Age to the Elizabethans*, 2 vols. (Newton Abbot, 1966).

GILLETT, EDWARD and KENNETH MACMAHON, *A History of Hull* (Oxford, 1981).

GIROUARD, MARK, 'Elizabethan Architecture and the Gothic Tradition', *Architectural History*, 6 (1963), 23–40.

——*Life in the English Country House* (New York, 1978; Harmondsworth, 1980).

——*Robert Smythson and the Elizabethan Country House* (New Haven, Conn., 1983).

——*Cities and People, a Social and Architectural History* (1985).

GLOAG, JOHN, *The Englishman's Chair: Origins, Design and Social History of Seat Furniture in England* (1964).

——*The Architectural Interpretation of History* (New York, 1975).

GODBER, JOYCE, *History of Bedfordshire, 1066–1888* (Bedford, 1969).

——and T. W. BAGSHAW, *Elstow Moot Hall* (Bedford, 1981).

GODFREY, W. H., 'The Lavenham Guildhall', *Archeological Journal*, 108 (1952 for 1951).

GOLDTHWAITE, RICHARD A., *The Buildings of Renaissance Florence, an Economic and Social History* (Baltimore, 1980).

GOTTFRIED, ROBERT S., *Bury St. Edmunds and the Urban Crisis 1290–1539* (Princeton, NJ, 1982).

GOULDING, R. W., *Louth, Old Corporation Records* (Louth, 1891).

GRADY, KEVIN, 'The Records of the Charity Commissioners, a Source for Urban History', *Urban History Yearbook* (1982).

GREAVES, R. W. (ed.), *The First Letter Book of High Wycombe* (Buckinghamshire Record Society, ii, 1956 for 1947).

GREEN, THOMAS ANDREW, *Verdict According to Conscience, Perspectives on the English Criminal Trial Jury, 1200–1800* (Chicago, 1985).

GRETTON, R. H., *Burford Records* (Oxford, 1920).

GUEST, Lady CHARLOTTE (ed.), *The Mabinogion* (1906).

GUILDING, J. M., *Reading Records*, 4 vols. (Reading, 1892 ff.).

GURR, ANDREW, 'The Elizabethan Stage and Acting', in Boris Ford (ed.), *The Age of Shakespeare*, ii, 2nd edn. (1982).

HABAKKUK, H. J., 'The Market for Monastic Property, 1539–1603', *Ec. HR*, 2nd ser. 10/3 (1958), 362–80.

HAMMER, CARL I., Jr., 'Anatomy of Oligarchy: the Oxford Town Council in the Fifteenth and Sixteenth Centuries', *Journal of British Studies*, 18/1 (1978), 1–27.

HANAWALT, BARBARA, 'Keeper of the Lights: Late Medieval English Parish Gilds', *Journal of Medieval and Renaissance Studies*, 14/1 (1984), 21–38.

HARBAGE, ALFRED, *Shakespeare's Audience* (New York, 1941).

HARDING, CHRISTOPHER, BILL HINES, RICHARD IRELAND, and PHILIP RAWLINGS, *Imprisonment in England and Wales, a Concise History* (1985).

HARDING, W., *A History of Tiverton*, 2 vols. (Tiverton, 1845–7).

HARDY, W. J., 'Remarks on the History of Seat Reservation in Churches', *Archaeologia*, 53 (1892), 95–106.

HARRIS, R. (ed.), *Weald and Downland Open Air Museum Guidebook* (Worthing, 1982).

HARTOPP, HENRY (ed.), *The Roll of the Mayors of the Borough of Leicester* [1935] (Leicester, n.d.).

HARTLAND, EDWIN S., *The Science of Fairy Tales* (1891).

HASLER, P. W. (ed.), *The House of Commons, 1558–1603*, 3 vols. (History of Parliament Trust, 1981).

HASTED, EDWARD, *The History and Topographical Survey of the County of Kent*, 2nd edn., 12 vols. (1797–1801).

HATCHER, JOHN, *Plague, Population and the English Economy, 1348–1530* (1977).

HEALES, ALFRED, *History and Law of Church Seats*, 2 vols. (1872).

HEARNSHAW, F. J. C. and D. M. (eds.), *Court Leet Records, 1603–1624* (Southampton Record Society, vol. i in 3 parts, 1905–7).

HEDGES, J. K., *History of Wallingford*, 2 vols. (1881).

HEINEMANN, MARGOT, *Puritanism and Theatre, Thomas Middleton and Opposition Drama under the Early Stuarts* (Cambridge, 1980).

HENDERSON, C. G., *Essays in Cornish History* (Oxford, 1935).

HENDERSON, EDITH G., *Foundations of English Administrative Law, Certiorari and Mandamus in the Sixteenth Century* (Cambridge, Mass., 1963).

HERRUP, CYNTHIA, *The Common Peace, Participation and the Criminal Law in Seventeenth Century England* (Cambridge, 1987).

HILL, CHRISTOPHER, 'William Perkins and the Poor', in *Puritanism and Revolution* (1958), 215–38.

——*The Century of Revolution, 1603–1714* (1961).

——*Society and Puritanism in Pre-Revolutionary England* (1964)

HILL, FRANCIS, *Tudor and Stuart Lincoln* (Cambridge, 1956).

——*A Short History of Lincoln* (Lincoln, 1979).

HILL, MARY C., *The History of Shropshire's Many Shire Halls* (Shrewsbury, 1963).

HILTON, R. H., 'Some Problems of Urban Real Property in the Middle Ages', in C. H. Feinstein (ed.), *Socialism, Capitalism and Economic Growth* (Cambridge, 1967), 326–37.

——'Rent and Capital Formation in Feudal Society', in *The English Peasantry in the Later Middle Ages* (Oxford, 1975), 174–215.

——'The Small Town and Urbanization: Evesham in the Middle Ages', *Midland History*, 7 (1982), 1–8.

HMC, *Sixth Report* (1877).

HMC 13, *Tenth Report* (1884).

HMC, *Various Collections, Fourteenth Report* (1895).

HMC, *Fifteenth Report* (1899).

HMC 55, *Various Collections* i (1901).

HITCHCOCK, HENRY-RUSSELL, *German Renaissance Architecture* (Princeton, NJ, 1981).

HODGE, BERNULF, *A History of Malmesbury*, 2nd edn. (Minety, Wilts., 1969).

HODGETT, G. A. J., 'The Dissolution of the Religious Houses in Lincolnshire', *Lincolnshire Architectural and Archaeological Society*, 4 (1951), 83–99.

HOHENBURG, PAUL M. and LYNN HOLLEN LEES, *The Making of Urban Europe, 1000–1950* (Cambridge, Mass., 1985).

HOLLAND, E., 'The Earliest Bath Guildhall', *Bath History*, ii (1988), 163–79.

HOMESHAW, E. J., *The Corporation of the Borough and Foreign of Walsall* (Walsall, 1960).

HORROX, ROSEMARY (ed.), *Selected Rentals and Accounts of Medieval Hull, 1293–1528* (Yorkshire Archaeological Society Record Series, 141, 1983 for 1981).

HOSKINS, W. G., 'The Rebuilding of Rural England, 1570–1640', *P and P* 4 (1953), 44–59.

——'English Provincial Towns in the Early Sixteenth Century', *TRHS* 5th ser. 6 (1956), 1–19.

——*The Midland Peasant* (1957).

——*Provincial England, Essays in Social and Economic History* (1963).

——*English Landscapes* (1973).

——*The Age of Plunder, the England of Henry VIII, 1500–1547* (1976).

——*The Making of the English Landscape* (1967, 2nd edn., 1989).

HOWARD, MAURICE, *The Early Tudor Country House, Architecture and Politics, 1490–1550* (1987).

HUGHES, PHILIP and LARKIN, F. J. (eds.), *Tudor Royal Proclamations*, 3 vols. (1964–9).

—— ——*Stuart Royal Proclamations*, i: *Proclamations of King James I, 1603–1625* (Oxford, 1973).

HUNT, WILLIAM, *The Puritan Moment: The Coming of Revolution in an English County* (Cambridge, Mass., 1983).

HURST, E. D., *History and Antiquities of Horsham*, 2nd edn. (1889).

HUTCHINS, JOHN, *The History and Antiquities of the County of Dorset*, 3rd edn., corrected by William Shipp and J. W. Hodson, 4 vols. (1861–73).

HYETT, F. A., *Glimpses of the History of Painswick* (Gloucester, 1928).

HYSLOP, C. W. CAMPBELL and E. S. COBBOLD, *Church Stretton*, 2 vols. (Shrewsbury, 1904).

IGNATIEFF, MICHAEL, *A Just Measure of Pain: the Penitentiary in the Industrial Revolution, 1750–1850* (1978).

INGRAM, MARTIN, 'The Reform of Popular Culture? Sex and Marriage in Early Modern England', in Barry Reay (ed.), *Popular Culture in Seventeenth Century England* (1985).

INGRAM, R. W. (ed.), *REED, Coventry* (Toronto, 1981).

JACOB, E., *The History of the Town and Port of Faversham in Kent* (1774).

JAMES, MERVYN E., 'The Concept of Order and the Northern Rising of 1569', *P and P* 60 (1973), 49–83.

——*Family, Lineage and Civil Society, a Study of Society, Politics and Mentality in the Durham Region, 1500–1640* (Oxford, 1974).

——'Ritual, Drama and Social Body in the Late Medieval English Town', *P and P* 98 (1983), 3–29.

——*Society, Politics and Culture, Studies in Early Modern England* (Cambridge, 1986).

JEFFERY, H. M., 'The Early Topography of Falmouth', *Journal of the Royal Institute of Cornwall*, 9 (1886–7).

JEWITT, LLEWELLYN and W. H. ST JOHN HOPE, *The Corporate Plate and Insignia of Office of the Cities and Towns of England and Wales*, 2 vols. (1895).

JOHNSON, D. J., *Southwark and the City* (Oxford, 1969).

JOHNSON, JOAN, *Tudor Gloucestershire* (Gloucester, 1985).

JOHNSTON, ALEXANDRA F. and MARGARET ROGERSON, *REED, York*, 2 vols. (Toronto, 1979).

JOHNSTON, D. M., *A Schedule of Antiquities of the County of Surrey* (Guildford, 1913).

JONES, E. L., STEPHEN PORTER, and MICHAEL TURNER, *A Gazetteer of English Urban Fire Disasters, 1500–1900*, Historical Geography Research Series, 13 (1984).

JONES, GARETH, *History of the Law of Charity, 1532–1827* (Cambridge, 1969).

JONES, W. A. B., *Hadleigh Through the Ages* (Ipswich, 1977).

JORDAN, W. K., *Philanthropy in England, 1480–1660, a Study of the Changing Pattern of English Social Aspirations* (1959).

——*The Charities of Rural England, 1480–1660, the Aspirations and Achievements of the Rural Society* (1961).

Journals of the House of Commons (1803 ff.)

KENT, JOAN, *The English Village Constable, 1580–1642, a Social and Administrative Study* (Oxford, 1986).

KERRIDGE, ERIC, 'The Movement of Rent, 1540–1640', *Ec. HR* 2nd ser. 6 (1953–4), 16–34.

KING, A. J. and WATTS, B. H. (eds.), *The Municipal Records of Bath, 1189–1604* (n.d.).

KITCHING, CHRISTOPHER, 'The Disposal of Monastic and Chantry Lands' in Felicity Heal and Rosemary O'Day (eds.), *Church and Society in England: Henry VIII to James I* (1977), 119–36.

KNAPPEN, M. M., *Tudor Puritanism, a Chapter in the History of Idealism* (Chicago, 1939).

KNIGHT, L. C., *Drama and Society in the Age of Jonson* (1937).

KNOOP, DOUGLAS and G. P. JONES, *The Medieval Mason, An Economic History of English Stone Building in the Later Middle Ages and Early Modern Times*, 3rd edn. (Manchester, 1967).

KOLVE, V. A., *The Play Called Corpus Christi* (Stanford, Calif., 1966).

KROEBER, A. L. and CLYDE KLUCKHOHN, *Culture* (Cambridge, Mass., 1952).

KUERDEN, R., *A Brief Description of the Borough and Town of Preston, originally composed between 1682 and 1686*, ed. John Taylor (Preston, 1818).

KURATH, H., KUHN, S. M., and REIDY, J. (eds.), *The Middle English Dictionary* (Ann Arbor, 1950–   ).

LAKE, PETER, *Moderate Puritans and the Elizabethan Church* (Cambridge, 1982).

LAMBERT, M. R. and R. WALKER, *Boston, Tattershall and Croyland* (Oxford, 1930).

LANCASTER, JOAN and E. H. R. DAVIDSON, *Godiva of Coventry* (Coventry, 1967).

LANDES, DAVID S., *Revolution in Time, Clocks and the Making of the Modern World* (Cambridge, Mass., 1983).

LANGLEY, THOMAS, *History and Antiquities of Desborough and the Deanery of Wycombe* (1797).

LEACH, A. F. (ed.), *Beverley Town Documents*, Selden Society, 14 (1900).

LEADBETTER, WILLIAM G., *The Story of Bromsgrove* (Bromsgrove, 1949).

LEGOFF, JACQUES, 'Au Moyen Age: Temps de l'église au temps du marchand', *Annales, SEC*, 15/3 (1960), 417–33.

——'Le temps du travail dans la "crise du xive s.": du temps médiéval au temps moderne', *Le Moyen Age*, 69 (1963), 597–615.

LEHMBERG, STANFORD E., *The Reformation of Cathedrals, Cathedrals in English Society, 1485–1603* (Princeton, NJ, 1988).

LEIGHTON, Revd W. A., 'Early Chronicles of Shrewsbury, 1372–1603', *Transactions of the Shropshire Archaeological and Natural History Society*, 3 (1880), 239–352.

LIPSCOMB, GEORGE, *History and Antiquities of the County of Buckingham*, 4 vols. (1847).

LITTLE, BRYAN, *The Buildings of Bath, 47–1947* (1947).

LLOYD, D., *The Making of English Towns* (1984).

LLOYD PARRY, H., *The History of the Exeter Guildhall and the Life Within* (Exeter, 1936).

LOADES, DAVID M., 'The Theory and Practice of Censorship in Sixteenth Century England', *TRHS* 5th ser. 24 (1974), 141–57.

LOBEL, M. D. (ed.), *Historic Towns, Maps and Plans of Towns and Cities in the British Isles, with Historical Commentaries from Earliest Times to 1800* (Baltimore, n.d.).

LOPEZ, ROBERT S., 'Hard Times and Investment in Culture', in *The Renaissance, a Symposium* (Metropolitan Museum of Art, New York, 1953), 19–34.

——'The Crossroads within the Wall', in Oscar Handlin and John Burchard (eds.), *The Historian and the City* (Cambridge, Mass., 1963), 27–43.

LYSONS, Revd DANIEL and SAMUEL, *Magna Britannia*, 9 vols. (1813–22).

MACCAFFREY, WALLACE, *Exeter, 1540–1640, the Growth of an English County Town* (Cambridge, Mass., 1958; 2nd edn. 1975).

MACHIN, R., 'The Great Rebuilding: A Reassessment', *P and P* 77 (1977), 33–56.

MAITLAND, F. W., 'Trust and Corporation', in H. A. L. Fisher (ed.), *The Collected Papers of F. W. Maitland*, 3 vols. (Cambridge, 1911).

MANNING, ROGER B., *Village Revolts, Social Protest and Popular Disturbances in England, 1509–1640* (Oxford, 1988).

MANSHIP, HENRY, *The History of Great Yarmouth*, 2 vols. (Great Yarmouth, 1854–6).

MARCUS, LEAH S., *The Politics of Mirth, Jonson, Herrick, Milton, Marvell and the Defense of Old Holiday Pastimes* (Chicago, 1986).

MARKHAM, C. A. and COX, Revd J. CHARLES (eds.), *The Records of the Borough of Northampton*, 2 vols. (Northampton, 1898).

MARKUS, T. A. (ed.), *Order in Space and Society, Architectural Form and its Context in the Scottish Enlightenment* (Edinburgh, 1982).

MARRAT, WILLIAM, *The History of Lincolnshire*, 3 vols. (Boston, 1814–16).

MARSH, H. E. W., *A History of the Borough and Town of Calne* (Calne, n.d.).

MARTIN, J. M., 'A Warwickshire Market Town in Adversity, Stratford-upon-Avon in the Sixteenth and Seventeenth Centuries', *Midland History*, 7 (1982), 26–41.

MARTIN-JAMES, Revd S., *Wymondham and its Abbey*, 7th edn. (Wymondham, 1953).

MATTHEWS, J. H., *A History of the Parishes of St. Ives, Lelant, Towednack and Zennor in the County of Cornwall* (1892).

MAY, G., *A Descriptive History of the Town of Evesham* (Evesham, 1845).

MAYO, C. H., 'Shaftesbury', *Proceedings of the Dorset Natural History and Antiquarian Field Club*, 15 (1894).

MCINTOSH, MARJORIE K., 'Local Change and Community Control in England, 1465–1500', *Huntington Library Quarterly*, 49/3 (1986), 219–42.

MELLOWS, W. T. (ed.), *Peterborough Local Administration, Parochial Government from the Reformation to the Revolution, 1541–1689*, 2 vols. (Northamptonshire Record Society, 9 and 10, 1937–9).

MERSON, A. L. (ed.), *The Third Book of Remembrance of Southampton, 1514–1602* (Southampton Records Series, 3 vols., 1952–9).

MESSANT, C. J. W., 'The Market Crosses of Norfolk', *East Anglian Magazine*, 2/1 (1936).

MORAN, GERALD, 'Conception of Time in Early Modern France: An Approach to the History of Collective Mentalities', *Sixteenth Century Journal*, 12/4 (1981), 3–19.

MOULE, H. J., *Descriptive Catalogue of Charters, Minute Books and Other Documents of the Borough of Weymouth and Melcombe Regis*, A.D. *1252 to 1800* (Weymouth, 1883).

MUIR, EDWARD, *Civic Ritual in Renaissance Venice* (Princeton, NJ, 1981).

MUMFORD, W. F., *Wenlock in the Middle Ages* (Shrewsbury, 1977).

NEALE, J. E., 'November 17th', in *Essays in Elizabethan History* (1958), 9–20.

NELSON, ALAN H., *The Medieval English Stage, Corpus Christi Pageants and Plays* (Chicago, 1974).

——*REED, Cambridge*, 2 vols. (Toronto, 1989).

NEWMAN, JOHN, *The Buildings of England, North East and East Kent* (Harmondsworth, 1969).

NOCKOLDS, HILDA, *Linton* (Royston, 1954).

O'CONNELL, M., *Historic Towns in Surrey* (Guildford, 1977).

O'DONOGHUE, EDWARD GEOFFREY, *Bridewell Hospital, Palace, Prison, Schools*, 2 vols. (1923–9).

OLIVER, B. W., 'The Long Bridge at Barnstaple', *Transactions of the Devonshire Association*, 78 (1946).

OLIVER, V. L., 'Tudor Building in Weymouth', *Proceedings of the Dorset Natural History and Antiquarian Society*, 62 (1941 for 1940).

OLSEN, DONALD, J., 'The City as a Work of Art', in Derek Fraser and Anthony Sutcliffe (eds.), *The Pursuit of Urban History* (1983), 264–85.

—— *The City as a Work of Art, London, Paris, Vienna* (New Haven, Conn., 1986).

ORMEROD, GEORGE, *The History of the County Palatine and City of Chester*, 2nd edn., 3 vols. (1852).

OSWALD, A., 'A Market Town with a Norman Plan, Appleby, Westmorland, II', *Country Life* (13 October 1966), 910–13.

OUTHWAITE, R. B., *Inflation in Tudor and Early Stuart England* (1969).

—— 'Who Bought Crown Lands? The Pattern of Purchases, 1589–1603', *BIHR* 44 (1971), 18–33.

PALLISER, D. M., *Tudor York* (Oxford, 1979).

—— 'Civic Mentality and the Environment in Tudor York', *Northern History*, 18 (1982), 78–115.

—— *The Age of Elizabeth, England under the Later Tudors, 1547–1603* (1983).

—— 'A Regional Capital as Magnet: Immigrants to York, 1477–1566', *Yorkshire Archaeological Journal*, 57 (1985), 111–23.

PALMER, CHARLES F., *The History of the Town and Castle of Tamworth* (Tamworth, 1844).

PARKER, JOHN, *The Early History and Antiquities of Wycombe* (Wycombe, 1878).

PARKER, VANESSA, *The Making of King's Lynn: Secular Buildings from the eleventh to the seventeenth century* (1971).

PATTEN, J., 'Rural–Urban Migration in Pre-Industrial England' (Univ. of Oxford, School of Geography, research paper no. 6, 1973).

PATTEN, JOHN, *English Towns, 1500–1700* (1978).

PATTERSON, ANNABEL, *Censorship and Interpretation, Conditions of Writing and Reading in Early Modern England* (Madison, Wis. 1984).

PEARL, VALERIE, 'Puritans and Poor Relief: the London Workhouse, 1649–1660', in D. Pennington and K. Thomas (eds.), *Puritans and Revolutionaries, Essays in Seventeenth Century History presented to Christopher Hill* (Oxford, 1978), 206–32.

PEGDEN, N. A., *Leicester Guildhall, a Short History and Guide* (Leicester, 1981).

PEVSNER, NIKOLAUS, *BoE, Shropshire* (Harmondsworth, 1958).

—— *BoE, South and West Somerset* (Harmondsworth, 1958).

—— *BoE, North-west and South Norfolk* (Harmondsworth, 1962).

—— *BoE, North-east Norfolk and Norwich* (Harmondsworth, 1962).

—— *BoE, Sussex* (Harmondsworth, 1965).

—— *BoE, Bedfordshire and the County of Huntingdon and Peterborough* (Harmondsworth, 1968).

—— *BoE, Northamptonshire*, 2nd edn, rev. Bridget Cherry (Harmondsworth, 1973).

—— *BoE, North-east and East Kent*, 2nd edn. (1976).

PEVSNER, NIKOLAUS, *BoE, Derbyshire*, 2nd edn. (1978).
——*BoE, Leicestershire and Rutland*, rev. Elizabeth Williams and G. K. Brandwood (Harmondsworth, 1984).
——and E. RADCLIFFE, *BoE, Suffolk*, 2nd edn. (1975).
——and DAVID VEREY, *BoE, Gloucestershire*, 2 vols. (Harmondsworth, 1970).
PHELPS, Revd WILLIAM (ed.), *The History and Antiquities of Somersetshire*, 2 vols.
(1836).
PHYTHIAN-ADAMS, CHARLES, 'Ceremony and the Citizen: the Communal Year
at Coventry, 1450–1550', in Peter Clark and Paul Slack (eds.), *Crisis and Order
in English Towns, 1500–1700* (1972), 57–85.
——*Desolation of a City, Coventry and the Urban Crisis of the Late Middle Ages*
(Cambridge, 1979).
——'Urban Decay in Late Medieval England', in P. Abrams and E. A. Wrigley
(eds.), *Towns in Societies, Essays in Economic History and Historical Sociology*
(Cambridge, 1978), 159–86.
PIGOT, Revd HUGH, *Hadleigh* (Lowestoft, 1860).
PLATT, COLIN, *The English Medieval Town* (1976).
PLATTS, A., *The History of Chippenham, 853–1946* (1948).
POLSUE, JOSEPH, *A Complete Parochial History of the County of Cornwall*, 4 vols.
(Truro, 1867–72).
POOL, P. A. S., *A History of the Town and Parish of Penzance* (Penzance, 1974).
POTTS, WILLIAM, *A History of Banbury* (Banbury, 1958).
POUND, J. F., 'An Elizabethan Census of the Poor; the Treatment of Vagrancy in
Norwich, 1570–1580', *Birmingham University Historical Journal*, 8 (1962),
135–51.
——*The Norwich Census of the Poor of 1570* (Norfolk Record Society, 11, 1971).
PRIESTLEY, URSULA and P. J. CORFIELD, 'Rooms and Room Use in Norwich
Housing, 1580–1730', *Post-Medieval Archaeology*, 16 (1982), 93–123.
PRIOR, MARY, *Fisher Row, Fishermen, Bargemen and Canal Boatmen in Oxford,
1500–1900* (Oxford, 1982).
PRYNNE, WILLIAM, *Histrio-Mastix, the Player's Scourge or Actor's Tragedy* (1633,
repr. 2 vols., New York, 1972).
Public Record Office, *List of Rentals and Surveys*, Lists and Indexes, XXV (1908).
PUGH, RALPH B., *Imprisonment in Medieval England* (Cambridge, 1968).
RAINE, A. (ed.), *York Civic Records*, Yorkshire Archaeological Society Record
Series, 8 vols. (1939–53).
RALPH, ELIZABETH (ed.), *Guide to the Bristol Archives Office* (Bristol, 1971).
RAMSAY, G. D., 'The Recruitment and Fortunes of Some London Freemen in
the Mid-Sixteenth Century', *Ec. HR* 2nd ser. 31/4 (1978), 526–40.
RATHBONE, M. G. (ed.), *A Descriptive List of the Wiltshire Borough Records*
(Devizes, 1951).
READER, F. W., 'Discovery of a Drawing of the Wendover Market House',
Records of Buckinghamshire, 13 (1934), 69–76.
REDFERN, FRANCIS, *History and Antiquities of Uttoxeter*, 2nd edn. (1886).
REYNOLDS, SUSAN, 'The Forged Charters of Barnstaple', *English Historical
Review*, 84 (1969), 699–720.
——*An Introduction to the History of English Medieval Towns* (Oxford, 1977).

RICE, M. A., *Abbots Bromley* (Shrewsbury, 1939).

RICHARDS, JEFFREY and JOHN M. MACKENZIE, *The Railway Station, a Social History* (Oxford, 1986).

RIDEN, P. and BLAIR, J. (eds.), *History of Chesterfield*, v (Chesterfield, 1980).

RIGOLD, S. I., 'Two Types of Court Hall', *Archaeologia Cantiana*, 83 (1968), 1–22.

RIX, S. W., 'An Account of the Guildhall at Diss', *Norfolk Archaeology*, 2 (1849).

RODDIS, R. J., *Penryn, the History of an Ancient Cornish Borough* (Truro, 1964).

ROFFE, DAVID, 'Walter Draguin's Town? Lord and Burghal Community in Thirteenth Century Stamford', *Lincolnshire History and Archaeology*, 23 (1988).

ROGERS, K. H., 'Salisbury', in M. D. Lobel (ed.), *Atlas of Historic Towns*, i, (Baltimore, n.d.).

ROSSER, GERVASE, 'The Anglo-Saxon Gilds', in John Blair (ed.), *Ministers and Parish Churches, the Local Church in Transition, 950–1200* (Oxford University Committee for Archaeology, Monograph no. 17, 1988).

ROWLEY, TREVOR, *The Shropshire Landscape* (1972).

Royal Commission on Historical Monuments, *Buildings of England, Bucks.* (1960).

——*Inventory of the Historic Monuments of Essex*, i (1916).

ROYCE, Revd DAVID, 'The Northleach Court-Book', *Transactions of the Bristol and Gloucestershire Archaeological Society*, 7 (1882–3), 90–116.

SACKS, DAVID H., 'The Demise of the Martyrs: the Feasts of St. Clement and St. Katherine in Bristol, 1400–1600', *Social History*, 11 (1986), 141–69.

SALTER, H. E. (ed.), *Oxford Council Acts, 1583–1626* (Oxford Historical Society, 1928).

SAMAHA, JOEL, 'Hanging for Felony, the Rule of Law in Elizabethan Colchester', *Historical Journal*, 21/4 (1978), 763–82.

SCARISBRICK, J. J., *The Reformation and the English People* (Oxford, 1984).

SCHAMA, SIMON, *The Embarrassment of Riches, Interpretation of Dutch Culture in the Golden Age* (New York, 1987).

SCROPE, G. POULETT, 'Abridgement of the History of the Manor and Ancient Borough of Castle Combe', *Wiltshire Archaeological and Natural History Magazine*, 2 (1855), 133–58.

SEABORNE, MALCOLM, *The English School, its Architecture and Organization, 1370–1870* (1971).

SHARP, BUCHANON, *In Contempt of All Authority, Rural Artisans and Riot in the West of England, 1586–1660* (Berkeley, Calif., 1980).

SHARPE, CUTHBERT, *A History of Hartlepool* (Hartlepool, 1851).

SHARPE, J. A., 'Enforcing the Law in the Seventeenth Century English Village', in V. A. C. Gatrell, Bruce Lenman, and Geoffrey Parker (eds.), *Crime and the Law, the Social History of Crime in Western Europe Since 1500* (1980), 90–109.

——*Crime in Early Modern England, 1550–1750* (1984).

SHEPHERD, SIMON, *Amazons and Warrior Women, Varieties of Feminism in Seventeenth Century Drama* (Brighton, 1980).

SHERWOOD, J. and NIKOLAUS PEVSNER, *BoE, Oxfordshire* (Harmondsworth, 1974).

SHORTT, HUGH (ed.), *The City of Salisbury* (Salisbury, 1957).

SIMON, JOAN, 'Town Estates and School in the Sixteenth and Early Seventeenth Centuries' in Brian Simon (ed.), *Education in Leicestershire, 1540–1940* (Leicester, 1968).

SIMPSON, ALAN, *The Wealth of the Gentry, 1540–1660* (Cambridge, 1962).

SLACK, PAUL, *The Impact of Plague in Tudor and Stuart England* (1985).

SLADE, C. F., 'Reading', in M. D. Lobel (ed.), *Atlas of Historic Towns* (Baltimore, n.d.).

SMALLEY, W., *Oundle's Story* (Oundle, n.d.).

SMITH, A. H., *English Place-Name Elements*, 2 vols. (Cambridge, 1976).

SMITH, HARRY PERCY, *The History of the Borough and County of the Town of Poole*, 2 vols. (Poole, 1949–51).

SMITH, T. P., 'The Early Schoolhouse of Dartford Grammar School', *Dartford Historical and Antiquarian Society Newsletter* (1977), 11–25.

SOUTHERN, RICHARD, *The Staging of Plays before Shakespeare* (1973).

SPARGO, J. W., *Juridic Folklore in England, Illustrated by the Cucking Stool* (Durham, N.C., 1944).

SPEDDING, JAMES (ed.), *The Works of Francis Bacon*, vol. 2 (1859).

SPUFFORD, MARGARET, *Contrasting Communities, English Villagers in the Sixteenth and Seventeenth Centuries* (Cambridge, 1974).

——'Puritanism and Social Control?', in A. Fletcher and J. Stevenson (eds.), *Order and Disorder in Early Modern England* (Cambridge, 1985), 41–57.

STALLYBRASS, PETER and WHITE, ALLON, *The Politics and Poetics of Transgression* (London, 1986).

STANFORD, MAUREEN (ed.), *The Ordinances of Bristol, 1506–1598* (Bristol Record Society, 41, 1990).

STATHAM, MARGARET, 'The Guildhall, Bury St Edmunds', *Proceedings of the Suffolk Institute of Archaeology*, 31 (1970), 117–57.

——*Jankyn Smith and the Guildhall Feoffees, 1481–1981* (Bury St Edmunds, 1981).

STATHAM, S. P. H., *History of the Castle, Town and Port of Dover* (1899).

Statutes of the Realm, ed. A. Luders, T. E. Tomlins, and J. Raithby, 11 vols. (1810–28).

STEDMAN, A. R., *Marlborough and the Upper Kennet Country* (Marlborough, 1960).

STEVENSON, W. H. (ed.), *Records of the Borough of Nottingham*, 3 vols. (Nottingham, 1882—5).

——'The Old Court House at Alfreton', *Journal of the Derbyshire Archaeological and Natural History Society*, 38 (1916), 127–30.

STONE, LAWRENCE, *Social Change and Revolution in England, 1540–1640* (1965).

——*The Crisis of the Aristocracy, 1558–1641* (Oxford, 1965).

——'Patriarchy and Paternalism in Tudor England: the Earl of Arundel and the Peasants' Revolt of 1549', *Journal of British Studies*, 13/2 (1974), 19–23.

——and STONE, JEAN C. FAWTIER, *An Open Elite? England, 1540–1880* (Oxford, 1984).

STRAUSS, GERALD, *Nuremberg in the Sixteenth Century*, 2nd edn. (Bloomington, Ind., 1976).

STRONG, ROY, *Splendour at Court, Renaissance Spectacle and Illusion* (1973).

STUBBES, PHILIP, *Anatomy of Abuses* [1583], ed. F. J. Furnival (1877–9).

SUMMERSON, SIR JOHN, *Architecture in Britain, 1530–1830*, 3rd edn. (1958).

SURTEES, ROBERT, *History and Antiquities of the County Palatine of Durham*, 4 vols. (1816–40).

SWABY, J. E., *A History of Louth* (1951).

SWINNERTON, Revd CHARLES, 'Stanley St Leonards', *Transactions of the Bristol and Gloucestershire Archaeological Society*, 44 (1922), 221–67.

TAYLOR, HENRY, 'The Ancient Crosses of Lancashire', *Transactions of the Lancashire and Cheshire Antiquarian Society*, 19 (1901).

THIRSK, JOAN (ed.), *The Agrarian History of England and Wales*, iv, *1500–1640* (Cambridge, 1967).

——*Economic Policy and Projects* (Oxford, 1978).

THOMAS, J. H., *Town Government in the Sixteenth Century* (1933).

THOMAS, KEITH, 'Work and Leisure in Pre-Industrial Society', *P and P* 29 (1964), 50–62.

——*Religion and the Decline of Magic* (Harmondsworth, 1973).

——'The Perception of the Past in Early Modern England', Creighton Lecture (London University, 1983).

THOMPSON, E. P., 'Time, Work-Discipline and Industrial Capitalism', *P and P* 38 (1967), 56–98.

THOMPSON, PISHEY, *The History and Antiquities of Boston* (Boston, 1856).

THOMPSON, T. R., *Materials for the History of Cricklade* (Cricklade, 1958–61).

THORPE, B., *Diplomatarium Anglicum Aevi Saxonici* (1865).

TILLYARD, E. M. W., *The Elizabethan World Picture* (1943, 1967).

TINDAL, W., *The History and Antiquities of the Abbey and Borough of Evesham* (Evesham, 1794).

TITTLER, ROBERT, *Nicholas Bacon, the Making of a Tudor Statesman* (1976).

——'Incorporation and Politics in Sixteenth Century Thaxted', *Essex Archaeology and History*, 8 (1976), 224–32.

——'The Incorporation of Boroughs, 1540–1558', *History*, 62/204 (1977), 24–42.

——'The Emergence of Urban Policy, 1536–1558', in J. Loach and R. Tittler (eds.), *The Mid-Tudor Polity, c.1540–1560* (1980), 74–93.

——'The Building of Civic Halls in Dorset, c.1560–1640', *BIHR* 58/137 (1985), 37–45.

——'The Vitality of an Elizabethan Port: The Economy of Poole, c.1550–1600', *Southern History*, 7 (1985), 95–118.

——'The End of the Middle Ages in the English Country Town', *Sixteenth Century Journal*, 18/4 (1987), 471–87.

——'The Sequestration of Juries in Early Modern England', *Historical Research* 61/146 (1988), 301–5.

TOULMIN SMITH, LUCY (ed.), *The Itinerary of John Leland*, 5 vols. (1907–10).

TOWNSHEND, GEORGE F., *The Town and Borough of Leominster* (Leominster, 1863).

TOY, H. S., *The History of Helston* (1936).

TREXLER, RICHARD, *Public Life in Renaissance Florence* (New York, 1980).

TUPLING, GEORGE HENRY, 'Lancashire Markets in the Sixteenth and

Seventeenth Centuries', *Transactions of the Lancashire and Cheshire Antiquarian Society*, 58 (1947 for 1945/6), 1–34 and 59 (1948 for 1947), 1–34.

TURNER, M. L., *Somerset* (1949).

TURNER, W. H. (ed.), *Selections from the Records of the City of Oxford* (Oxford, 1880).

TWEMLOW, J. A. (ed.), *Liverpool Town Books*, 2 vols. (Liverpool, 1918 and 1935).

UNDERDOWN, DAVID, 'The Chalk and the Cheese: Contrasts Among the English Clubmen', *P and P* 85 (1979), 25–48.

——*Revel, Riot and Rebellion, Popular Politics and Culture in England, 1603–1660* (Oxford, 1987).

Valor Ecclesiasticus, ed. John Caley and Jos. Hunter, 6 vols. (1810–34).

VCH, Bedfordshire, iii (1923).

VCH, Berkshire, i (1924), iii (1923), and iv (1924).

VCH, Buckinghamshire, iii (1925) and iv (1927).

VCH, Essex, v (1966).

VCH, Durham, iii (1928).

VCH, Gloucestershire, viii (1968), xi (1976).

VCH, Hampshire and the Isle of Wight, iii (1908, repr. 1973).

VCH, Hertfordshire, ii (1908), iii (1912).

VCH, Huntingdonshire, ii (1932).

VCH, Leicestershire, iv (1958).

VCH, Northamptonshire, iii (1930).

VCH, Oxfordshire, iv (Oxford, 1979); vi (1959), vii (1962), x (1972), and xi (1983).

VCH, Somerset, iii (1974).

VCH, Staffordshire, iv (1979), vi (1979), and xvii (Oxford, 1976).

VCH, Surrey, ii (1905), iii (1911), and iv (1967).

VCH, Sussex, iii (1946), iv (1953), and vii (1940).

VCH, Warwickshire, ii (1908), iii (1945, repr. 1965), iv (1947), and viii (1969).

VCH, Worcestershire, ii (1906) and iii (1913).

VCH, Wiltshire, ii (1955), vi (1962), x (1975), and xii (1983).

VCH, Yorkshire, East Riding, i (1969), vi (Oxford, 1989).

VCH, Yorkshire, North Riding, ii (1923).

VOWELL (*alias* Hooker), JOHN, *The Description of the Citie of Excester* (1575), ed. W. J. Harte, J. W. Schopp, and H. Tapley-Soper, 3 vols. (Devon and Cornwall Record Society, 1919–47).

WALKER, WENDY, *Essex Markets and Fairs* (Chelmsford, 1981).

WASSON, JOHN (ed.), *REED, Devon* (Toronto, 1986).

WATKINS, ALFRED, 'The Freeman's Prison at the Boothall, Hereford', *Transactions of the Woolhope Naturalists' Field Club* (1938 for 1934), 49–53.

——*An Essay Towards the History of Bideford* (Exeter, 1792).

WAYNE, DON E., 'Drama and Society in the Age of Jonson, an Alternative View', *Renaissance Drama*, 13 (1982), 103–29.

WEBB, JOHN, *Poor Relief in Elizabethan Ipswich* (Suffolk Record Society, 9, 1966).

WEBB, SIDNEY and BEATRICE, *English Local Government, the Manor and the Borough*, 2 vols. (1908).

WEEKS, W. S., *Clitheroe in the Seventeenth Century* (Clitheroe, n.d.).

WEINBAUM, MARTIN, *British Borough Charters, 1307–1660* (Cambridge, 1943).

WELCH, EDWIN (ed.), *Plymouth Building Accounts of the Sixteenth and Seventeenth Centuries* (Devon and Cornwall Record Society, NS 12, 1967).

'W. H. R.', *An Account of Swaffham Markets and Fairs* [1832] (Swaffham, n.d.).

WICKHAM, GLYNNE, *Early English Stages, 1300–1660*, 3 vols. (1959–81).

WILLAN, T. S., *The Inland Trade* (Manchester, 1976).

WILLIAMS, JOHN, 'Northampton's Medieval Guildhalls', *Northamptonshire Past and Present*, 7 (1983–4), 5–9.

WILLS, C., *A Short Historical Sketch of the Town of Barnstaple* (Barnstaple, 1855).

WILSON, F. P., *The English Drama, 1485–1585* (Oxford, 1969).

WILSON, SIDNEY, *A Saunter Round Faversham* (Faversham, 1936).

WOLSEY, S. W. and R. W. P. LUFF, *Furniture in the Age of the Joiner* (1968).

WOOD, MARGARET, *The English Mediaeval House* (1965).

WOOD, P. D., 'Topography of East Grinstead', *Sussex Archaeological Collections*, 106 (1968), 49–62.

WOODRUFF, C. EVELEIGH, *A History of the Town and Port of Fordwich* [1895] (Canterbury, n.d.).

WOODWARD, D. M., '"Swords into Ploughshares": Recycling in Pre-Industrial England', *Ec. HR* 2nd ser. 38/2 (1985), 175–91.

WORSFIELD, A. F. de P., 'The Court Hall, Rye', *Sussex Archaeological Collections*, 66 (1925), 208–18.

WRIGHTSON, KEITH, 'Aspects of Social Differentiation in Rural England, c.1580–1660', *Journal of Peasant Studies*, 5 (1977), 33–47.

—— 'Two Concepts of Order: Justices, Constables and Jurymen in Seventeenth Century England', in J. Brewer and J. Styles (eds.), *An Ungovernable People?* (New Brunswick, New Jersey, 1980), 21–46.

—— *English Society, 1580–1680* (1982).

—— and DAVID LEVINE, *Poverty and Piety in an English Village, Terling, 1525–1700* (New York, 1979).

WRIGLEY, E. A. and R. S. SCHOFIELD, *The Population History of England, 1541–1871, a Reconstruction* (1981).

YAXLEY, SUSAN (ed.), *History of Hemel Hempstead* (Hemel Hempstead, 1973).

YOUINGS, JOYCE, *Sixteenth Century England* (1984).

Index

Wylles, Henry, yeoman of Evesham 94
Wymondham 7, 32
  hall in 31, 45, 121

yeldehall 6–7
  see also guild halls
York 115, 137, 145–7, 152

administration of 40
prisons in 40, 124, 126
public buildings 40, 115, 126, 146–7, 152
Yorke, Mr, of Marlborough 65–6
Yorkshire 75
  West Riding 2, 51